1992

PROFESSIONAL DEVELOPMENT AND PRACTICE SERIES

Ann Lieberman, *Editor*

Editorial Advisory Board: Myrna Cooper, Nathalie Gehrke,
Gary Griffin, Judith Warren Little, Lynne Miller,
Phillip Schlechty, Gary Sykes

Exploring Teaching

Reinventing an Introductory Course

Edited by
Sharon Feiman-Nemser
Helen Featherstone

Teachers College, Columbia University
New York and London

Published by Teachers College Press, 1234 Amsterdam Avenue
New York, NY 10027

Chapter 3 is an expansion of an article originally published in the *Journal of Teacher
Education*. Reprinted with permission from the *Journal of Teacher Education, 41*(3),
12–20.
Chapter 7 is an expansion of an article that originally appeared in *Kappan 72*(3),
204–209. Reprinted with permission.

Library of Congress Cataloging-in-Publication Data
Exploring teaching: reinventing an introductory course / edited by
  Helen Featherstone, Sharon Feiman-Nemser.
      p.   cm. — (Professional development and practice series)
    ISBN 0-8077-3164-1 (alk. paper) — ISBN 0-8077-3163-3 (pbk. :
  alk. paper)
      1. College teaching — Michigan — Ann Arbor — Case studies.
  2. Teaching. I. Featherstone, Helen, 1944–   . II. Feiman-Nemser,
  Sharon. III. Series.
  LB2331.E96   1992   91-39353
  378.1′25 — dc20   CIP

Printed on acid-free paper

Manufactured in the United States of America

98 97 96 95 94 93 92   8 7 6 5 4 3 2 1

Contents

143,778

v

Foreword

The purpose of the Professional Development and Practice series is to present research, narratives, and descriptions of innovative work that leads to deeper understanding of educational practice and how to improve it. The intent is to provide descriptions of, discussions about, and possible actions for the problems of educational practice at a time when we need fresh insights, experimentation, and new conceptions. Those who willingly undertake the struggle to rethink our nations' schools are represented in this series.

Exploring Teaching takes on one of the oldest and most difficult problems in education — how to introduce the study and practice of teaching to beginners. Feiman-Nemser and Featherstone take the reader on an intriguing journey through an introductory course, organized around three questions:

What does it mean to teach?
What are schools for?
What do teachers need to know?

We travel with a sensitive group of teacher educators and their students as they all collectively think, question, observe, and try to make sense of what teaching is and what it could be. The students observe elementary classrooms in person and on videotape, and what they see becomes the grist for their class discussion. Because teaching is so familiar to the new candidates, the course seeks to confront initial beliefs that often need to be enriched or transformed. We, the readers, join the students and their teachers in unwrapping the skills, attitudes, beliefs, and knowledge that are a part of being a teacher.

Under the leadership of a group of teacher educators who work not only to provide prospective teachers with an important introduction to the teaching field, but also offer to create "a learning community" for themselves, every aspect of teaching is held up for examination, discussion, and understanding.

This course, a vehicle for examining teaching, becomes the reader's guidebook to a deep and intense education in how people learn, what means teachers use to teach others, and the role of beliefs in constraining or expanding the view teachers hold of students. And in ending the book with a discussion of their enduring dilemmas as teachers and teacher educators — of the ways in which, for example, they find themselves sacrificing demands for critical thinking in order to encourage wider student participation, and vice versa — the authors model for us, the readers, as well as for their students, the real meaning of teaching.

Ann Lieberman
Series Editor

Foreword

When Sharon Feiman-Nemser first came to Michigan State University in 1980, I asked her to assume responsibility for the course we offered to undergraduates who had not yet been admitted to the College of Education but who wished to explore the possibilities offered by a career in teaching. I hoped that she would reinvent the course, making it a place where college sophomores who had spent 13 years of their lives in schools and thought they knew all about teaching could learn to look at their assumptions afresh. Sharon agreed to take on this challenge, on two conditions. She insisted that the course be taught in sections of no more than 25 students, and that faculty with reputations for excellence in teaching should teach most of the sections. I agreed, believing that a course taught in this way could significantly influence the way our teacher candidates thought about their future university preparation, as well as their future work as teachers.

I have not been disappointed, and neither have the students. The work that teachers and students in Exploring Teaching (TE-101) have been doing in the last 10 years is the essential work of the current educational reform movement. They have been asking what it means to teach, what schools are for, and what a teacher needs to know—the very questions that teacher educators, school boards, politicians, policymakers, and thoughtful citizens have been grappling with. They have been trying to identify their own assumptions about these important questions, to examine these assumptions and the ways that they have come to hold them, and to decide whether the assumptions make sense. Their classroom conversations, their papers, and their examination bluebooks indicate that students often conclude that the practices and ideas that they accepted unquestioningly when they entered the course need considerable revision. As a result, our students move on to their professional training with many more questions about teaching, learning, schooling, and their own needs as prospective teachers than they had when they entered TE-101.

These questions, along with the conviction that quality teaching is a complex undertaking, lead our students to look carefully at the four alternative teacher education programs we offer them, and to choose in large numbers (larger than we can actually accommodate) programs that are difficult and demanding. When they leave TE-101, they know that they have a lot to learn and they are excited about trying to learn it. They are beginning to develop the sorts of dispositions that all teachers must have if we are truly to reinvent schooling.

The faculty and graduate students who teach TE-101 help tomorrow's teachers to break with outdated conceptions of teaching and learning. They also initiate novice teacher educators into the challenging work of preparing thoughtful teachers. Graduate students who are invited to teach TE-101 have already distinguished themselves in their first years of graduate study; they are eager to challenge unexamined notions about schooling and to share with their students their own enthusiasm for teaching. Before they teach TE-101 they "apprentice" with a faculty member or graduate student who has taught the course several times before, observing class meetings, reading student journals and papers, and perhaps teaching a few classes or joining small group discussions. They also attend the weekly staff meetings in which those who are teaching the course reflect together on their practice and on their students' learning. By the time the novices take responsibility for their own section of the course, they have had many opportunities to talk and think about the problems of challenging conventional notions of teaching and to hear what experienced teacher educators are thinking about their own practice. In the community of the TE-101 staff, our graduate students become innovative and reflective teacher educators.

The essays by graduate students give a glimpse of how that happens. Susan McMahon has used her teaching journal to reconstruct the thoughts she had as she watched Suzanne Wilson teach the course and the ways she used what she learned to teach her own section. She allows us to see how her observations, the readings and discussions of her graduate courses, and her classroom experience interacted as she constructed, and reconstructed, her own version of TE-101. Margery Osborne shows us how she thinks about her role in orchestrating the classroom conversation, and how her ideas about schooling and college teaching grew out of her experiences teaching college science. And Michelle Parker and Linda Tiezzi, who wrote their essay after they had taught the course for several years and moved on to explore other roles as teacher educators in MSU's Professional Development Schools, contribute their insights to the current debate over the use of cases in teacher education.

This sort of writing about teacher education — the writing of teacher educators about their own practice — serves several vital functions. At the most obvious level, it allows teacher educators to view the work of their colleagues and promotes thoughtful dialogue about the improvement of college teaching — dialogue that is now in short supply even in colleges of education. It also allows other teachers, both in and out of universities, to see how particular teacher educators are *thinking* about their teaching; these reflections of thoughtful teachers may be as valuable as the more concrete images of actual practice. And it makes those doing the writing think carefully — writing leads us to new insights about our students and about our practice.

But perhaps most important, this sort of writing allows teacher educators to join with schoolteachers in a new sort of collegiality: one based on their common concerns as teachers. For teacher educators, like their colleagues in the schools, have classes to teach, papers to grade, excuses to evaluate, lessons to plan, group work to orchestrate. Like other teachers they must ask themselves at the end of a class period, "What did these students actually learn today?" When college professors describe their practice, they open the door to a real conversation: Schoolteachers can evaluate and comment on their goals and strategies. They can make suggestions, based on their own knowledge of teaching.

For too long the dialogue between schools and colleges has been painfully one-sided: College professors have criticized schools and told teachers how to do their jobs better; school people have responded defensively, noting that few college professors have recent firsthand knowledge of teaching. There has been much anger and little productive dialogue. But now a growing number of universities, including those in the Holmes Group, are committed to changing the terms of this conversation, to bring the wisdom of schoolteachers into the university, and to bring college professors into the schools. Books like this one, which remind us that teacher educators are teachers with something to learn from and something to teach other teachers, help to set the stage for a new conversation, and a new way for school and university people to talk together about the improvement of practice.

Judith E. Lanier
Dean, College of Education
Michigan State University

Acknowledgments

More than 20 professors and doctoral students have been involved in designing and teaching Exploring Teaching (TE-101) since 1980. Eleven have written chapters for this volume. But others have helped to shape the course over the years, adding to the collective wisdom of the TE-101 staff. They include Henrietta Barnes, Joyce Cain, Douglas Campbell, Bruce Cheney, Nora Evers, Susan Florio-Ruane, Diane Holt-Reynolds, Magdalene Lampert, Tim Little, Douglas MacIsaac, Shirley Miske, Paul Ongtogook, Lynn Paine, Gemette Reid, Sharon Rushcamp, Nancy Wiemers, John Zeuli. We value their conceptual and practical contributions to the course.

We are grateful to Judy Lanier, dean of the College of Education, and Henrietta Barnes, chair of the department of teacher education, for giving us support to develop this course. We also thank them for enabling many graduate students to serve an apprenticeship for a term in which they had no formal teaching responsibilities. Their willingness to divert scarce resources to an introductory course demonstrates their strong commitment to undergraduate instruction.

This book is a product of our personal and professional friendship. We conceived the idea walking to work together and nourished it along over lunch and around the edges of our other responsibilities. Talking and writing together about our teaching has been a continuing source of stimulation and enjoyment.

Besides the cooperation of our fellow authors, we benefited from the word-processing skills of Nora Murphy and Jan Knight, who entered in numerous changes and printed out various versions. We thank them for their patience and assistance.

Carole Saltz, Ron Galbraith, and Cathy McClure at Teachers College Press have given us enthusiastic support and careful guidance. We especially want to acknowledge Ron Galbraith's encouragement before his untimely death. Ron knew just how to inquire about our progress without making us feel behind schedule. Cathy McClure has worked patiently with us through the final stages of putting the manuscript together.

More than anyone else, our students have pushed us to shape and reshape Exploring Teaching. Some of them are quoted in these pages, but those who are not have also left their mark.

1

Introducing Teaching

Sharon Feiman-Nemser
Susan Melnick

Before I walked into TE-101, I had no idea how much I
needed to know in order to be a good teacher. I thought teaching was going to be easy. I would instruct, and my students
would merely absorb the material. I didn't realize there was
much more knowledge I needed to know in between these two
steps. (TE-101 student)

How should we introduce undergraduates to the study and practice
of teaching? As instructors of an innovative introductory education
course, we have given considerable thought to the kind of initial
learning opportunity we want students to have and to the messages
about teaching and learning to teach that we believe a first education
course should convey. Over the past 10 years we have developed a
course that differs from traditional introductory courses in the arts
and sciences as well as in education. Called Exploring Teaching (or
TE-101), the course aims to loosen the grip of unexamined beliefs
about teaching that students have built up through years of teacher
watching and growing up in the general culture. In pursuing this
aim and the intellectual habits that support it, the course exemplifies
the values of liberal/professional education.

This chapter provides an introduction to the Exploring Teaching course—how it evolved, what it is like, how it differs from
conventional introductory courses in education. Subsequent chapters offer a more detailed look at particular aspects of the course.
Some describe the teaching and learning surrounding a major assignment or instructional sequence. Others examine the challenges
and dilemmas associated with being a teacher in this setting. To-

gether they open a window on the pedagogical thinking and practice of teacher educators who wish to change prospective teachers' ideas about teaching.

THE UNIVERSE OF INTRODUCTORY COURSES

Introducing undergraduates to teaching as a field of inquiry and professional practice presents unique challenges. More than any other profession, teaching socializes prospective members from childhood. Students in elementary and secondary schools learn the norms of teaching by watching teachers for 12 years. This fact has important implications for the goals, content, and pedagogy of introductory education courses.

Typically introductory courses for prospective teachers take one of two forms. Either they are organized around a series of topics covered in an introduction to education textbook or they revolve around an early field experience. The first approach aims to introduce prospective teachers to the complexities and demands of teaching "from the other side of the desk" through exposure to a wide variety of topics and issues related to teaching, learning, and schools. Proponents of the second approach argue that prospective teachers need to revisit classrooms in order to find out whether teaching is an appropriate career choice either through firsthand experience or through encounters with cases of school teaching.

Survey Courses

Textbooks tend to drive Introduction to Education survey courses. A single course might deal with such diverse topics as school architecture, instructional planning, the purposes of schooling, management and discipline, teacher salaries, career opportunities in education, federal, state, and local governance, learning styles. Because many of these subjects have little relevance to beginning education students, the course may convince them that teacher education has little practical value. Furthermore, relying on a textbook means that students encounter fragmented and predigested ideas.

Early Field Experiences

Considered a major innovation in the 1970s, introductory courses based on early field experiences give prospective teachers a chance to determine whether teaching is for them at the beginning of their professional studies rather than at the end during student teaching. Still the impact of such courses can be problematic.

Firsthand Experience. With no preparation and minimal supervision, beginning education students tutor individual pupils, lead reading groups, grade papers, put up new bulletin boards. If all goes well, they may conclude that teaching requires little preparation. If it goes poorly, they may conclude prematurely that they lack what it takes to teach. Such experiences tend to confirm students' faith in the primacy of firsthand experience in learning to teach and to reinforce their preoccupation with what Dewey (1904) called "the outer forms of behavior." Rather than challenging students' entering beliefs, early field experiences reinforce them (Calderhead, 1988; Feiman-Nemser & Buchmann, 1986b).

Vicarious Experience Through Cases. A recent variation on the early field experience approach emphasizes the use of decision-oriented cases of teaching (Merseth, 1991). In such a course, students imagine themselves in the teacher's shoes as they try to figure out what should be done in various problematic situations. Good cases capture some of the complexities of teaching. They freeze the action, giving prospective teachers a chance to consider the situation from various perspectives. From such opportunities, education students may begin to appreciate the dynamic and multifaceted nature of teaching.

Some decision-oriented cases raise critical questions about teaching and learning (e.g., Who is responsible for motivating students? What is the impact of ability grouping?); others ask students to decide what to do about discipline or homework or to diagnose a reading problem (examples taken from Kowalski, Weaver, & Henson, 1990). Like early field experiences, however, early encounters with such cases can easily play into students' preoccupation with the control of student behavior. Moreover, the expectation that beginners can solve complex pedagogical problems without any preparation confirms the belief that teaching requires little special knowledge. Lacking other resources, beginning teacher education students understandably rely on their own schooling for guidance.

Defining the Problem

If a vast body of definitive knowledge about teaching existed, it might make sense to construe the task of introducing teaching as a problem of knowledge transmission and adopt a survey approach.

If education students had no idea about what schools were like and what teachers do, it might make sense to construe the task of introducing teaching as a matter of exposing them to the "real world" of classrooms through some kind of early field experience. In fact, there is little consensus about the state of the knowledge base despite recent advances in research on teaching and efforts at codification (Reynolds, 1989; Richardson, 1987). Furthermore, prospective teachers can hardly be considered "blank slates" when it comes to teaching. From growing up in the culture and attending school, they have built up strong beliefs about teaching and learning, subject matter and students. These beliefs powerfully influence what prospective teachers learn during teacher preparation and what they do as teachers. Teacher educators cannot afford to ignore them or to leave them unexamined.

RESEARCH ON TEACHER CANDIDATES' ENTERING BELIEFS

Researchers at the National Center for Research on Teacher Education at Michigan State have found that undergraduates often enter teaching with a limited view of their role as teachers. They see teaching as a matter of telling pupils what they know and assessing their recall of that information. They view learning as a process of memorizing and practice, not as a process of constructing meaning from new ideas (Ball, 1988a; McDiarmid & Ball, 1987).

Beginning teacher education students, especially at the elementary level, tend to emphasize the affective rather than the academic sides of teaching. They cite patience, warmth, and caring as the most important attributes of a good teacher (Weinstein, 1989) and they believe that enhancing pupils' self-esteem is more important than maximizing their achievement (Book, Byers, & Freeman, 1983).

Beginning teacher education students also have limited views about learners who are different from themselves (McDiarmid & Ball, 1987; Paine, 1990). They believe that some children cannot master basic skills in reading and math (Brousseau & Freeman, 1989; Freeman & Kalaian, 1989). They attribute school failure to poor home environments, limited abilities, and poor student attitudes, thus sidestepping the issue of responsible teacher action.

Many teacher candidates believe that they already know enough to begin teaching (Freeman & Kalaian, 1989). "I feel com-

fortable about being a teacher," wrote one beginning teacher education student. "It's natural. . . . I don't feel like it is new. I know
how classrooms operate and . . . I'm sure I could do a better job,
right now as a teacher, than most of what I see out there" (Crow,
1987, p. 9). Elementary candidates expect to learn little from their
education courses (Crow, 1987). Nor do they see how liberal arts
courses contribute to their preparation for teaching. Mostly they
assume that what they need to know will be acquired from student
teaching and on-the-job experience (Weinstein, 1989).

Such beliefs will discourage prospective teachers from giving
serious attention to pedagogies that rest on different views of teaching and learning. Ultimately, their pupils will feel the consequences,
especially those ill-served by conventional schooling (Good, 1987;
Peterson, Fennema, Carpenter, & Loef, 1989).

These facts suggest that teacher preparation, if it is to open
possibilities and promote greater responsiveness to the challenges of
teaching, cannot simply add new knowledge and experience to existing stores. It must also help prospective teachers to transform initial
beliefs so that they can envision richer possibilities for teaching and
learning than those derived from their own schooling. But this is
easier said than done.

People tend to hang on to familiar ways of thinking, ignoring
conflicting ideas or reinterpreting them to fit their current views.
Prospective teachers are no exception. Studies show that conventional teacher education changes few beliefs (Tabachnick &
Zeichner, 1984). Perhaps teacher educators fail to challenge students' entering beliefs. Perhaps their efforts are too limited. Still,
teachers often leave their preservice preparation with initial beliefs
intact.

Research on the process of conceptual change suggests some of
the conditions that must exist if people are to change their minds.
First, they must be dissatisfied with their existing beliefs. Second,
they must see and value compelling alternatives. Third, they must
figure out some way to integrate the new beliefs with their earlier
conceptions (Posner, Strike, Hewson, & Gertzog, 1982). These
ideas have important implications for teacher preparation.

If prospective teachers are to expand their perspectives on
teaching, they must be provoked to reexamine their own schooling
and question the beliefs derived from these experiences. Encounters
with new forms of teaching and learning can help them imagine
alternatives, provided these encounters are vivid, concrete, and detailed enough to challenge the models internalized since childhood.

But the success of these encounters requires that prospective teachers see how the new possibilities and perspectives address the inadequacies of former beliefs and images.

For the past 10 years we have been experimenting with ways to transform and extend our students' views of teaching and learning, schools and subject matter. Our experiences underscore the centrality and tenacity of prior beliefs in learning to teach. They also yield concrete ideas about ways to challenge and extend these beliefs and the sorts of pedagogical dilemmas that arise when teacher educators work toward this goal.

HISTORY AND CONTEXT

In 1980, Judy Lanier, then acting dean of the College of Education at Michigan State, asked a group of faculty to redesign TE-101, an introductory course required of all students entering the elementary teacher education program. Like other forward-looking colleges in the 1970s, MSU had instituted an early field experience course to help students decide whether they really wanted to be teachers. Students spent one day a week assisting teachers in a local elementary or middle school classroom and then met once a week on campus in sections to discuss the experience. Although arranging field placements for the 600 students who took the course every year posed a major challenge, over the years there emerged a cadre of loyal classroom teachers eager for an extra pair of hands and the chance to influence a future teacher. Despite their willingness to have students in their classrooms, the pitfalls of early field experience remained (Feiman-Nemser & Buchmann, 1986b).

In the early 1980s, Michigan State created four new thematic teacher education programs as alternatives to the existing program (Barnes, 1987). One program highlights the creation of classroom learning communities; a second focuses on conceptual teaching of academic subjects; a third emphasizes teaching in heterogeneous classrooms; and a fourth focuses on the teacher as decision maker. Designed by groups of faculty, each program offers a coordinated set of courses and field experiences to cohorts of students. The substantial clinical component in the alternative programs reduced the pressure for field experiences in the introductory course and gave us the opportunity to rethink what introducing students to teaching and learning might mean.

We thought that an introductory, undergraduate course should contribute to students' liberal and professional education and promote a view of teaching and learning to teach as serious intellectual work. We hoped to counter the expectation that education courses, particularly the 101 variety, offered meager intellectual fare. We also sought to broaden students' conception of relevant sources of knowledge in learning to teach, so they would make good use of their time at the university.

Believing that our students—mostly white, middle-class, females from small, homogeneous communities and highly conventional schools—would hold rather limited views of teaching and learning, we decided that the course should aim, first and foremost, to confront these beliefs. At the beginning, we had rather vague ideas about how to do this: We thought we would put students in touch with their own learning experiences by resurrecting memories of schooling, use the course itself to exemplify new roles for teachers and students, and make the familiar strange by having students study the culture of elementary school classrooms.

We had clearer ideas about the necessary structure. Although 500 to 600 students must take the course each year, we insisted that faculty reputed to be good teachers teach it in sections of no more than 25 students. Besides increasing the likelihood that the course would be well-taught, the involvement of strong faculty ensured a seriousness of purpose. Since then we have offered between five to eight sections of the course each quarter. About half of the sections are taught by faculty and half by advanced graduate students.

The second condition—small sections allowing for active participation and the exchange of ideas—was indispensable to the kind of liberal learning we wanted to promote. Schwab's (1954) observations on the role of discussion in liberal education provide an eloquent rationale for this requirement:

> Discussion in one form or another—with others or with one's self—is indispensable to a good liberal education. For in the last analysis, discussion is not merely a device, one of several possible means by which a mind may be brought to understanding of a worthwhile object. It is also the *experience* of moving toward and possessing understanding, and a liberal education is concerned with the arts and skills of understanding. (p. 54)

The first version of the course had a small field component. Students spent four days as participant-observers in an elementary classroom. Each time they went to the field, they completed an assignment that focused their attention on some aspect of classroom life (Florio-Ruane, 1989). After several years, we developed a version of the course that substitutes peer-teaching and analysis of videotapes and lesson transcripts for field experience. Except for Chapter 3, which describes a unique approach to the field, all chapters focus on some variation of that version. An example of a recent syllabus used by Feiman-Nemser and adapted by many other instructors can be found in the appendix.

As the following chapters reveal, individual instructors often change the course in major and minor ways. These range from reordering the focal questions to replacing a section of the course with a new assignment. Weekly staff meetings, shared goals, and a common pool of readings, assignments, and videotapes help ensure that the variations still serve the intended purposes of the course. Below we provide a general introduction to the course by describing the goals, content, and pedagogy.

THE TE-101 ALTERNATIVE

Goals

Exploring Teaching aims to challenge students' entering beliefs, to broaden their ideas and images of what teaching and learning in schools could be like, and to foster an inquiring disposition. In principle, these three goals complement one another. As students encounter new ideas and images of teaching, they are more likely to see the limitations of their initial beliefs and appreciate the value of keeping an open mind. In practice, however, they often pull us in opposite directions. On the one hand, we want students to ask their own questions and make their own connections. At the same time, we want to give students options for thinking about teaching and learning in new ways. This means helping them grasp the concept of "hidden curriculum" and "pedagogical content knowledge" or the differences between "knowledge reproduction" and "knowledge transformation." And so we often ask ourselves, in the limited time we have, is it more important to clarify the ideas students bring or the texts we supply? Should we follow the lead of students' questions or revisit vaguely understood concepts? In Chapter 10, we discuss some of the practical dilemmas that arise in trying to meet the goals of the course.

Content as a Network of Ideas

We organize TE-101 around three broad questions: What does it mean to teach? What are schools for? What do teachers need to know? These questions frame a set of issues we explore through personal reflection, analysis of case studies, and videotapes of classroom teaching, discussions, readings, simulations, and so on. Both the questions and the issues reflect our evolving picture of students' entering beliefs and the kind of intellectual foundation that will orient students to serious professional study.

What Does It Mean To Teach?   At the beginning of the course, most students think of teaching as a simple and straightforward activity that results in learning. Teachers teach; students learn. Teaching is telling. Learning is listening to what the teacher says and giving it back more or less intact. Accustomed to "frontal teaching" (Cuban, 1984) and subject-matter knowledge defined by textbooks, students often cannot imagine any other approach. And they see themselves as perpetuating this view. Describing the way she imagined herself as a teacher when she entered TE-101, this student speaks for many:

> I would be at the head of the class in front of a bunch of neatly aligned rows of students sitting at their desks. I would have gotten most of my ideas from the materials I remember using as an elementary student, for example, basal readers, SRAs, spelling books from levels A through H . . . I pictured myself meeting with separate groups for reading and math . . . I just thought that both teaching and student learning would come naturally.

The first question — "What does it mean to teach?" — invites students to consider the nature of teaching and its relationship to learning. How can one tell when teaching is occurring? Can there be teaching without learning? We pose these questions to highlight the reciprocal yet uncertain relationship between teaching and learning. We want students to understand that teaching means taking responsibility for pupils' learning. At the same time, we want them to appreciate that, from moment to moment, teachers cannot know with confidence whether they are teaching and their students learning.

To broaden students' understanding of teaching, we consider Jackson's (1986) description of two dominant traditions — knowledge reproduction and knowledge transformation. According to Jackson, when teachers treat knowledge as a commodity to be transferred to students, they test to find out whether pupils can reproduce it more or less faithfully. When teachers treat knowledge as something learners construct for themselves, they ask questions to help pupils transform knowledge to fit prior understandings and experience or revise their prior knowledge to fit their new understandings. This distinction helps our students realize that teachers have different purposes which, in turn, shape their practice.

We also read David Hawkins's (1967/1974) essay, "I, Thou, and It," which presents a model of the relationship of teacher, learner, and subject matter. According to Hawkins, worthwhile subject matter provides the common meeting ground for teachers and students. Whereas parents "love" their children, good teachers "respect" their students as potential artisans of their own learning. Such teachers create rich learning environments to engage students' interests and then intervene appropriately to support, deepen, and extend their learning. Hawkins challenges our students' assumption that loving children is reason enough to want to teach and forces them to consider the centrality of subject matter in teaching.

What Are Schools For?   The second organizing question focuses on teaching as a form of work carried out in a particular institutional setting, the U.S. public school. Typically our students have given little thought to the contexts of teaching — either the larger societal context or the features of communities, schools, and classrooms — and their impact on teaching and learning. To help them begin to appreciate how these contexts influence what teachers do and what they ought to do, we explore three issues — the purposes of schooling, the policies and practices of ability grouping and tracking, and the hidden curriculum.

The multiple and often conflicting purposes that society holds for schools complicate the work of teachers. Rising expectations about what schools should do and the failure of policymakers and parents to establish clear priorities increase teachers' uncertainties about what to teach and their vulnerability to criticism (Goodlad, 1984). Glimpsing these larger issues broadens students' conception of their role and lays the groundwork for them to consider the relationship between school and society.

Ability grouping and tracking offer compelling examples of how school practices embody societal expectations. Beginning early in the century, these organizational arrangements evolved to address the diversity of pupils swept into public schools by the tide of immigration. While tracking and ability grouping may simplify the work of teachers and administrators, in practice they ensure that pupils encounter quite different knowledge (Goodlad, 1984; Cohen, 1984; Oakes, 1986a, 1986b). Many parents and teachers believe that ability grouping and tracking enable schools to address the individual needs of each child, but researchers like Goodlad (1984) and Oakes (1986a, 1986b) raise questions about the purposes these practices actually serve. Their assertions shock most of our students, who have grown up with these practices and tend to take them for granted.

Jackson's (1968) analysis of the "hidden curriculum" of schools also opens students' eyes to features of classrooms they have never considered—to the fact that teachers and pupils must manage a space that is crowded, an environment that is explicitly and implicitly evaluative, and relationships that are characterized by the uneven distribution of power. In TE-101, students examine for the first time the interaction between the official curriculum and the way teachers manage "crowds, praise, and power"—the norms and expectations that govern life in classrooms.

What Do Teachers Need To Know?   When we ask students why they want to teach, they are much more likely to cite their love of children than their love of learning. To stimulate thinking about preparing to teach and to influence the way students approach courses in both education and arts and sciences, we explore the nature and variety of teacher knowledge and the role that this knowledge plays in generating instructional representations. For example, we introduce the distinction between "content knowledge" and "pedagogical content knowledge" (Wilson, Shulman, & Richert, 1987). Content knowledge encompasses central concepts, modes of inquiry, and standards of evidence in a given field, whereas pedagogical content knowledge includes the examples, demonstrations, metaphors, and analogies teachers generate to explain critical concepts and their interrelationships. We also consider what teachers need to know about learners—their culture, interests, prior experience with subject matter—to create appropriate representations of subject matter.

Pedagogy

Although different people teach the course differently, there are some common elements in the pedagogy of TE-101. These include an emphasis on discussion and the use of cases in conjunction with theoretical readings. In a real sense, the pedagogy is also part of the content of the course. To enhance students' understandings of key concepts and ideas, we often focus on their experiences as learners (and teachers) in the course.

Discussion.   A central feature of liberal learning, discussion plays a critical role in TE-101. Because we want students to become active learners, we work hard to create a classroom learning community where they can make public and personal meaning through reading and writing, speaking and listening. Often this requires instructors to model and coach intellectual skills that are not well developed in our undergraduate students. In their chapters Tom Bird and Margery Osborne describe efforts to cultivate such skills.

To increase participation and provide opportunities to clarify thinking and rehearse ideas, we frequently have students work in small groups as a prelude to whole-class discussions. Over the years we have experimented with different ways to form and structure these groups. For example, we used to vary the composition from meeting to meeting but found that permanent groups tend to build a level of trust and work more productively over time. Although the advantages of group work seem to outweigh the disadvantages, we puzzle about the tendency of groups to avoid disagreements and seek consensus. (See Chapter 10 for a discussion of this point.)

The expectation that students will reveal their uncertainties, explain and defend their ideas, and pose their own questions often intimidates students used to sitting passively and listening to the teacher. In their chapters, Suzanne Wilson and Tom Bird examine some of the problems that arise when instructors ask "good" students to function as active and collaborative learners.

Connecting Cases and Theoretical Readings.   Many of the discussions center around cases of school teaching drawn from a variety of sources. These cases serve as a stimulus, drawing out students' beliefs for examination and reflection. Because many of the cases portray kinds of classrooms that our students have not experienced, they also expand ideas and images of what teaching could be like. Finally, the cases provide a concrete vocabulary for clarifying personal beliefs and a context for exploring and illustrating concepts from the readings. In Chapter 5, Linda Tiezzi and Michelle Parker describe the teaching and learning surrounding our use of cases.

Cases of unconventional teaching will not by themselves alter beliefs. Because students also need new ways of thinking about these teachers and their work, we study the cases in conjunction with theoretical and empirical readings. What would Hawkins (1967/ 1974) say about Paley's teaching? Do you think that Leslie Stein is more interested in "knowledge reproduction" or "knowledge transformation" (Jackson, 1986)? What different kinds of knowledge does Herb Kohl (1984) draw on in teaching *MacBeth* to 7- to 10-year-olds? Puzzling together over such questions, students begin to make sense of key concepts and to see specific instances of teaching in new ways.

Reflections on Personal Learning.   We also ask students to write and talk about the teaching and learning they experience in TE-101. When Suzanne Wilson asks, "Did I teach today?" (see Chapter 7), she is challenging her students to connect an argument about the nature of teaching with their immediate experiences as learners. On days when Suzanne talks a lot, the students are more likely to say "yes"; on days when the class simulates a school board meeting, they are not so sure.

To help students explore new aspects of teaching and learning, some instructors have developed projects that involve students in learning and then teaching new content. In the permutations project (Chapter 2) and the moon project (Chapter 4), students construct their own understanding of unfamiliar material, then try to explain and represent it to someone else, and, finally, write about these experiences. These projects make vivid and concrete many of the "big ideas" explored in the course.

The chapters that follow illustrate how the goals, content, and pedagogy come together to create particular kinds of learning opportunities for beginning teacher education students. But TE-101 is more than an introductory education course. It is also a practicum site for preparing future teacher educators and a laboratory for all of us to study teacher learning and the pedagogy of teacher education.

THE LEARNING COMMUNITY OF EXPLORING
TEACHING TEACHERS

Over the past 10 years, TE-101 has evolved continually as new instructors have joined the staff, and we have learned more about our students and our subject matter. Weekly staff meetings provide a forum for discussing readings and assignments, sharing ideas and dilemmas, refining our goals, and deepening our understanding of how the various elements of the course contribute to one another.

Learning From Teaching

Common problems encountered in teaching TE-101 force us to examine what we are doing and to consider alternatives. Over the years, both individually and as a group, we have made various changes in the course based on our collective teaching experience. We have also generated knowledge about students' entering beliefs and their likely reactions to particular issues, questions, and assignments. Passed on to new staff, this knowledge helps us plan more effectively.

Changing the Questions. We designed the first revision of TE-101 around the following questions: Why do I want to teach? What is teaching like? What are schools for? The sequence reflected an underlying logic. First students would look inward, analyzing their reasons for wanting to teach. In the process, they would begin to uncover and articulate their assumptions about teaching. To help students test those assumptions, we placed them in classrooms as participant/observers where they tried to find out how teachers thought about their practice and how students experienced school learning. Finally, we tried to set classroom teaching in a broader context by raising questions about the multiple and conflicting purposes of schooling.

For their first assignment, students wrote a letter to someone they knew explaining their reasons for wanting to teach and for thinking that teaching suited them. Many students said that they wanted to teach because they liked being around children. Few mentioned a love of learning or a desire to get students excited about a particular subject. Some said they were pursuing a teaching career against the wishes of their parents or friends. Others wrote that parents and friends considered them a "natural."

Having invited students to express their personal beliefs, we worried about how to respond to these limited views of teaching. It seemed unfair to criticize them; in addition, we suspected that too much probing or questioning so early in the course might discourage participation. On the other hand, we wanted students to appreciate that, in teaching, "love is not enough."

After several years, we decided to change the first focal question from "Why do I want to teach?" to "What does it mean to teach?" in order to put the emphasis on underlying views of teaching. To challenge students' thinking about the importance of "loving students as learners," we added the Hawkins (1967/1974) essay that argues that parents love their children but teachers need to "respect" students as "artisans of their own learning." We also introduced a focal question about what teachers need to know. These curricular changes grew out of our experiences with the course. They also reflected changes in the field such as renewed interest in teachers' subject-matter preparation.

Generating Knowledge. Like all teachers, we have also learned a lot about how our students think about teaching and how they are likely to respond to particular readings, cases, and questions. For instance, when we read excerpts from *Wally's Stories*, we expect some students to argue that Paley is irresponsible for "allowing" her pupils to continue believing that stones melt. When we view a videotape of Maggie Lampert's fifth-grade class discussing the meaning of two graphs, we expect that some students will question why she permits the discussion to go on for so long. We anticipate these reactions because our students generally believe that good teachers tell students what they need to know and correct their mistakes or misconceptions. Similarly we know that students will most likely substitute their own ideas about "respect" for Hawkins's ideas. They will also need help in constructing their own arguments about the meaning of teaching, the purposes of schooling, and the pitfalls of experience in learning to teach.

Learning From and With Each Other

Exploring Teaching is a popular practicum site for doctoral students in teacher education. Out of a total of 8 to 10 sections each quarter, about half are taught by graduate students. Before taking over a section, each graduate student spends a term observing and talking with a more experienced 101 teacher about the goals, content, and pedagogy of the course. In Chapter 8, Sue McMahon

describes her apprenticeship with Suzanne Wilson. The regular in-
duction of new staff creates a steady source of new ideas. It also
forces veterans to reflect continually on their practice in order to
explain how and why they treat particular readings, manage specific
activities, anticipate and respond to students' comments or questions
in certain ways.

The fact that we are all teachers with experiences to share
makes us a community of equals. Good ideas-in-use have their own
authority. Professors learn as much from graduate students as graduate students learn from professors. For example, Margery Osborne's success in fostering thoughtful discourse in small groups
persuaded most of her colleagues to try assigning students to permanent groups at the beginning of the course (see Chapter 6).

At the same time, the meetings can be difficult. We continually
struggle against the tendency for those with more power and status
to dominate. And because some people are teaching TE-101 for the
first time while others have years of experience under their belts,
needs and interests vary widely. We vacillate between helping novices to survive and addressing the concerns of more experienced
instructors. When the agendas merge, which often happens, we all
become teachers and learners.

We recently had such an experience when, at the request of
the TE-101 staff, Dennis Gray (1989), a visiting educator interested
in "Socratic" seminars, led a seminar on Hawkins's (1967/1974) essay "I, Thou, and It." Because of our common interest in teaching
through discussion, we wanted to experience Gray's approach firsthand. Although we do not all adopt a "Socratic" stance in our teaching of TE-101, we certainly share the goal of "enlarging understanding" that Gray associates with his version of "Socratic seminars."

> Adding to students' storehouses of information and organized
> knowledge is not the main purpose of seminars, although such
> byproducts are certainly common. Nor is the purpose of semi-
> nars to add muscle to the skills of learning, although seminars
> do give strenuous practice in close reading, careful listening,
> clear speaking, and precise thinking. Understanding the intellec-
> tual complexities of important ideas demands ever-growing
> knowledge and skills to be sure, but enlarged understanding
> remains the primary goal of seminars. (p. 17)

On the day of the seminar, 12 participants, including faculty
and graduate students, veterans, and novices at teaching TE-101
gathered around a large table, copies of the text in hand. Gray

opened the discussion with the question: "What are some synonyms for 'I,' 'thou,' and 'it?'?" Listening hard, he followed each answer with a question, allowing time for speakers to reflect and to seek support from the text. One question led us down a path none of us had ever considered: "When we draw the I-Thou-It triangle, does it matter what we put on top?" A newcomer to our group argued persuasively that the "it" should be at the top so that the "I" and the "thou" (or teacher and student) would be on the same plane. This new interpretation truly enlarged our understanding of this central text, suggesting new issues to explore with our own students. We closed with a critique of the seminar itself—the pace of the discussion, the uneven pattern of participation, the fact that participants had differential knowledge of the text, the question of whether such occasions favor people with certain intellectual propensities.

The seminar offered new readings of a core essay and raised fascinating questions both about pedagogy and about our learning community. It reminded us, as we undertook final revisions on this volume, that as long as we teach the course, we shall continue to explore the curriculum and pedagogy of Exploring Teaching.

2

The Permutations Project: Mathematics as a Context for Learning About Teaching

Deborah Loewenberg Ball

Recently, teacher educators and policymakers have been raising a host of questions about what teachers need to know in order to "teach for understanding" to a diverse student population — and about how prospective teachers can best learn those things (Kennedy, 1991). The discourse has focused mainly on the subject-matter preparation of teachers (Ball & McDiarmid, 1990; Carnegie Task Force, 1986; Holmes Group, 1986; Shulman, 1986). However, the essential challenge of preservice teacher education is, of course, to find ways to help prospective teachers develop both subject-matter understandings and pedagogical vision, knowledge and skills. We also need to learn to help them learn to interweave these kinds of knowledge (Ball, 1988a; Feiman-Nemser & Buchmann, 1986b; Shulman, 1987; Wilson et al., 1987). To do this we must design and try out multiple arrangements for combining, imaginatively, opportunities for learning about subject matter and learning about pedagogy. In this chapter I describe my effort to use mathematics as a context for learning about teaching and learning how to teach.

I have developed a sequence of activities related to the mathematics of permutations that I use in my section of Exploring Teaching. In order to help prospective teachers examine their assumptions about teaching, learning, and learning to teach, I chose mathematics as the subject matter precisely because so many prospective elementary teachers dislike it and dread teaching it. It seemed ideal because they were likely to have brought considerable "baggage" with them about mathematics and about how it is taught and learned, and about themselves in relation to mathematics, based on their past experiences with it. As such, I thought it would provide a fertile ground for their inquiry.

Based on the literature on precollege and college mathematics teaching and learning (Schoenfeld, 1983), research on prospective teachers (Ball, 1988a; Kalaian & Freeman, 1988), and my own experience as a mathematics student, elementary teacher, and staff developer, I made some predictions about what prospective teachers might already know, think, believe, and feel. These predictions guided the development of the unit. I focused on permutations because I expected that many elementary teacher education students would never have studied it formally; consequently, they could engage genuinely as learners in the activities. If they had previously encountered the concept in a mathematics class, their understanding was likely to be procedural (Hiebert, 1986); that is, they would know to "use the formula" (i.e., calculate a factorial).

I predicted that students might believe the following:

- Mathematics does not have much relationship to the real world. Mathematics primarily involves manipulating symbols; story problems are a pain.
- Knowing mathematics means knowing "how to do it." If someone gets the right answer, that is evidence that they know it.
- Teaching mathematics involves telling or showing students how to do different kinds of problems.
- Teachers ask questions to elicit the correct answers. If a teacher questions your answer, it means you have done something wrong.
- Good teachers try to make mathematics *fun* for students.
- Elementary school mathematics teaching does not require much knowledge of math—anyone who can add, subtract, multiply, and divide knows enough mathematics to teach little kids. Learning to teach, therefore, is mainly a matter of acquiring techniques.
- Love of children, not knowledge of subject matter, is the basis of elementary school teaching.
- Young children are trusting and eager to learn but are not yet capable of thinking about complicated mathematical ideas or solving real problems.

- I do not like mathematics, it makes me anxious, and I have never been good at it. I just don't have a "mathematical mind."

I designed the content, activities, and approaches of the unit to bring these and other ideas to the surface for examination and analysis.

CONTENT AND ACTIVITIES

The unit extends over 2 weeks, including four 1½-hour class sessions and additional out-of-class work. Over the course of the project, the prospective teachers first learn about permutations themselves, then observe me help a young child explore the concept, and finally try their hand at helping someone else (child or adult) learn about permutations. During each of the phases of the project, I encourage them to pay close attention to what they are thinking, doing, and feeling.

Three readings accompany the unit. The first, an essay by David Hawkins (1967/1974) entitled "I, Thou, and It," highlights the distinctive relationship that teachers have with students around subject matter. According to Hawkins, the teacher's role is to respect students' thinking and to provide a "feedback loop" that helps pupils to construct knowledge and understanding for themselves. The prospective teachers also read Herbert Kohl's (1984) *Growing Minds: On Becoming a Teacher* and an excerpt from Vivian Paley's (1981) *Wally's Stories*. Paley and Kohl illustrate the centrality of subject-matter knowledge in teaching and the importance of respecting children's thinking. Both also show how, when seen through children's eyes, adult assumptions about the reasonableness of subject matter often prove insufficient (Hawkins, 1967/1974).

Phase One: Learning

For the first two class periods, the students participate as learners of mathematics. As a teacher, I try to pique their curiosity by challenging them to make sense of the fact that the 25 students in our class could sit in 1,551,121,000,000,000,000,000,000 *different* seating arrangements.[1] I explain: If they switched seats steadily every 10 seconds, trying to make all these arrangements, it would take them almost 5 quintillion years. This demonstrates the absolute incomprehensibility of these numbers. The class backs up to 15, or even 10 people, hoping that smaller numbers will result in a more manageable number of seating arrangements.

These smaller numbers still yield an amazing number of possibilities (e.g., even just 10 people can be seated in 3,682,000 *different* arrangements — 10! = 10 × 9 × 8 × 7 × 6 × 5 × 4 × 3 × 2 × 1 = 3,628,800).* In order to try to understand what is going on, next we explore the concept from the simplest cases, starting with just two people, and then three and four. In some classes we act out the problem by setting up chairs in a row and having people move around in the seats until everyone is satisfied that all possible arrangements have been formed. In other classes students have used symbols and manipulated the arrangements on paper: ABC, ACB, BAC, BCA, CAB, CBA. Sometimes I introduce objects — such as Cuisenaire rods — that they can use to represent the situation concretely. The discussion is often lively and students propose a variety of explanations and ideas. I solicit alternative approaches and ask questions such as, "Do you see a pattern here?" or, "Why are you multiplying those numbers?" My purposes are twofold: to make them come to see what they *do not* understand and to encourage them to talk about what they think is going on in order to help them understand permutations for themselves.

For homework, I distribute a set of varied problems and ask the students to try the problems with two goals in mind: to extend their own understanding of permutations and to pay attention to the role the homework plays in their learning — how they tackle it, how they feel about it, and why. In class, we discuss the problems and the students' thoughts about them. Some problems parallel what we have done in class — for example: "How many ways are there to arrange four books on a shelf?" Others require the students to extend the ideas explored in class: calculating the chances of holding the winning number in a lottery, for instance. Some students become frustrated because they cannot immediately plug in a formula and get the answer; they want me to tell them what to do or to verify that what they are doing is right. Instead, I ask them questions — for example: "What does what you have written down here — 5,040 — mean in the context of this problem?" When I encourage them to collaborate with other students, some are annoyed; they

---

*The notation that mathematicians use for the factorial is !. In other words, 4! (read "four factorial") represents 4 × 3 × 2 × 1. Many calculators have a ! button. If you press 7, followed by !, the calculator will compute 7 × 6 × 5 × 4 × 3 × 2 × 1, which is the number of orders in which seven objects can be arranged.

confront their assumptions that the *teacher* is supposed to *teach*—that is, to tell them what to do. I expect them to explain and justify their solutions; in their past mathematics classes getting a number from using the formula had been enough. As we discuss the problems, many students are completely astonished to discover the variety of approaches that people have taken to solve the problems: They explain that they have always assumed that in mathematics there is just one right answer, one approach. We discuss the role played in their learning by the homework problems and the rationale for their various types and design.

Over these two class periods, most students gradually figure out the pattern of permutations and develop some understanding of its underlying logic. Still, some students feel very tense, even though how well they "get it" has no bearing on their course grade. Every term, two or three students who have taken more mathematics than the rest think they understand the concept and try to explain it to their classmates. These students are surprised to discover that this is much more difficult to do than they realized, and they stumble. They draw diagrams that make sense only to them, they give explanations that no one can follow, they find themselves repeating things louder and louder in vain attempts to get their classmates to see things as they do. As one student wrote later, "I tried to present my theory in hopes of helping the rest of the class, but as my mouth opened, I found it very difficult to put into words what came easily to mind."

Phase Two: Observing Learning and Teaching

During the next phase of the project students get another view of learning and teaching mathematics by observing me helping a young child explore permutations. The children I have brought to class have ranged between 6 and 9 years of age and, although the context may sound intimidating, all the children have been remarkably relaxed and have talked aloud freely about their theories and ways of thinking about the problems.* I use several different repre-

---

*Some terms I have had the students observe me work with a whole class of elementary school children—usually third grade—in the elementary school where I teach. This alternative has trade-offs: On one hand, the teacher candidates have an opportunity to observe the topic being taught and learned in a real classroom in which children may learn through discourse with one another. On the other hand, the classroom context adds "noise" and maintaining a clear focus on learning and on the teacher's role in helping someone else learn is more difficult.

sentations with the children (e.g., lining people up; forming two-, three-, and four-digit numerals; ways of distributing candy to friends*) and model the same kind of teaching that I used with teacher education students. I ask questions to help the child develop his or her ideas about possible choices and arrangements of objects. As they watch, the prospective teachers pay attention to my interactions with the child; what kinds of representations I select and how these are structured and why; and the child's thinking—what he or she is doing and saying. Many of the students think further about the subject matter, and several have reported later that it is during this period that they learned the most about the pattern and logic of permutations.

Before the class ends, the prospective teachers have an opportunity to ask questions of the child. Some ask about particular things the child said or did, trying to understand more clearly what he or she might have been thinking. Others try to ask about the concept in some other way to see how the child is understanding it. Still others ask how the child felt about the experience. Many of the students find it very difficult to frame their ideas as questions; instead, they lead. For instance, trying to get a sense of how the child reacted to different kinds of tasks, one student asked 6-year-old Rachel, "Don't you think it was easier to do it with candy bars than with blocks?" In the next class the students discuss this observation, exploring both the teaching and the learning that occurred. They talk about what they saw as they watched the child and what they thought about it. They ask me questions about things I did or said, and together we analyze the choices I made.

Phase Three: Teaching

In the final stage of the project, the students take on the role of teacher and try to help someone else explore the concept of permutations. Some choose children, others work with their roommates or parents. We spend some time in class, usually in small groups, discussing preparations for this. Many try to model their approach after what they have seen me do with the child; others draw on what helped *them* understand the concept.

Afterwards, as teachers, they discuss what they learned about

---

*For example: You have one Hershey bar, one bag of M&Ms, and one Sugar Daddy. How many different choices do you have if you want to give one piece of candy to each of two friends and yourself?

their learner, about the subject matter, and about teaching. Many report how strong their inclination was to tell their learners "the answer" instead of helping them to construct their own understandings. Others confront the limits of their own knowledge and the effect of that lack on their effectiveness as teachers.

To conclude the project, students write a paper entitled a "Case Study of Teaching and Learning" in which they integrate their experiences across these different experiences. Although they can construct this case study in any way they choose, I ask them to include their experiences both as learner and teacher and to draw some tentative conclusions about mathematics, about the teaching and learning of mathematics, and about learning to teach.

PROSPECTIVE TEACHERS' RESPONSES TO THE PERMUTATIONS PROJECT

Students' writing about the permutations project has provided me with valuable glimpses of what prospective elementary teachers know and believe when they enter teacher education. It has also helped me expand my own understandings of the pedagogical possibilities and pitfalls in teacher education. The experience in the permutations project appears to challenge successfully some of the ideas that prospective teachers bring to TE-101. It has helped them to recognize and, then, to question their assumptions. Their papers provide windows onto the ideas and ways of thinking they bring and onto the changes some of them have begun to make.* They show them reassessing their ideas about mathematics, about teaching and learning, and about themselves.

Subject-Matter Understandings: Mathematics

For some of the students, a powerful aspect of the experience is confronting their own knowledge and feelings about mathematics. This experience is unusual: Facing off with subject matter is not typical in preservice teacher education. Teacher educators tend to take prospective teachers' subject-matter knowledge for granted, fo-

---

*Quotations in this paper are drawn from papers written by elementary teacher education students at the conclusion of the permutations project over four terms during the academic years 1985–86 and 1987–88.

cusing instead on pedagogical knowledge and skills (Ball & Feiman-Nemser, 1988). Similarly, many prospective elementary teachers assume that "common sense and memories of their own schooling will supply the subject matter needed to teach young children" (Feiman-Nemser & Buchmann, 1986a, p. 245). In the permutations project, many of the teacher education students discover that there is more to understanding subject matter than they assumed. Frequently they comment on the difference between knowing a rule or formula and *understanding*. For example, one student wrote:

> I learned the method of using factorials to figure out permutations, but I still cannot explain fully why we use multiplication instead of another numeration [*sic*].

And another reflected that she "found out that knowing a formula and understanding it are two different things." For many of the prospective teachers, knowing math had always meant being able to produce the answer the teacher wanted, paying scant attention to *why* the algorithms worked, as one student indicated:

> I'm learning about mathematics in this class. . . . Math isn't just memorizing formulas — it is knowing *why* a problem is done the way it is. . . . In high school, [it was] memorizing formulas, theorems, and definitions.

Confronting this new way of knowing was not always easy for the students, especially for those who had been successful in school. One explained:

> I have always been a good math student, so not understanding this concept was very frustrating to me. One thing I realized was that in high school we never learned the theories behind our arithmetic. We just used the formulas and carried out the problem solving. For instance, the way I learned permutations was just to use the factorial of the number and carry out the multiplication. . . . We never had to learn the concepts, we just did the problems with a formula. If you are only multiplying to get the answer every time, permutations could appear to be very easy. If you ask yourself *why* do we multiply and really try to understand the concept, then it may be very confusing as it was to me.

Another prospective teacher reflected that although she had always enjoyed math, she now realized that she had "learned to understand mathematics by memorizing formulas . . . [and had been] conditioned to looking for formulas instead of the processes to obtain the answers."

These comments suggest that, besides knowledge *of* the subject, prospective teachers also bring ideas of what mathematics *is* — what it is about, what it is good for, what knowledge is and where it comes from, as well as how right answers are established — that shape their understanding of and approach to the subject.

These insights about subject-matter knowledge and understanding typically emerge from the prospective teachers' efforts to help others understand. They discover that they cannot see the subject matter from someone else's perspective, nor figure out alternative ways to guide or respond. One student concluded,

> When I decided to be a teacher, I knew there were a lot of things I had to learn about teaching, but I felt I knew everything there was to teach my students, until we began our permutations project. During the permutations activities, I found I was as much a learner of subject matter as I was a learner of the art of teaching. . . . I found that my education in the future will not be limited to "how to teach," but what it is I'm teaching. My knowledge of math must improve drastically if I'm to teach effectively.

***What Does It Mean To Know Mathematics For* Teaching?**   For some students, the experience of learning permutations themselves challenged their prior ideas about knowledge. Others, who felt comfortable with their understanding during the learner phase, became unsettled when they tried to teach the concept of permutations to another person. For example, one wrote:

> I was trying to teach my mother permutations. But it turned out to be a disaster. I understood permutations enough for *myself*, but when it came time to teach it, I realized that I didn't understand it as well as I thought I did. Mom asked me questions I couldn't answer. Like the question about there being four items and four positions and why it wouldn't be $4 \times 4 = 16$. She threw me with that one and I think we lost it for good there.

One student, who had been very active in class during the learner phase, analyzed a difficulty she had encountered:

> I was trying to explain my understanding of [permutations] to those who did not yet understand. I had to keep rearranging my perspective, that is, approach the idea from different angles in order to try to present the concept in a way that would help others understand it. The problem was that I could not see what link was missing. . . . My understanding of it was so straightforward and simple that I didn't know how else to approach it. I was not able to articulate the concept in a way that increased their understanding. . . . I understood the material and found myself searching for the phrase or diagram that would make it as self-evident for them as it was for me.

During this teaching phase, many of the prospective teachers realize that subject-matter understanding for teaching may be different from that needed for personal use. They often characterize this distinction as the difference between knowing permutations "for yourself" and knowing permutations to be able to help someone else learn it. This distinction grows out of the requirements of teaching, as one student commented:

> There isn't a universal explanation [for permutations]. We needed many different versions; different people understood different examples. . . . You really have to know your subject matter well enough to be able to play around with it. If you can only give one explanation, many of your students won't understand. . . . If you know your subject matter well (inside and out), it is easier to find different explanations and examples. You can't be tied down to just one way of doing a problem.

Teaching and Learning

As the prospective teachers' comments about mathematics indicate, they also come to teacher education with ideas about mathematics teaching and learning. For several of the teacher education students, the permutations project challenged their conception of what it means to *teach* as well as what it means to *learn*. Many brought an image of math teaching in which the teacher "tells knowledge" and asks questions to check up on students. Commenting on my teaching, one student observed, "It seemed strange to me that you asked us *why* we multiply. Whenever I have been taught mathematics, I was never asked why. I was always just told to multiply."

The prospective teachers started to see that questions could be a valuable tool if learners were to discover or create understanding for themselves. One student wrote:

> By the end of our time together, I had learned not only how valuable questions were to teaching, but I realized that how I asked them and when I asked them made a big difference. I started to get a feel for when to let Joni talk herself into a circle, and when frustration would back her into a corner and I should help her. I could steer her with the word "Why?" and although it was very subtle, it made her look deeper. How exciting! All I did was help Joni to find a few doors, and she could do the opening all by herself.

Related to this was the issue of confusion and the teacher's responsibility for teaching. This same student noted that "a certain amount of frustration" was productive; others noted the feeling of satisfaction they had from having worked out their "stuckness" — previous math teachers had always *given* them "the formula."

Many of the prospective teachers are astonished when they observe the young child in class. They want to know if the child is "gifted" because they cannot believe that a 6- or an 8-year-old can think or reason in this way. Their surprise reveals their assumptions about young children's capacity to reason and make sense; the experience of observing a young child provokes some of them to revise their thinking:

> One thing I noticed from watching Rachel is that children are good thinkers. Teaching isn't just to tell children what you know and expect them to learn it. We tend to think of children as a clean slate [and] the teacher's role is to fill up this so-called slate.

The permutations project also seems to challenge some students to reexamine their assumptions about *themselves* as learners. For example, one student remarked, "Most of all, I realized that I *do* have the ability to learn mathematics when it is taught in a thoughtful way."

Feelings About Oneself as a Knower and
Learner of the Subject Matter

Although some prospective elementary teachers enjoy and feel competent in math, many have had negative experiences with mathematics and they do not feel successful as learner of math. Most are women: We should not be surprised that they feel as they do about mathematics, given what we know about girls' experiences in school mathematics. As teacher educators, however, we ought to worry about their bringing these feelings about themselves with them to teacher education. One student reported that she felt "very insecure" at the beginning of the permutations project, explaining, "Math, in whatever form, has always come in a painstakingly slow manner and scenes from Math 108 and Accounting 201 seem always to haunt me." A second told me later, "When you told the class that we were going to be using math for the next project, I froze — my palms got sweaty, and I didn't hear anything you said for the rest of that hour." A third wrote, most graphically:

Armed with a pencil as my sword and paper as my shield, I was thrust into the conflict, sent to meet the threatening foe face to face. Math was the enemy to be conquered. Against incredible odds, I prepared for the task. The teacher clearly stated the goal: I was to attempt to achieve an understanding of permutations. Panic settled quickly as I recalled how uncomfortable and incompetent I was when it came to mathematics.

Teacher educators need to acknowledge these feelings in exploring what prospective teachers bring with them to their formal preparation to teach, as such feelings affect what students learn from teacher education. For example, one said afterwards,

[I] got lost . . . got nowhere [and] did not enjoy the permutations activities because I was transported in time back to junior high school, where I remember mathematics as confusing and aggravating. Then, as now, the explanations seemed to fly by me in a whirl of disassociated numbers and words.

This student's emotional reaction to the subject affected her engagement in the experience. What does this promise for her first experiences as a teacher of elementary mathematics? Confronting and beginning to untangle this reaction is critical to helping her become prepared to teach math. Designing such projects in other subject areas — science, writing, or history, for example — will undoubtedly bring to the surface related reactions among other prospective elementary teachers.

REFLECTIONS ON THE PERMUTATIONS PROJECT: LEARNING FROM TEACHING

The permutations project has provided a fruitful context for my students to begin reconsidering some things they had firmly believed or assumed — about teaching, learning, and children, about learning to teach, and about themselves. For some, it has been an occasion to connect experiences of learning with their hopes for teaching. For others, it has provided an eye-opening glimpse of young children's competence. Others have become aware of some of their own tendencies and habits and began wondering about those. For example, during the teaching phase of the permutations project, some of the prospective teachers became aware of their strong inclination to *tell*. Although they wanted to let their learners figure things out for themselves, many of them found it difficult not to jump in and do it for them. Although they were, in principle, convinced that they should help students *understand* math and not just tell them, "This is the way to do it," some discovered that "teaching for understanding" is tough. Because they did not learn mathematics this way when they were in school, they found themselves falling back on rules and algorithm rhymes. They began to wonder about what they would need to learn in order to be able to act on commitments to teach meaningfully.

Herein lies a danger inherent in using mathematics — or perhaps any subject matter — as context. My students leave TE-101 recognizing for the first time that their anxiety with mathematics is due, at least in part, to the way in which they were taught. They realize that they are not incapable of learning mathematics, and they take pleasure in this new-found discovery, as women and as prospective teachers. Yet they also feel frustrated, for now they would like to learn some mathematics. Convinced that they will need to understand mathematics differently from the ways in which it was proffered to them, they ask me what to take. Few courses exist that can open up mathematics to them in the ways they need and deserve. I feel as though I have helped them open a door that leads nowhere, and I am frustrated too.

A second danger is embedded in helping prospective teachers see young children's inventiveness and intelligence. On one hand, this is wonderful and they are struck with the children's ingenuity and brightness. They begin to see that they may have underestimated children and this is exciting. On the other hand, it is also scary. If children are this smart, some of my students worry, how will I ever be prepared to teach them? The children seem at times to learn more quickly, to grasp ideas that confuse and intimidate the prospective teachers. Florio-Ruane and Lensmire (1990) report from their experiences in a writing methods course that prospective teachers were delighted to learn to see children as writers. The children's competence with their written texts was engaging. I am not sure that close encounters with children's mathematical sophistication affect my students so positively.

A third danger, one that also embeds the first two, rests with trying to make learning to teach look too complex. Some students think they are ready to teach, like one who wrote at the beginning of TE-101, "I think I could step into a high school classroom and teach. I enjoy talking and things like that . . . I don't think I'll have any problem." Students like this one do need to begin to see practice as more complicated and learning to teach more involved. Still, making it seem too complicated and uncertain may leave students feeling discouraged and overwhelmed (see Floden & Clark, 1988, on dealing with dilemmas of representing uncertainty in teacher education).

As teacher educators, what are next steps we might take in thinking about the potential of using subject matter as a context for learning about teaching? It would be interesting to experiment with units similar to the permutation project, but using other subject matters. For instance, a project involving U.S. history might help prospective teachers begin to locate their assumptions about diverse people's experiences of and participation in American society. Questions of "fact" in history might also be productive for rethinking assumptions about knowledge. And taken-for-granted faith in texts might also be challenged in this context. We could undoubtedly construct other fruitful possibilities in science or literature, each of which might offer other potential terrains for beginning professional preparation for teaching. The moon project (see Chapter 4) is exemplary of such a unit. Each subject matter might offer different possibilities in dealing with the dangers I sense alongside the promise. Continuing conversation about the balance between success and risk will also contribute in important ways to our growing repertoire and understanding.

NOTE

1. *Permutations deals* with the mathematics of combinations: specifically, the number of distinct orders in which a set of objects can be arranged. For example, if the set consists of two numerals—5 and 7—then there are *two* unique arrangements possible: 57 and 75. With three numerals—5, 7, and 9—*six* arrangements are possible: 957, 975, 759, 795, 579, 597. Notice that these six arrangements are formed by placing one number in the first position (the hundreds place) and then switching the other two around. The number of permutations of three objects can be described as 3 × 2 (because there are three objects, each of which can be placed in the hundreds place for two "turns" while the other two are switched around. With four—5, 7, 9, 1—the four numerals can be placed in the first position (now the thousands place) while the other three numerals are switched around. Thus, you have 4 × 6 because there are six ways to rearrange three objects.

This is all fine, and it probably makes sense, but the problem is that, in order to calculate the number of permutations of a given set of objects, you would always have to know the number of permutations for the previous number of objects. For example, to figure out how many arrangements there are for eight objects, you would need to know how many there are for seven and then multiply that times eight. To get around this, the mathematics of combinations is helpful here. Consider the tree diagram for three objects:

$$
\begin{array}{lll}
& \diagup\, \text{B}-\text{C} & \text{ABC} \\
\text{A} & & \\
& \diagdown\, \text{C}-\text{B} & \text{ACB} \\
\\
& \diagup\, \text{A}-\text{C} & \text{BAC} \\
\text{B} & & \\
& \diagdown\, \text{C}-\text{A} & \text{BCA} \\
\\
& \diagup\, \text{A}-\text{B} & \text{CAB} \\
\text{C} & & \\
& \diagdown\, \text{B}-\text{A} & \text{CBA}
\end{array}
$$

For the first position, you have three choices: A, B, and C. After you select one, then you have two choices remaining for the second position. Then, for the last position, you have just one choice. Thus, the permutation for six can be described like this: 3 × 2 × 1. For four objects, you have four choices, followed by three, then two, then, finally, one choice:

```
        B—C—D      ABCD
       /
  A—C—D—B          ACDB
       \
        D—B—C      ADBC


        A—C—D      BACD
       /
  B—C—D—A          BCDA
       \
        D—A—C      BDAC


        A—B—D      CABD
       /
  C—B—D—A          CBDA
       \
        D—A—B      CDAB


        A—B—C      DABC
       /
  D—B—C—A          DBCA
       \
        C—A—B      DCAB
```

So 4 × 3 × 2 × 1 describes the permutation for 4 and is called the *factorial* of 4.

3

Tilting at Webs of Belief: Field Experiences as a Means of Breaking With Experience

G. Williamson McDiarmid

Twenty-two undergraduate teacher education students are sitting on folding chairs or an old sofa at the back of a typical third-grade classroom. They are enrolled in the introductory teacher education course at Michigan State University. The discussion they are currently having with the third-grade mathematics teacher is part of their field experience. In 5 minutes, the third graders at Forest Elementary School will return from recess. The teacher, Deborah Ball, has been describing her plans and goals for the upcoming lesson and has passed out to the university students a three-staged "mystery number" worksheet she has devised. The students are present in Ball's classroom because their university instructor (that's me) knows that they will see mathematics and learners treated in ways that will not accord with their prior experience. In addition to teaching third graders mathematics each day, Ball is a researcher and scholar who has written extensively about what she terms "mathematical pedagogy" (Ball, 1988a).

One of the university students raises his hand and says, "There's a mistake in this which makes it impossible to solve."

Ball and the other students study the sheet again.

"You're right," she says. "What do you think I ought to do about it?"

Ball and the university students discuss the pros and cons of using the assignment as is. The students worry that the third graders will become confused and frustrated or may learn things that are incorrect. Ball listens and points out that this is an example of the kinds of dilemmas teachers frequently face:

Should she, at the 11th hour, scrap the assignment and her plans or give them the assignment, trusting in their capacity to figure out what is wrong with it? As the first third grader comes through the door, Ball announces, "I'm going to use it."

After a lively 40-minute discussion of adding and subtracting positive and negative numbers, the third graders divided up into groups of three to work on the mimeographed mystery number assignment. Within a few minutes, several of the groups discover it is unsolvable. Regathering as a large group, the teacher asks what her pupils thought of the problem. A few seem angry that the problem has no solution — one pupil even calls it a "foolish joke." Most of the pupils seem unperturbed and several suggest changes in the directions that would enable them to find a solution.

After the bell rings signaling gym class, a few of the university students, feeling the discussion they witnessed supported their initial belief that the pupils should not be given the worksheet, ask the teacher if she thinks she did the wrong thing and she responds:

> I don't know. On the one hand, pupils like Ahmed who take a lot of satisfaction from solving puzzling problems were upset. But, as you saw, most of them took it in stride. And it became an occasion for us to talk about operations with positive and negative numbers and whether or not zero is positive or negative. The question for me is what may pupils understand now about positive and negative numbers that they may not have understood before.

The primary value of this incident lay in its power to force my students to voice and reconsider one of their many unexamined beliefs about teaching (which I discuss below). In discussing the use of the flawed assignment, students manifest their beliefs that teachers should protect children from confusion and that young children are not capable of figuring out difficult problems for themselves — two strands in a web of beliefs about teaching. The field experience that is part of my Exploring Teaching course is structured so that students will encounter evidence calculated to challenge these unexamined beliefs and orientations.

Early field experiences, which have been the rage in teacher education for over a decade and a half or so (Waxman & Walberg,

1986), are rarely occasions for prospective teachers to confront their web of beliefs about teaching. Rather, such experiences are frequently mere extensions of what Lortie (1975) terms "the apprenticeship of observation" and serve principally to reinforce these beliefs, understandings, and attitudes—to reinforce what Buchmann (1987) has termed the folkways of teaching, "ready-made recipes for action and interpretation that do not require testing or analysis while promising familiar, safe results" (p. 161). Learned by "tradition and imitation" and authorized by "custom and habit" (pp. 154–155), the folkways provide prospective teachers with orientations that accord with their experience of schools and also seem to work.

THE ROLE OF EARLY FIELD EXPERIENCE

Early field experiences can be seen as a response to charges by policymakers, teachers, and teacher education students that teacher education programs are too abstract and academic (Waxman & Walberg, 1986; Webb, 1981). According to this point of view, the practical and the theoretical in introductory courses will be brought into closer alignment if students are exposed to high doses of "reality"—that is, observing, assisting, and teaching in classrooms. Moreover, early field experiences will alert prospective teachers to the relevance of subsequent education courses, thereby addressing what Katz, Raths, Mohanty, Kurachi, and Irving (1981) have termed the "feedforward" problem; that is, beginning teachers tend to believe they were not taught essential knowledge—for example, knowledge about how to manage a classroom—regardless of whether or not they were actually exposed to the information. When asked how the quality of their preservice program could be improved, recent graduates offer suggestions like the following: "more hands on experience . . . more field experience . . . more student teaching . . . more practical experience . . . more practical applications . . . gear more to practical concerns . . . more experience in schools . . . a wider variety of school situations . . . " (Fotiu, Freeman, & West, 1985, p. 15). The explanation offered for this phenomenon is that as students, prospective teachers do not see the relevance of much of what they are taught and, consequently, do not attend to knowledge for which they have no immediate need.

Teacher educators who teach introductory courses with a field experience face a dilemma: On the one hand, experiences in school classrooms are memorable and powerful and are considered eminently credible by prospective teachers; on the other hand, such experiences are fraught with pitfalls, not the least of which is that what students see serves largely to confirm their faith in the folkways of teaching. As Feiman-Nemser and Buchmann (1986a) have written:

> These pitfalls [of experience] arrest thought or mislead prospective teachers into believing that central aspects of teaching have been mastered and understood. Premature closure comes from faulty perceptions and judgments that are supported, even rewarded, by trusted persons and a salient setting. . . . What makes these perceptions pitfalls is that future teachers get into them without knowing it and have a hard time getting out. What makes them even more treacherous is that they may not look like pitfalls to an insider, but rather like a normal place to be. (p. 71)

BEGINNING TEACHERS' BELIEFS ABOUT TEACHING AND LEARNING

As an educator of beginning teacher education students, I have become familiar with the web of beliefs that the mostly white, mostly middle-class, and mostly female students bring with them to introductory teacher education courses. Research on prospective teachers attests to the prevalence of these beliefs (see Ball, 1988b; Brousseau & Freeman, 1989; Broussesau, Freeman, & Book, 1984; Feiman-Nemser, McDiarmid, Melnick, & Parker, 1989; Fotiu et al., 1985; Freeman & Kalaian, 1989; Gomez, 1988; McDiarmid, 1989; Neufeld, 1988; Schram, Wilcox, Lanier, Lappan, & Even, 1988).

For instance, beginning teacher education students believe that teaching subject matter is largely a matter of telling or showing — the view of teaching prevalent not only in schools but in the broader culture (Cohen, 1988; Cuban, 1984; Jackson, 1986). They assume that, as an article of faith, every child is unique — or special — and deserves an education tailored to his or her particular needs (McDiarmid, 1991).[1] Consequently, most prospective elementary teachers believe different objectives and standards should be applied to different students (Freeman & Kalaian, 1989). Many prospective teachers believe some children are not capable of learning basic skills in reading and math (Brousseau & Freeman, 1989; Freeman & Kalaian, 1989). Half of them think that students are responsible for their own school failures: They lack either the right home environment, the right attitude, or the right ability (Freeman & Kalaian, 1989; Paine, 1990); that is, at least half of all prospective teachers are disposed to think that if children don't succeed, "it's their own fault."

For most prospective teachers, learning means committing to memory what they are told or have read, although their views may vary by subject matter. Not only did their high school and elementary experience convey this view of learning, but their experience in college courses — in both liberal arts and education — confirms it (Ball & McDiarmid, 1990). They believe that learning depends on practice, because this will help pupils remember rules, procedures, and facts (Ball, 1989). The more practice learners get in spelling words, doing computation problems, choosing the correct adverb to fit the blank, answering end-of-the-chapter questions or worksheets, and so on, the more they will learn.

Many prospective teachers believe that subject matter at the elementary level is "simple" (Ball, 1988b) and that they probably already know enough to start teaching before they even begin their professional studies (Freeman & Kalaian, 1989). Some methods and a little classroom management — that is, discipline — would be nice, but they feel they know enough about what they are going to teach and how (Fotiu et al., 1985). And where do they believe they will learn this bit they don't know? In classrooms. This belief is reinforced by veteran teachers who tell them the primary benefit of teacher education is the opportunity to do fieldwork (Fotiu et al., 1985).

Rather than challenging students' initial beliefs, teacher educators tend to focus on issues that they and their students already agree on (Brousseau & Freeman, 1989). As a consequence, most prospective teachers complete their teacher education programs without having examined, much less questioned, their most fundamental beliefs about teaching, learners, learning, subject matter, and the role of context. I would argue, in fact, that teacher education students rarely become aware of the assumptions under which they operate. Instead, they either reconfigure ideas and information they encounter to fit their initial beliefs and understandings — or they simply reject what doesn't fit. In this regard, they are no different from younger students (Resnick, 1983; Wittrock, 1986).

THE EXPLORING TEACHING FIELD EXPERIENCE

To challenge the lessons of prospective teachers' past experiences with schools and teaching, I have tried to design a field experience that forced students to give voice — either in discussion or in writing — to their assumptions and what called their assumptions into question. In thinking about the field experience, I was guided by my knowledge of their opinions about teaching, learning, learners, subject matter, context, and learning to teach — that which constitutes a web of beliefs. For instance, the view that mathematics consists of rules and procedures is reinforced by the view that learning mathematics means remembering the correct algorithm and teaching involves giving learners lots of practice to help them remember and testing frequently to determine if they can get the right answers.

These views of the subject matter, teaching, and learning are interwoven with the belief that listening to other pupils' explanations and ideas is confusing, that finishing the textbook or covering the curriculum signals successful teaching, and that what children need, especially poor children and those of color, is to master the basic skills, meaning computation. A field experience intended to force prospective teachers to rethink their understandings of teaching and learning should, consequently, confront students' assumptions not separately but as the web they constituted.

Description of the Experience

I arranged for the prospective teachers in my introductory course to observe, as a group, Deborah Ball, an experienced teacher, who I knew taught in ways that were likely to challenge my students' assumptions and beliefs. I chose her less because she "modeled" good practice and more because her practice played havoc with much that passes for conventional wisdom in teaching. Through the creation of a learning community (Schwab, 1976) in her classroom, moreover, Ball enabled all pupils — regardless of language or cultural background or gender — to participate on an equal footing in a conversation about mathematics that does not end and to voice their understandings relatively free of worry about ridicule from their classmates.

Before observing Ball's classroom, my students puzzled over, wrote about, and discussed the same piece of subject matter that

Ball's third graders would be discussing: operations with positive and negative numbers. Before and after each of the four classes they observed, they interviewed Ball about her purposes, goals, plans, her reactions to events and students, and her rationale for her behaviors. They observed her class discussing positive and negative numbers and working on problems together in small groups and, subsequently, responded in writing to specific questions about what they had observed. Ball, my students, and I jointly developed a clinical interview that my students then used to explore the third graders' understandings of operations with positive and negative numbers. They discussed with Ball pupils' responses to the interview in their effort to assess pupils' understandings. The prospective teachers then attempted to teach someone — a roommate, friend, or relative — about operations with positive and negative numbers. Finally, they wrote a "case study" of the teaching and learning of the subject matter.

The entire sequence occurred over a 4-week period and involved 4 hours of observation in Ball's classroom, another 4 hours of discussion with her, and about 10 hours in the university classroom. Below I describe in more detail each of these elements of the field experience, my rationale, and my students' reactions.

THE UNIVERSITY CLASSROOM: EXAMINING SUBJECT-MATTER UNDERSTANDING

I chose to focus on mathematics because of prospective teachers' typical attitudes. Most prospective elementary teachers are not fond of mathematics and believe themselves lacking an aptitude for the subject (Ball, 1988a; Schram et al., 1988). One of my student's feelings and attitudes were shared by most:

> As a learner in Deborah's class I was not very comfortable
> . . . because I have always had a deep dislike for . . . math.
> When I was growing up and taking math classes I always did
> very well until high school where I went downhill and avoided
> it like the plague. When I walked into Deborah's classroom for
> the first time I wanted to continue to avoid it and try to observe without actually thinking about the topic.

Another student wrote:

> Mathematics is a subject many people love to hate. I can re-
> member so many times in high school Algebra when the class
> looked forward to coming into the room to complain about
> why math was an impossible subject to learn. . . . Our teacher
> would simply walk in, demonstrate how to work through dif-
> ferent problems, then assign us homework. . . . I am able to
> do math only because I am able to memorize rules. I have
> never been asked to understand the concepts of why a mathe-
> matical solution makes sense.

Finally, many of my students do not see any value in learning
mathematics:

> In my eyes, mathematics was useless. I could never under-
> stand where in my lifetime I would ever use math formulas
> again. In a checkbook? On a resume? What was the purpose of
> learning it? From the beginning, my understanding of math
> was to memorize the laws and formulas to get the answer. I
> didn't have to know the concepts of math. I didn't even know
> mathematics had concepts!

At the same time, they don't believe their dislike for mathematics or their lack of aptitude is a handicap because the mathematics
they need to know is simple: addition, subtraction, multiplication,
division, fractions, decimals, ratio, percentages, and so on (Ball,
1988a). Prospective teachers conclude that they can safely depend
on the mathematics learned in school and in college and can focus
on methods. I reasoned that if I could get my students to realize the
inadequacy of their knowledge of mathematics for teaching even
young children "easy stuff," I could convince them of the importance
of a genuine understanding of all subject matters for teaching.

In choosing a topic to study, I wanted as simple a piece of
mathematics as I could find. Fortune once again smiled on me:
During the time my students would be visiting her class, Ball
planned to work on operations with positive and negative numbers.
This seemed ideal: My students would almost certainly feel confident about their knowledge of this topic.

During the class that followed their first visit to Ball's classroom, we talked about the kind of teaching and learning they had
experienced previously in school and college, comparing their recollections with the teaching they had seen in the third-grade classroom. They prepared for this discussion by reading about opera-

tions with integers in a mathematics methods book recommended for its conceptual explanations. I also asked them to solve the equation $-8 - (-2) = ?$ and to explain in writing what they understood this answer to mean.

For many, the experience was unnerving. Most were unaccustomed to explaining their answers. As one student wrote, "The answer is -6 but I don't know why. I was taught that when you subtracted a negative number, it is just like adding a positive. That's all. I don't know why it works." In class, a student volunteered to read his explanation. He came to the front of the room, wrote his answer on the board, and stated that subtracting a negative is the same as adding a positive. When someone asked him why, he repeated his first explanation, more slowly — a technique he no doubt learned from observing his own teachers.

"I still don't get it," complained a student. "I mean your answer is the same as mine but your explanation is just the same thing I was taught in school. Why is it -6 and not -10?" Frustrated, the first student drew a number line on the board — an idea he subsequently admitted he got from his first day observing in Ball's classroom when several of her pupils used the number line to justify their answers. Pointing to the negative 8 on the line, he explained that "taking away" negative 2 means moving towards zero.

Consternation deepened on many of the faces in the room.

"Why do you move toward zero on the number line?"
"Aren't you taking away even more?"
"Wouldn't the answer be more negative?"
"What's a number line? How does that 'explain' this answer?"

The first student looked from the number line to the questioners and shrugged his shoulders.

When I asked if anyone had another way of explaining the answer, a young woman came forward and drew a circle. In the circle she drew eight negative signs and crossed out two of them. "Let's say you have eight negative markers in a bag. If you take away — subtract — two of them, you'd have six negative markers left." This was the example used in the methods textbook my students had read. Several of those visibly puzzled by the number line example unfurrowed their brows.

After she answered some of the questions put to her, I asked the class, "Did anyone come up with a story that would represent what negative 8 minus negative 2 means?" After a long silence, a student said, "I don't know if this works exactly, but here goes: Suppose a South American country owed U.S. banks $8 billion and the banks decided to cancel $2 billion of the debt. That would leave $6 billion in debt." This example provoked a lot of discussion because the Latin American debt issue had recently been featured prominently in the news and because this was the first "real world" application that anyone had suggested. Most of the discussion focused on whether the banks were actually contributing something (i.e., adding a positive) or taking away from a negative and how important the distinction was mathematically and politically. As class ended, someone was making the point that deciding whether this was addition of a positive or subtraction of a negative might depend on point of view — the debtors might construe it one way and the creditors the other. We had spent over an hour discussing one "simple" problem: $-8 - (-2) = ?$

In reaction to this class, one student wrote:

> Learning about integers and operations with negative and positive numbers in this class taught me how much I do not know! My background in math goes up through calculus and I had trouble with several of the concepts we touched upon. There is a difference between learning the rules and really visualizing and understanding what is behind those rules.

Another student described her experience as follows (her use of "theorem" here illustrates the difficulty students have in finding language to describe their understandings):

> When I first learned about positive and negative integers I was given a bunch of theorems and taught to apply those theorems to the problems we were given. . . . I was never asked how the theorems were derived. . . . I got my answers because that was how the rules said to do it, and that was that. When I learned about positive and negative integers this second time, in our class, I had to support my answers with ideas other than theorems. If I tried to explain it with a theorem, I was asked to explain how I got the theorem. So I, like the students [in Ball's class], not only had to understand my answer, but the answers behind the theorem too. . . . At first I had a hard time explaining my answers without saying "that's just the way it is," but the more we discussed it in class, the more I began to analyze it.

The Field Setting

Beliefs About Learners, Learning, Teaching, and Context.   The discussion described above forced my students to confront their notions about what mathematics is and what it means to do mathematics. Most thought that mathematics was a body of rules and procedures to be remembered and appropriately applied and that doing mathematics meant solving computational or word problems by yourself. As the comments above indicate, students confronted other dimensions of teaching, particularly their views of themselves and others as learners, their understanding of the learning process, their assumptions about teaching, and the role of others in that process — classmates and teacher.

Their observations in Ball's third-grade classroom further forced them to consider their views of learners, particularly young learners, the learning process, and teaching. To describe a typical class, I will crib from one of my students. Note that this individual's observations have been supplemented by the discussions students had before and after each class with Ball:

> Deborah uses three types of forums. First, there is what I call individual study time. Second, there is what I call group discussion. Lastly, there is what I refer to as partner work.
>
> During individual study time [at the beginning of each class] students are given a problem to work on individually. For example, on October 26th, the problem that students worked on was as follows: "1) Write down at least 10 numbers. 2) Then add 20 to each number. 3) Now circle all the answers that are even."
>
> This individual study time allows each student the opportunity to think about the problem and practice skills individually with limited influence from other students and from Deborah. Deborah utilizes this time period to assist students that have questions, and to motivate students that are having problems getting started. . . .
>
> During the group discussion time students are given the opportunity to share with the class answers to the problems that they worked on individually. It appears that initially each answer is treated with the same degree of validity. That is, Deborah does not tell the student whether the answer is correct or incorrect. Deborah allows the rest of the students an opportunity to challenge all answers given. Deborah stresses that it is

essential to ask for challenges to all answers. This will not prejudice any response and will not discourage students from participating because they fear they may have a wrong answer. Another point that Deborah stressed about challenges to her students is that it is not acceptable to say, "No way!" when a challenge or answer that seems incorrect is given. This was made clear when Hilary made a challenge that was incorrect; a large number of students said, "No way!" to Hilary's statement that $11 + 20 = 21$. . . . Deborah is concerned with keeping a mutual respect among the students. Perhaps a mutual respect will allow students to learn and understand math without being concerned about taking risks of giving incorrect answers. . . . [This approach] will enhance curiosity about math that will encourage them to ask more questions and thus allow them a greater understanding. . . .

Another important aspect of discussions is the right of revision that each student has. If a student is convinced by others in the class that the answer he or she has given is incorrect, the student has the opportunity to revise that answer . . .

In partner work Deborah has paired the class into groups of two students. . . . During my interview with Brian, he said that he liked working with partners the best because this gave students the opportunity to help each other. Brian's observation is very important because in essence what he is saying is that in some cases peers are able to help each other understand mathematics better than the teacher can. Possibly Deborah recognizes the importance of what Brian has said. In the three forums that she has created she has placed a great degree of emphasis on peers helping one another. In the group discussions her role is basically one of motivating class participation, she tries to get the students to direct conversation toward one another and not toward her. . . .

Something else that is important to Deborah is that her students learn that what mathematics consists of is people getting together and agreeing on conventions. . . . During the first few minutes of discussion [of the problem described above] there was a rather extended debate as to what "at least" meant [in the sentence, "Write down at least 10 numbers"]. Hilary said that she thought in this situation it means that she could only use 10 numbers. Ivy challenged her and said that it meant you could write 10 or more numbers. The majority of the class agreed with what Ivy said.

This experience required my students to reconsider what it means to teach something. Most of them believed that the teacher's role is to tell, show, or explain procedures, facts, ideas, and so on. Although Ball told children how to behave — how to disagree with someone, for instance — and how to go about an activity, she rarely told them whether answers or representations were wrong or right. Rather, she created and encouraged discussions about problems in mathematics. To illustrate her teaching, one student recorded her utterances during a brief exchange with her pupils:

> "Find a sentence [you wrote] that you want to talk about. Dan, explain your sentence and how it works." [Other students start to raise their hands and interrupt Dan while he is responding.] "Quiet down. Does anyone else have any ideas or challenges? Why does or doesn't this sentence make sense? Can anyone give me some reasons? Dan, would you like to revise your explanation? Does anyone have any suggestions?"

Several students remarked that she frequently redirected her pupils' comments away from her and toward the individual whose idea was being discussed. They also noticed how Ball both developed her pupils' ability to reason about mathematics and enabled them to "save face":

> When an answer was given, Deborah did not say whether it was right or wrong but instead encouraged her students to challenge one another. If Deborah sensed students were heading in the wrong direction, she would ask them if they wanted to "revise" what they had just said instead of simply telling them that they were wrong. By doing this, she was allowing them the opportunity to THINK through what they had just said and perhaps realize their mistake.

My students noted how this encouraged pupils to continue participating and communicated to them that doing mathematics was a thoughtful activity facilitated by the ideas and feedback of others.

My students may have been most surprised by the level of discussion and debate among the third graders they observed and interviewed. Believing that young children don't know much and aren't capable of understanding complicated ideas, they expressed surprise at the level of intellectual sophistication (Kohl, 1984) they encountered:

I was amazed by how well Deborah's students understood positive and negative integers. The students were all basically enthused about discussing the math problems and their explanations for their answers were all thought [through]. When Deborah gave students a problem to do that had no correct answer [a reference to the Mystery Number problem described at the beginning of the paper], I was surprised by how quickly the students realized this and by how many of them knew what was wrong about it. . . . Lawrence and his partner had already figured out that something wasn't right about it within the first 5 minutes. . . . Another girl approached Deborah, telling her the problem wasn't possible and exactly why it wasn't. The students knew they could make a mistake and that is why they weren't afraid to challenge others, even the teacher's math ditto.

In particular, the prospective teachers were impressed by the third graders' use of representations in their discussions. After describing how different pupils had used the number line, bundles of sticks, and the minicomputers[2] to substantiate their answers, one of my students observed, "The way I saw these tools used was not as learning devices, but as tools to help the students explain their answers."

Believing part of the teacher's role is to praise and correct pupils, they were not prepared for the lack of public evaluation in Ball's classroom. As one of my students explained,

Even wrong answers and strange explanations are discussed because they might bring up an interesting subtopic or an area of confusion for the class, such as the properties of zero [the university students observed a lengthy debate as to whether zero was odd or even]. They are also discussed to show that speaking up in class is accepted and good. Her students are taught to evaluate their own answers and others' answers, which is a valuable skill for any subject and can be extended to everyday problems.

In group interviews with Ball after the observations, my students asked her how she could cover the district curriculum for third-grade mathematics if she spent several days or even a week on the same problem. In response, Ball then asked them to consider the various topics that her pupils had considered in their discussion of integers: addition and subtraction, even and odd, the nature of zero, ratio and proportion, estimation and mental calculation, and so on. Her pupils, in figuring out a single problem, had used many of the ideas and operations that constitute the third-grade curriculum. Because of their own experience in discussing $-8 - (-2) = ?$ in our classroom — a discussion that involved them in thinking about the relationship of subtraction to addition, as well as the nature of numbers — the university students could readily credit Ball's claim.

They also noted the importance of the "community" of the classroom Ball created around the learning of mathematics. The focus of the community was understanding mathematics. Although Ball communicated and displayed both affection and concern for her pupils — and they for her — these sentiments fortified the community but were not its basis. The following excerpt reveals one of my student's effort to grapple with the connections among the classroom context, pedagogy, and subject matter:

> Discussion, then, allows the students as a "community" to express their ideas and thoughts amongst themselves, and through the challenge method come up with agreement as to what could be possible hypotheses or theorems in accordance with the content that is being covered.

Encountering a classroom community built around a mutual engagement with content is an occasion for prospective elementary teachers to confront what 9 out of 10 claim is their primary reason for teaching: Love of children. Kohl (1984) distinguishes between loving all students and loving students as learners. He argues that love is not boundless, that teaching is but a part of one's life, and love engages "all parts of one's life," and that "it isn't possible to love so many people you know so little about and will separate from in six months or a year" (p. 64). Teachers do, however, argues Kohl, "have an obligation to care about every student as a learner" (p. 66).

Students also noted how Ball's approach enabled children from a variety of cultural backgrounds and females as well as males to be a part of the conversation and the community. A student who interviewed a Chinese pupil who joined the class after the school year began noted that, although unsure of herself and limited in her ability to express herself orally in English, she could do and explain the problems on the clinical interview and she "enjoys Deborah as her teacher, the class as a whole and she loves mathematics." Others noted the lack of grouping by ability and the fact that children from a range of cultures — Zimbabwean, Chinese, Pakistani, as well as several in the United States — participated in discussions and communicated directly with each other about their ideas.

A major topic in the Exploring Teaching course is how differentiation within schools and classroom results in different students learning different subject matter, which prepares them for different futures in school and society. Poor students and those of color are more likely than are white middle-class students to find themselves in low reading groups and in general vocational tracks. Most prospective teachers who attended large comprehensive public schools benefit from ability grouping and from being members of the "college" track; consequently, for them ability grouping and tracking are part of the natural order. Ball's use of groups organized on bases other than ability — such as students' preferences or her judgment about mutual compatibility — presented an occasion to discuss the uses and effects of ability grouping.

Teaching and Telling. After wrestling with mathematics in their university classroom, observing third graders deal with the same content, interviewing both the teacher and the pupils, the beginning teacher education students now had to teach someone else subtraction with negative numbers using their newfound understanding. This presented students an opportunity to confront their assumptions about teaching and learning, as well as their views of mathematics, deeply embedded in our culture.

Some students found their understanding inadequate to the task:

> I started off by having my college-age roommate explain to me what negative and positive integers meant to her. She automatically referred to the number line, indicating that the numbers on the right of zero were positive and the numbers on the left were negative. Then I proceeded with some problems; $8 + (-4)$; $-8 + (-4)$; $-8 - (-4)$; $8 - (-4)$. In the first problem there was no real difficulty. We figured out the problem, and I used the number line to substantiate the answer. The farther we got in the problems the harder it became for me as a teacher to explain without using the saying, "It's a rule, that's why!" From this experience I learned I need to become more acquainted . . . with different ways of explaining without just stating rules.

Most students, like this one, still thought their role was to explain or show the learner their rationale for the answer, not to draw forth the learner's understanding. Even students who noted that Ball enabled her pupils to develop their own rationales for their ideas reported that, faced with a similar situation, they, not their learner, explained the answer:

> I worked with a friend of mine, Monique, and told her that I needed her to help me with a project. I explained to her that we were going to work with subtracting negative numbers and she jokingly said, "Fine." I then proceeded to give her a problem, "What is $-6 - (-2)$?" She readily responded, "Negative four." When asked why, she said, "Well . . . because . . . when you subtract a negative it is just like adding a positive and $-6 + 2$ is -4."
>
> I then asked her, "Why?"
>
> She looked at me rather perplexed and then said, "Well, because it is!"
>
> I asked again, "Why? I don't understand, how does the rule work?"
>
> I could tell at this point I was upsetting her so I explained to her how we get so misled by learning rules without reasoning. I then proceeded to explain how this could be shown. I drew a circle and put six "chips" in it and told her all the chips in the circle were negative. Then, I told her we were going to subtract two negative chips from the six and asked her how many negative chips were left.
>
> Again she replied, "Negative four," but this time she understood why.

Also evident in this response is the persistent tendency to confuse teaching with what Ryle (1949) terms a "task verb" and teaching as an "accomplishment verb."

Some students did resist the temptation to tell and get it over with. One, after describing how she had worked with her roommate, asking her learner to show her on a number line why she thought $-8 - (-2) = -6$, eventually getting her to articulate her understanding of subtraction, wrote the experience "helped me realize that it can be frustrating, because you want to tell them how to do it, but it is also rewarding because you lead them to the answer and I was able to get her to realize that her first solution was faulty [and] she went back and revised it." Another wrote: "While I was teaching

Devon, my feedback to him consisted of answering his queries as if
his answer was right. When he was giving his reasons, I resisted the
strong urge to give him a way to represent his ideas."

The dominant theme that emerged from students' descriptions
of their attempts to teach operations with positive and negative integers was, however, their realization of the relationship between their
own understanding of the concept and their capacity to help someone else understand. One student who felt she had muffed her first
effort but succeeded quite well as her own understanding developed
during her second attempt wrote, "It became evident that I could
not teach concepts that I did not myself understand." Another wrote
of her effort,

> I went on to show [the learner] the chips model in the handout
> [taken from the mathematics methods text]. This only added
> to the problem because we both became confused. We worked
> with the chips model for some time but did not accomplish any
> more. . . . This experience showed me the importance of
> knowing and being able to express verbally both the how and
> the why of these problems and concepts.

Realizing that they lack an understanding of seemingly "simple"
subject matter is unsettling for some students, particularly those
who are about to graduate and cannot grasp at the hope that somehow their remaining university courses will provide them with the
knowledge and understanding they lack.

What Do They Learn?   How do I know that this field experience forced my students to confront their initial beliefs and conceptions and begin to change them? I don't. I do not wish to imply that
I am content with my uncertainty, yet the only reliable test of
changes in belief is what these students will do in their own classrooms. In the meantime I must be satisfied with what I can infer
from the discourse in my own classroom and from students' written
work. Like Deborah Ball, I try to create a classroom where students
are comfortable expressing their beliefs, doubts, puzzlements, and
understandings, whatever they may be, and in which they are
equally comfortable changing these. Unless I know what my students are thinking as well as what they understand about the ideas
and experiences they encounter in the course, I will make decisions
about means and goals blindly. Knowing that not all students are
comfortable discussing their views and understandings publicly, I

use "fastwrites" (impromptu, 5-minute, unproofed written reactions to questions or statements), responses to study questions on the readings, and formal papers as other sources of information on my students' thinking.

For those among my readers who pride themselves on being hard-nosed, I will conclude with some sample responses to a question on the final examination. To prepare for this question, students watched a videotape of a teacher teaching his fourth graders operations with integers. This teacher, whom we called "Bob," conformed closely to the view of good teaching most of my students brought with them to Exploring Teaching: He stood at the front of the room, exuding confidence and organization, wrote math problems on the board, maintained pupil attention, asked questions for which right and wrong answers existed, explained solutions, used a representation—the Logo "turtle" on a video screen—of operations with integers that was both high tech and arguably interesting to fourth graders. I chose Bob for my students to observe because he conformed closely to many people's notions of an effective teacher. Here, I thought, is a teacher very like the teacher many prospective teachers aspire to be.

On the final, I asked them to compare Bob's and Deborah's goals, hidden curriculum, opportunities to learn, as well as their representations of operations with integers. I reasoned that I could gauge their understanding in a crude fashion by their ability to identify and discuss the issues raised by the representations used in each classroom. Finally, I asked them to speculate on the sources of the differences they saw between the two teachers.

Below, I provide an example from a response to the final:

Bob's representation of subtracting negative numbers involved the use of the computer and the Logo "turtle." Each step in the problem was seen as a command for the turtle to follow. If the problem read $8 + (-5)$, we would break it into parts and commands for the turtle to get our answer,

    8 = Move the turtle in direction [turtle is] facing,
    + = No change in turtle direction
    − = 180-degree turn in turtle's direction
    5 = Move five spaces in direction [turtle is] facing

  • • • • • • • • • • •
  0 1 2 3 4 5 6 7 8 9 10

If we were to do the following problem:

$8 - (-5) = ?$ we would do the same procedure with
our turtle.

$8 =$ Move eight places in the direction [turtle is] facing
$- =$ 180-degree change of direction
$- =$ 180-degree change of direction
$5 =$ Move five places in the direction [the turtle] is
facing

• • • • • • • • • • • • • • • •
0 1 2 3 4 5 6 7 8 9 10 11 12 13 14 15

In doing the problem this way, we got the right answer, but do
we know why? Is it only because that is where the turtle
stopped? And will this tool be useful if we had a much larger
number? Could the kids still move the turtle 115 spaces . . .
and then change directions and go 85 spaces (i.e., 115 +
-85)? It soon becomes too complicated to use.

As a teacher educator, I find this response encouraging because
of the focused, thoughtful analysis of the representation that reveals
evidence of emerging pedagogical judgment. Teachers must judge
the value and appropriateness of various representations of the subject matter at their disposal—textbooks and other materials, computer software, activities, stories, analogies, examples, manipulatives, and so on (McDiarmid, Ball, & Anderson, 1989). In making
such judgments, teachers draw on their knowledge not merely of
the subject matter but of their learners—their prior experiences and
understandings—and the learning process, as well as of the context
of the school and community. In this particular response, the student brings to bear both his understanding of mathematics and
his sense of the computer's practicality as a tool for helping pupils
understand this piece of mathematics.

Bob also referred to "Eli's magical peanuts" in explaining subtraction of negative numbers. Apparently this representation is
much like that used by the student in my class who explained subtraction by taking negative chips out of a circle. One of my students
criticized this representation:

This [representation] gives a sense of mysteriousness about
math to the children. Deborah's idea of math was more concrete with her use of many tools. She used the minicomputer,
the number line, and the bundles of sticks to represent numbers and operations. These gave more meaning to the kids.
She used these tools as evidence.

As for the turtle, this student wrote:

> I did not like this representation because it strictly involved memorizing rules and there is no emphasis on the process [of getting answers]. In Deborah's class she made sure the kids would justify their answers. . . . Ahmed once said that the answer was "getting more negative" and this to me displays more of an understanding than using the turtle. The turtle was also a bad representation because it didn't have any negative numbers on it and the number line only went up to 8.

Students also criticized Bob for being the arbiter of representations:

> Bob, "the authority," said, "I don't think that this is a good model to use," referring to Eli's bag of peanuts to solve the problem, $5 - (-3)$. However, the students in Deborah's class were encouraged to use any method of solving a problem that made sense to them, including the number line, the minicomputer boards, et cetera. I have learned through Deborah's class that each student is capable of learning and that there are many ways to represent [concepts] so that all levels of ability have an opportunity to learn. . . . Bob, not having a complete understanding of the concept of negative integers, limits possible representation models.

Finally, in speculating on the differences between the two classrooms, students wrote about differences they thought they detected in the two teachers' knowledge about learners and about mathematics. As one student noted, when "Bob attempted to use his computer to show that two 'negatives' make a 'positive,' he completely forgets the fact that one of those 'negatives' was actually a subtraction sign instead. He, therefore, demonstrated $5 + [-(-3)]$ rather than $5 - (-3)$." This student was noting that Bob had defined the "$-$" sign as a "180-degree turn in the turtle's direction" but used as an illustration a problem that involved subtraction. Rather than helping students understand the difference between the minus sign used to signify negative numbers and the same sign used to indicate the subtraction procedure, Bob may have further confounded this distinction in his pupils' minds. Another student pointed out that telling pupils that the turtle turns 180 degrees whenever it encounters a negative sign "is just another way of saying that $- + - = +$." That is, saying that the turtle does an about-face each time it encounters a minus sign is not a conceptual explanation but rather describes a procedure.

That prospective teachers, at this early stage in their professional studies, can discuss the pros and cons of various specific
representations of a mathematical concept, can generalize about the
characteristics of appropriate representations, can see the importance of multiple representations to create access to the subject matter for all children seems to indicate that they have begun to think
about what teachers need to know about learners, subject matter,
and pedagogy.

REFLECTIONS

In thinking about this course, the primary question that occurs
to me is whether such a focused, in-depth experience with one topic
in mathematics taught by an atypical teacher in a single third-grade
classroom can have much effect on the way beginning teacher education students think about teaching other subject matter to other
learners in other settings. In discussions and in their papers, I encountered evidence of students' resistance to generalizing the lessons
of their experience in Ball's classroom: Some students claim that
Ball's pupils must be gifted; others claim that the school's proximity
to the university makes it an atypical setting (many of the pupils'
parents are students at the university) and explains why Ball is able
to achieve what she does; still others claim that Ball's knowledge of
mathematics or of children is exceptional and beyond the capacity
of other mere mortals. Except for the assumptions that the pupils
are gifted—by several standards, they appear no more so than most
third graders—the other claims are not totally unwarranted. For
students intent on keeping their beliefs and orientations intact, these
claims are their refuge.

For those students who are willing to revise their understandings and beliefs about teaching, I also wonder about their capacity
to transfer the lessons they learned about the teaching and learning
of mathematics to other subject matters. Do they come to see spelling instruction—and such drills exercises in pure memorization and
free-floating, contextless memory bites of language—or vocabulary
drill—in a new light? Do they think children are as capable of making sense of the Freedom Rides as they are of making sense of
$-6 - (-4)$? Do they understand that ability grouping, however
sanctioned by time, custom, and folk wisdom, is as discriminatory
and invidious in reading as it is in math?

Students who realize the inadequacy of their knowledge in most
subjects lose much of the blithe confidence they exhibit at the begin-

ning of the term. Asked to analyze their knowledge for teaching and to speculate on how and where they might learn what they feel they lack, many nonetheless exhibit an abiding faith in their college classes:

> If I were to take Deborah's place in teaching integers to her third graders I would need to know a lot more about the subject matter. I could learn more about positive and negative integers if I were to take some mathematics classes in college.

Evidence that prospective teachers' liberal arts and professional courses will afford them the opportunity to develop the kind of subject-matter understanding that Deborah Ball demonstrates is lacking (Ball & McDiarmid, 1990). If anything, the evidence on college classrooms indicates that teaching and learning are just as mechanical, disconnected, and fragmented at this level as they are at the precollegiate level (Bennett, 1984; Boyer, 1987; Kimball, 1986, 1988; Kline, 1977; McDiarmid, 1990).

Despite our discussions about the kind of knowledge needed to help pupils develop understanding of critical concepts, some students persist in believing that more knowledge (read "more courses") will furnish the understanding that they feel they lack. In part, they continue to believe this because, as proponents of the power and rectitude of schools, they associate knowledge and learning with formal course work; in part, future courses represent a hope to which they can cling. Many students leave Exploring Teaching aware that their subject-matter understanding is insufficient but confident that exposure to more college courses will rectify the problem.

Yet, one theme in our discussions was the almost complete lack of attention their liberal arts professors paid to students' understanding of the subject matter. Trapped in large lecture classes, subjected to tedious textbooks, and faced with multiple-choice exams, students expressed frustration with the kind of knowledge they had the opportunity to learn. Whether their awareness of how mechanical and disembodied learning and teaching in most university courses are was translated into demands for different approaches to teaching, I don't know. That many of them recognize what they are presently learning will be of little value in teaching does, however, seem to justify confronting their unexamined beliefs. Some may do something about it: seek out smaller courses run as seminars, such as those typically found in honors programs at large universities; demand more explanation and discussion in their courses; create study groups in which they can talk about key ideas in a course; reflect on their own understanding to judge whether or not it is sufficient for teaching.

For those students who are near the end of their college career, confronting them with how little they know and understand may appear even less justified. Teachers do, however, learn and gain understanding of their subject matter on their own. Critical to such learning may be recognizing what constitutes genuine understanding for teaching. That is what our struggles with $-6 - (-4)$ are intended to do.

Yet, despite abundant evidence that prospective teachers do reconsider their initial beliefs and orientations, that they begin to understand the folkways of teaching they have learned are not merely unreflective but, in some respects, downright damaging, I am skeptical about the effects of the course. Like the web of the great spider Shelob in Tolkien's (1965) *Lord of the Rings*, the strength of each individual strand of belief—about teaching, learning, learners, subject-matter knowledge, and context—is formidable. But interwoven as they are, the various strands constitute a web of remarkable resilience; severing one strand barely diminishes the overall strength of the whole. And I feel often like Samwise Gamgee, Frodo's Sancho Panza, attacking the web:

> "Cobwebs!", he said. "Is that all? Cobwebs! But what a spider! Have at 'em, down with 'em!"
>
> In a fury he hewed at them with his sword, but the thread that he struck did not break. It gave a little and then sprang back like a plucked bowstring, turning the blade and tossing up both sword and arm. Three times Sam struck with all his force, and at last one single cord of all the countless cords snapped and twisted, curling and whipping through the air. (pp. 420–421)

NOTES

1. The beliefs underlying folkways are not patently false. Indeed, most, like this one, incorporate crucial elements of empirical reality and moral commitment. Who but W. C. Fields-like curmudgeons would deny that "each child is unique"? This explains the power, prevalence, and tenacity of such beliefs. The issue for teacher education is: What are the pedagogical consequences of such beliefs? In this case, for instance, I would argue that this belief has served to justify the "tailoring" of opportunities to

learn subject matter and of standards that have denied children of color and poor children equal chances to learn equal knowledge (McDiarmid, 1991). Apparently "good" beliefs about teaching, if examined, can and do lend themselves to perverse results.

2. The minicomputers, produced by CEMREL as part of its Comprehensive School Mathematics Program, were developed by a Belgian mathematician, Georges Papy. They are $8\frac{1}{2}$ " $\times$ 11 " pieces of cardboard on which are printed two equal squares, each of which is subdivided into four squares of different colors. Each of the smaller squares represents a number; students place various combinations of positive or negative markers on these squares to represent numbers. Pupils use the minicomputers for various operations — addition, subtraction, multiplication, division. Like electronic computers, the minicomputers thus allow pupils to do various calculations. In addition, the squares can be used to represent place value.

4

The Student, the Teacher, and the Moon

Helen Featherstone
Sharon Feiman-Nemser

Stepping off the curb during an early morning run, Mary DeShino, a first-grade teacher and 8-year veteran of the Boston Public Schools, had a powerful insight. For the past 2 years she had been observing the moon as part of an experimental project for teachers at the Massachusetts Institute of Technology. For a long time she felt more frustrated than enlightened in trying to make sense of changes in the moon's appearance and location. That morning, Mary DeShino understood what happened to the moon, where it was, and where it would be, in relation to the sun, why one side was lit during the waning stages and the other side during the waxing stages.

All her life DeShino had believed that other people had better answers than she because they knew more. That morning she recognized that she could figure things out for herself. About her newly gained understanding, she wrote: "I would never forget what I now knew. I understood my knowledge. Nothing, even time, could take this knowledge away from me. I had discovered it on my own" (DeShino, 1987, p. 24).

This episode marked a turning point in DeShino's view of herself as a person, a learner, and a teacher. In a moving account of her own development, she describes her transformation from a "dispenser of knowledge" to a "facilitator of learning": "I came to value, with a profound respect, the ability in each of us to think, to be intelligent. . . . If I could observe the moon, collect data, and come to understandings that became an integral part of me, it now seemed obvious that I should apply the same processes to my work with children" (p. 24).

Eleanor Duckworth, one of the coordinators of the project that Mary DeShino participated in and a professor of education at Harvard, continues to engage teachers in moon watching as a way of reconnecting them to their capacity for intellectual productivity. She adapted this activity from a moon-watching teacher's guide developed by the Elementary Science Study where she worked in the 1960s. Duckworth believes that when teachers discover their ability to construct knowledge for themselves, they will be more likely to trust this capacity in children.

Duckworth puts teachers in contact with interesting materials and encourages them to explain their thinking. In trying to make their thoughts clear, teachers come to see that learning is complex, that understanding involves more than using the "right" words, that they can learn a lot from each other, that knowledge is a human construction (Duckworth, 1986).

Duckworth has inspired us in two ways. First, as a teacher educator writing about her practice, she has shown us how concretely helpful such reflective essays can be—leading us toward this volume. Second, her project led several TE-101 instructors to design a major assignment around the activity of moon watching. We thought that putting our students in touch with their own learning could produce powerful insights about teaching. As the project evolved, it became a vehicle for bringing together ideas about teaching, learning, knowledge. In this essay, we describe the moon project, discuss its impact on students' thinking, and consider ways to modify it in the future.

THE MOON PROJECT

Early in the course we told students to start observing the moon and to keep track of their observations and questions in a "moon journal." Because these would become the basis of their second paper, we recommended looking at the moon every night and recording what one saw. Later we discovered that many students found the assignment puzzling or even "stupid." After all, this was an education course, not a course in astronomy!

Phase 1: Learning About the Moon

After students had observed the moon for 4 weeks, we asked them to bring their moon journals to class. Some students had made regular and detailed entries, including the time of the observation, a description of the weather, a sketch of the moon. Others had not taken the assignment seriously and had less to share with the group. The three excerpts below illustrate the range in terms of personal involvement and detail.

Student 1: Kara

1/19   6:25 PM. There was a haze around it. Thicker on the bottom than top.

1/21   7:15 PM. It was a little more full than before. There was less haze around it. It was higher up in the sky and more to the right.

1/24   6:20 PM. It was around on the other side. The moon seems to go in a clockwise direction.

1/25   8:30 PM.

1/27   7:30 PM.

1/31   11:40 PM. Very clear. Bright full moon. For the first time I can see it from my window so it still is going clockwise.

2/1   10:55 PM. Lower and farther than last night. Could still see it from window. There is a lot of haze around it.

Student 2: Ellen

I started looking for the moon the first week in October. I was bothered to find that the moon was not visible during this time. I was then very excited and careful to write down a fair amount of information the first few times I was able to see the moon. This though became after one week difficult to do. I began looking for the moon while I was on my way to work or class and keeping accurate data was not quite accomplished. Despite the fact that my journal is not as complete as it could be, I feel that I did a decent job. On the last page is a visual description.

Oct. 7   About 8:00 PM. The moon seemed to me fairly high in the sky. I don't know directions very well so I am unable to state where it was. The moon was a half moon. It glowed.

Oct. 8   Did not see moon. May have been cloudy. I did not record.

Oct. 9   7:35 PM. Fairly cloudy. Moon little over half full. No points. Light pouring off both ends. Only one star visible. Clouds continuously passing over moon, shading it. Not high overhead.

Oct. 10   10:48 PM. The sky was clear when I looked. Moon appeared 2/3 full; little more bright and glowy. Not high in the sky; shaped like a football. No stars close by.

Oct. 11   10:00 PM. Low in the sky; closer to being full; was colored; dimmed glow.

Oct. 12   8:30 PM. Full moon; still not high overhead; could see dark spots on the moon.

Oct. 13   10:45 PM. Full moon; bright and radiant. Followed me all over town.

Oct. 14   Moon still appeared full; was covered in a sheath of clouds; light was dulled because of clouds. Man in the moon winked at me.

Oct. 15   Time? Continues to be a big moon, but not as full.

Oct. 16   Cloudy; no moon seen.

Oct. 17   Moon isn't full anymore; saw it in the AM. I started looking for the moon the first week (see Figure 4.1).

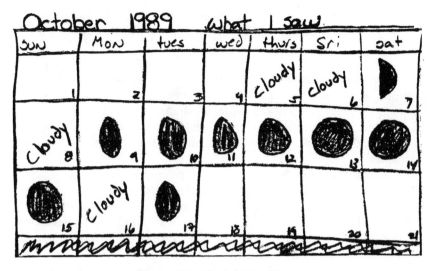

Figure 4.1 Ellen's Moon Chart

Student 3: Laura

Oct. 2: Couldn't see the moon.

Oct. 5: Clear but I couldn't find it; assuming it's a new moon; I was extremely frustrated. I kept searching the sky over and over, thinking that perhaps I was just missing it because I saw so many other stars.

Oct. 9: 12:45 am — The moon was very eerie tonight. It was very low in the south and very large.

Oct. 9: 8:00 pm — The moon looked bright tonight and similar to the way it looked this morning, only it was smaller and higher in the southeastern sky.

Oct. 10: 9:50 pm — The moon was in quite a predictable spot, high in the south eastern sky, the light area was a bit larger than last night.

Oct. 11: 7:30 pm — I saw the moon and it was still daylight. It was almost directly in the eastern sky. This time only a little bit south.

Oct. 12: 10:00 pm — Almost full!

Oct. 14: 2:30 pm — FULL MOON! Shone right on me through my bedroom window. I thought it was a light. Almost directly overhead. Where are the moon, sun and earth in relation to each other? Where does it start and finish?

Learning Alone and With Others. We divided the class into groups of five students and directed them to share their observations, pool their ideas about what was happening to the moon, and figure out what information they needed to gather in order to explain the changes they had observed and answer questions that had come up.

The group work was affected by the composition of the groups, the quality of the moon journals, and students' prior knowledge and involvement in the project. In most cases, students worked well together. In a few instances, group work was hampered because one student dominated or because the observations were too limited to reveal any patterns.

During the initial phase of the project, we wanted students to think about themselves as learners — whether they could put together what they saw with what they already knew about the moon, what questions still puzzled them, how they approached the task compared with others in their group. To encourage their reflection, we asked students to write down their thoughts about the following questions after the groups had met for the first time:

- What did you know about the moon before the project and how did this knowledge influence your understanding?
- What did you notice about the moon?
- When you compare how you approached this task with the way others did, what can you say about yourself as a learner?
- Were you able to put together what you saw with what you already knew?
- What are your hunches or hypotheses about the moon? What questions remain?

What students knew about the moon varied greatly. Some recalled learning a few basics in elementary school; others had taken astronomy in college.

I knew the moon revolved around the earth and the earth revolved around the sun. I knew the moon only reflected the sun's light and did not generate light on its own. I don't remember when or where I learned these things. I am pretty sure it was in elementary school.

Several acknowledged that they had always taken the moon for granted:

> When I began observing the moon for this project, I realized that I did not know anything about it. The observations brought about questions as well as information. I began to be interested in the project at this point and wanted to know and understand the moon which had been, until then, 'just there.'

In writing about themselves as learners, students made revealing comments whose import they only later came to appreciate.

> As a learner I am motivated by some internal fear of not getting something completed more than for the sheer joy of learning.

> I tend to look inward, deep into my own mind's resources. I tend to get frustrated with myself rather than go right to outside resources to find answers.

> I see myself as a hands-on learner, one who needs to see or have examples of something in order to fully understand it.

Before the next group meeting, students were supposed to find out answers to the questions they had generated. Some groups assigned different students to track down specific information. Other groups took a more laissez-faire approach. One group relied entirely on the "expert" who had dominated the discussion to gather appropriate resources. Students, including those who had not done so before, continued to record their observations.

Phase 2: Planning and Teaching About the Moon

Two weeks later, the groups reconvened to share what they had found out and to plan a lesson about the moon that each student would teach to someone outside of class. Some students had consulted astronomy books and other materials. One student had even called the director of the University planetarium. In most groups, students talked excitedly about what they had learned, drawing diagrams, poring over reference books, using balls of paper to show the relationship of the earth, moon, and sun. In a few cases, when students had not come prepared, groups had trouble getting started and ended up going to the library.

In planning their lessons, the groups were supposed to agree on a common goal, decide what types of learners they would teach, and plan appropriate activities. Most groups decided to focus their lesson on the phases of the moon ("the waxing and waning") and to teach roommates or siblings. One group decided to try out the lesson on learners of various ages.

After the second group meeting, we again had students write about their learning, focusing this time on the contribution of the group. To guide their reflections, we provided the following questions:

- What did you do since the last moon meeting to clarify your confusions and check out your hunches?
- How did other people contribute to your learning?
- What did you do to help the group resolve its questions?
- Have you learned anything new about yourself as a learner?
- What do you know (or suspect) about the moon that you didn't know when this project began?

These "fastwrites" sensitized us to the differential effects of the groups, especially the power of others to energize or limit learning.

For many students, the moon groups served as the main arena of learning. Students shared data and confusions, provided explanations, raised questions, tested their own understanding.

I felt that I learned a considerable amount about the moon in my moon group. . . . I was able to give reasons and explanations to members of my group so that I could see, as could they, if I had a correct understanding of what I had learned.

Each student eventually taught the group lesson to someone outside of class—often a roommate, boyfriend, or sibling. One woman taught her Sunday school class of 4-year-olds and another herded five neighborhood kids into her basement for a lesson about the moon.

Most lessons focused on the phases of the moon and involved the use of diagrams, calendars, and demonstrations. The lessons varied in their emphasis on teacher explanation or active involvement of the learner. Some teachers asked learners to predict the shape of the moon, others had learners participate directly in a demonstration using flashlights and tennis balls. Most groups created some kind of chart to illustrate their explanation of the moon's phases.

Reflecting on the Experience. After teaching their lessons, students reconvened in moon groups to talk about their experiences and plan a presentation for the rest of the class. In their presentations, we asked each group to teach its lesson and then discuss the similarities and differences that members encountered in their teaching, and the issues and questions raised by the experience. The presentations not only expanded students' thinking about ways to teach about the moon; they also expanded students' knowledge about the moon as they encountered different representations. Comparing experiences helped students develop insights into learning and teaching. These insights provided the basis for a major paper in the course. The assignment gave students an opportunity to think about the interaction of teaching, learning, and subject matter by reflecting on their experiences in the moon projects.

WHAT STUDENTS LEARNED

Obviously, we cannot be sure what our students learned. The course readings and the syllabus provide clues about what we *hope* they will learn, and it would be naive to assume that these students would not reflect those ideas in their writing. From teaching many sections of TE-101, we know that students often cling tightly (and loudly) to old beliefs about teaching and learning in the face of abundant evidence about more favored views, so we read their papers and fastwrites with great interest, and perhaps without sufficient skepticism. We will, therefore, begin by discussing what students wrote and defer to the final section of the essay our reflections on the limitations of these data.

Fastwrites and papers suggest that the moon assignment gave flesh to many of the ideas we had explored together in the course, and to much of what students had read. As they worked their way through teaching and learning about the moon, many reported that their ideas had changed dramatically, that they were seeing teaching and learning in more complex ways. Beyond this, the project also seemed to have catalyzed some new learnings.

In talking and writing about their experiences, students drew on almost every important idea in the course; however, a few themes emerged over and over. These fell into five different categories: lessons about learning in general, lessons about themselves as learners, lessons about cooperative groups, lessons about teaching, and lessons about what teachers need to know.

Learning

Writing about their own learning and that of their pupil, TE-101 students made several observations about the process of learning. They noted that ideas took time and multiple exposures to develop; that they often understood a concept better when it was presented in several different ways; that learning occurs most surely when the learner actively searches for resources and answers. Caitlin's narrative contains many of the general points that students made:

> The first step of my learning involved watching the moon and writing down what I saw each day. The first couple of days it was perfectly clear out, but I didn't see the moon. I realized the reason was because it must [be] out during the day, but I had just assumed that it was out every night, and if it was clear, you could see it every night. Soon it came back to being out during the night. Sometimes I would look at the moon several times a night to watch its path across the sky, and a pattern started developing. A pattern also showed up in the shape of the moon and which way the open section pointed.
>
> Then I got together with a couple of classmates and discussed what we had seen and knew. . . . Kay brought in a picture of the phases of the moon and how the sun's reflection on the moon formed these phases. When I saw this chart is when I think knowledge transformation* took place. When I was just looking at the moon, I was just noting, not really understanding because I couldn't relate it all together. But that chart pulled all the loose ends together. *I could relate what I had actually seen in the sky to this chart and really understand why I saw the phases that I did.*
>
> I didn't reach my knowledge transformation all at once, though. Kay brought up the synotic and sidereal months. She tried to explain it to me several times, but it didn't work. I just couldn't understand it at this point. I guess it was just too far beyond my present knowledge at that point. Each time our group got together, she brought it up, and each time I asked

---

*This term comes from a reading by Jackson (1986). It refers to a process by which "knowledge is assimilated or transformed or otherwise adapted to fit within the learner's system of habitual thought or action."

her to explain it. Finally, a couple of weeks later, it finally kicked in. I understood that it took 27 ⅓ days for the moon to rotate on its axis, and 2 more days for it to catch up to the earth, which had rotated around the sun in the meantime.

Like Caitlin, many students noted that their learning took time and multiple exposures to ideas. Ruth drew some conclusions for her future teaching:

When our group met for the first time to share observations and knowledge about the moon, I was shocked at how little I knew compared to everyone else. During the discussion I learned many little facts. One member explained the phases . . . and the path of the moon. At this time I did not understand what she was talking about, but I started to look for some of the things she talked about and I became more interested about learning.

During the next meeting these ideas were explained again and they made more sense and I remembered more than I thought I had. *This showed me that since I did catch on to the concept the second time, the first exposure was important in preparing me for learning the material the second time.* When I was teaching my roommate these same concepts her experience was similar. *This is important for me to know as a teacher so I give children some exposure to concepts that may seem too confusing for them to help prepare them for later learning.* Another way this experience helped me was to show me not to become frustrated if the students do not understand a concept the first time, or even the second time it is given.

Many students observed the way their own understanding of the moon moved through stages, and related their observations of themselves to Maja Apelman's (1980) comments about the extended process of learning. Linette explained:

I agree strongly with Apelman's statement, "Learning is a gradual, continuing process; understanding does not come all at once. You need time for ideas to sink in and you need a chance to go back to your teacher, to ask the questions which arise only as you begin to think about a new idea." I know this is true from my experience as a learner and as a teacher. While

learning about the moon I was surrounded by a lot of information, too much to possibly collect all at once. I know more
about the moon than I did before this project, and I am confident because of this basic knowledge I will make more connections and eventually know even more about the moon.

Closely linked to the idea that real understanding of new ideas
takes time and several exposures was the notion that multiple representations of the same material deepened and broadened understanding. Even though the students had already studied the moon
on their own for 7 weeks, had discussed their questions and the
patterns they observed with classmates on at least three occasions,
and had planned and taught a lesson on the moon to someone
outside of the class, almost all reported that they had learned from
the presentations other groups made of their lessons. Reflecting on
the presentations in an in-class fastwrite, Ruth noted, "They were
taught in different ways and if I didn't understand it the first time I
usually did the second time." She saw this even more clearly when
she tried to explain the path of the moon to her roommate.

> At first I tried explaining the path by reading and explaining
> my notes to her. She rolled her eyes and laughed because she
> could not understand anything I was telling her. Next I tried
> drawing the path on paper which she seemed to understand a
> little better but not completely. Then I got out objects that she
> could see and I showed her exactly what I meant. Finally, she
> understood. If I would not have had those various ways of
> showing her the concept, it would have taken a longer time to
> get the information that I was presenting across to her.

For Mary, the lessons about learning were, in a sense, even more
fundamental. Unable to make any sense out of the lunar patterns
she observed, she set off for the library and looked for relevant
books.

> The majority of my knowledge on the moon came from these
> books that I located and read on my own. This led me to a dis-
> covery that I had never even considered before; that some-
> times the responsibility to learn falls on the student. I guess I
> had always taken for granted that the knowledge a student re-
> ceived was the responsibility of the teacher.

The experience of successfully—and apparently for the first time—assuming responsibility for her learning allowed Mary to see why Maja Apelman (1980) had advocated a shift from teaching by instructing to teaching by facilitating. Certain that she would have learned almost nothing about the moon if she had continued to wait for enlightenment from above, she declares herself in full agreement with Apelman. And she sees *herself* somewhat differently: "I also believe that because I took the responsibility to learn on my own, it has helped me to value my own thinking a little more highly."

All these points about learning—that it takes time and often occurs gradually and after repeated exposure to a new idea, that multiple representations and active involvement assist the learner— bear directly on teaching.

The Self as a Learner

Some students, reflecting on what they saw as they watched themselves at work on the moon project, drew conclusions about themselves as learners. For Megan the picture was heartening. "I have learned that I am open to new information. I really enjoyed looking up data and getting information about the moon. It introduced me to something I didn't know anything about. It was exciting learning something new and interesting."

Others were less pleased by what they saw. Ginny gave up after several nights of not finding the moon at all, and then went off to the library to see if she could figure out why she had failed. Looking back over her efforts she notes—

It was strange to examine myself as a learner, and to compare my learning to that of others. I guess I never thought of my learning as a style. It was just what happened when teachers taught. Now I see that I like structure and organization in learning, such as outlined material and the "right" answers. I also realize this may not always be the most effective way to learn.

Linda's self portrait contains the seeds of an important insight about the solitary, individualistic nature of American schooling:

In the time that elapsed between our meetings, I came to realize something about how I learn and have always learned. I went home and got my astronomy book because I really wanted to figure out the phases. As I read, re-read, and read a third time, I still didn't understand. Rather than being compelled to search for the answer elsewhere, I became extremely frustrated and angry with myself for not understanding. I gave up. As I look at the incident now, I realize that it summarizes how I have always been. I have always relied on myself to find answers. I rely on my brain and my brain only to work through problems. When posed with a problem I hold the expectation that I have to and can, find the answer on my own. I have always studied alone with a book, never taking part in a study group. I almost always go right to a book to find answers that I want, and I am annoyed when I need to ask someone else to help. I'm not sure if this is a sign of egoism or just a result of never experiencing any emphasis on group work in my academic career. I like to believe it is the latter.

Groups

Most students reported that working on the project in a group had helped them to learn. This happened in four different ways: The groups motivated students to learn more about the moon; group leaders shared the work of gathering data, locating resources, and making sense of confusing ideas; students learned from "teaching" others in their group; finally, by comparing themselves to others in their group, students learned about their own learning style.

Many students reported that, although they had been observing the moon regularly for 4 weeks, they had had little interest in the project until they met with their moon group for the first time and began to talk about what they had seen. "Before I started this project I knew very little about the moon and I wasn't really very curious about it until I started watching it and especially after I got together with my group," observes Rebecca in her first in-class fastwrite. The other group members seemed to know considerably more about the moon than she did; after listening to them speculate about the changing shape and location of the moon, she felt she would understand the patterns she observed a bit more in the future.

Mary, who rarely spoke in full-class discussions, found that the group provided a comfortable setting for learning from others:

I learned in my group by listening to what other people had to say. Being able to talk things over and ask questions in my group really helped my learning about the moon. I think sometimes students are afraid to participate on a larger scale, and by dividing them into smaller groups it might help them become more actively involved and therefore get more out of the lesson.

Groups explained, gathered and shared information, and arrived at new hypotheses and new questions together. Linda, the solitary learner, reported that at the first meeting of her moon group she had listened quietly, unwilling to admit that she could not make sense of the moon's phases.

As I listened I started making connections in my mind, and I started asking questions. I felt comfortable letting other people help me with my uncertainties. I was also able to add in my knowledge to help others to understand. I noticed that visual aids of any sort, whether they be pictures or objects, helped me extremely in my understanding of the positioning. I also found that if I re-explained a concept back to someone, it reinforced my understanding even more. It was a very unusual way of learning for me. At first, I had a strange feeling about it, but it evolved into a great feeling. I felt like leaving the class, singing the praises of Cohen!*

Annette describes the ways in which other group members helped her to interpret the patterns she observed:

The group members separated, gathered more information on their own, then met again to discuss our newly acquired knowledge. This time we were able to achieve an understand-ing of how the phases of the moon worked. One group mem-ber seemed to catch on quicker, therefore she was able to help the others by putting the information into words that we could understand. She also brought diagrams in where we could see the phases drawn with pictures. I would not have received this further understanding if I never had the opportunity to inter-act with the group.

Besides serving as a collection of fact finders and explainers, the groups gave students an audience, providing a comforting dress

---

*Students read material by Elizabeth Cohen (1986) on cooperative learning.

rehearsal for later "teaching." "By explaining and talking in front of my classmates, I was able to increase my speaking skills and my confidence in presenting my material to others," wrote Annette. More important, explaining to others got students actively involved in making sense of new ideas. Linda found that "if I re-explained a concept back to someone, it reinforced my understanding even more." It also forced some people to redefine what it means to understand. Rena, for example, noted that her responsibilities as a group member required her to push for a deeper understanding than she would ordinarily seek.

> It's easier to be the learner for oneself than the learner for a group. As a learner for myself all I had to do was concentrate on my grasping the material and being able to retain that information for knowledge reproduction situations. When learning with intentions of interacting with a group there's a need to be more prepared. I really wanted to know the material so I could be an asset to the group. As I was learning (re-learning) about the moon, I kept thinking, "Am I understanding completely what the books are saying?" I wanted to be able to explain if the group was puzzled about any point. I was really excited about the material.

Several students noted that close work with other students gave them a baseline for comparing their own approach to learning with that of other people and thus learn something new about themselves. Megan learned that she was "open to new information." A few of her classmates found that they were not as curious or as aggressive in seeking answers to their own questions as others in their groups.

Although most students claimed to have found the group work helpful, a few used the paper assignment to reflect on unproductive group dynamics. Barbara bravely analyzed how her enjoyment of expert status kept others in a passive role where they learned less than they otherwise might have.

> Because I had the most recent astronomy class, the group turned to me with their questions. I enjoyed answering them because it gave me a kind of "high" feeling when I knew more on a subject than someone else. But because of the attitude of confidence that I started the group project with, the group expected me to be able to answer their questions, which I could most of them because everyone had fairly simple questions.

When a question arose that I could not answer, instead of de-facing myself by just admitting I did not know and that they should find the answer out themselves, I acted confident and just told them that I would find the answer out and tell them at the next grouping. My ego, which made me want to look good in front of everyone, is one reason why my group did not learn very much about the moon. . . . My acting led my group to rely on me for the project instead of themselves, which is one reason that they did not learn very much.

While Rebecca, Mary, Rena, and others noted that the group had enhanced their learning by arousing their curiosity, and putting them in a variety of relationships to the new ideas, Barbara found that one individual could sabotage the learning of others by casting them always in the same role — in this case a passive one. The lessons, apparently quite different, rested on some similar discoveries about teaching.

Teaching

Many students enter TE-101 with simple and somewhat naive views of what teachers do. Rena writes:

Teaching always appeared to be so cut and dry and simple, es-pecially at the elementary level. It seemed as if all that was needed to know in order to teach K-5 were the things I had previously learned in elementary school. I never gave thought to an approach on how to present material to a variety of young minds. It just seemed as though my teachers just came into class and introduced some new material. We learned it, went over the lesson a few times and that was it. The lesson was done. I didn't realize that teachers learned in preparation for their lesson plan. It seemed as if everything was already laid out in their "teacher's copy" books. Either their teaching style was so good that I didn't even notice I was being taught, or they just plain taught like this (which could explain my handicap in math now).

For Rena and her classmates, the moon project provided an oppor-tunity to reexamine this view, and to think more deeply about what teaching actually involves.

Some lessons about teaching grew out of students' experiences as learners. The quarter before Melissa enrolled in Exploring Teaching, she had taken an astronomy course. Having spent three full weeks of the course studying the moon, she began her moon journal somewhat lackadaisically: "I really thought I knew everything I needed to know for this project." Before long, however, she began to suspect that she knew a good deal less than she had thought. And at the end of the quarter she announced that she had learned "ten times more about the moon in this class than I learned in Astronomy 119." She was angry when she began to see how little she had gotten out of her astronomy course. As she tried to figure out what had gone wrong, she kept returning to the distinction Wilson et al. (1987) draw between teachers' subject matter knowledge and their "pedagogical content knowledge," knowledge of ways to transform and represent subject matter in order to teach it.

> Content knowledge means having an understanding of the concepts in one's area of interest whereas pedagogical content knowledge means having knowledge of how to take one field and embody as many resources as possible, such as analogies, illustrations, examples, explanations, etc., so that it is comprehensible by others. Professor Tate had to have had content knowledge in order to be a certified professor at Michigan State University, but as far as pedagogical content knowledge, he was definitely lacking. For example, in studying the moon for this class (TE-101), I got out my old astronomy folder and reviewed the lecture notes and tests. We spent three weeks studying the moon, and we never once set foot outside to look at it. There were about five to six questions on the exam related to how the seasons and the phases are intertwined. I remember being very confused about that, yet after observing the moon in this class, it was all so easy. The illustration our group used in our presentation . . . made complete sense to me and it was as if the missing piece was there and I could finally say, "I understand." Professor Tate never made use of diagrams, illustrations or any props to explain what he was lecturing about that certain day. I cannot help but think that the relation between the seasons and the phases would have made more sense to me if an illustration would have been used.

Melissa drew her lessons about teaching from her experiences as a learner: As she really began to understand the relationship between the moon's position and seasonal changes, she became deeply dissatisfied with the teaching that had taught her so little. As she examined her experiences as a learner in the astronomy course, she saw the limitations of unsupplemented "telling." Shulman's distinction between content knowledge and pedagogical content knowledge gave her a language and a framework for discussing what was missing from her astronomy professor's teaching.

Other class members drew similar lessons from their teaching: Their students seemed badly confused when they simply "told" how the moon's rotation related to the observable phases. Many were powerfully affected by uncertainties about students' level of understanding — uncertainties that had seemed quite manageable when they had read about them in Philip Jackson's (1986) essay "The Uncertainties of Teaching." Teaching their lesson to the whole class, they realized, left many students with undiagnosed and unresolved confusions. Says Ruth:

> In our small group teaching one another and in a one-to-one situation with our experimental students, the students are able to freely ask a question whenever they have one. In the larger group, the setting was more structured and very few people asked questions. We did not know what the students knew before we started so we did not know where they got confused or why. Even when students did ask questions about what was confusing them, it was usually too late for either them or us to get a coherent message across. This was a cause of the frustration we all felt.

Many students were startled to find themselves abandoning carefully crafted lesson plans as they and their students became more deeply involved with the material.

> I had an outline of the objectives I wished to cover. In all my planning, I never thought to consider my pupils' own questions or thoughts. When I actually began to teach my lesson I was faced with another individual capable of thought and questioning. She expressed agreement, disagreement, and puzzlement. My lesson plan was suddenly forgotten, and while we did cover the material I had planned, we did so at the pace my student determined.

This experience helped Linette to see why she had admired Herb Kohl's (1984) commitment to his students' individual needs, and

why Kohl had decried rigid adherence to textbooks or other pre-
fabricated curriculum. And Annette, caught between her desire
to reshape her lesson in response to her 9-year-old student's
knowledge and interests, and her feeling that she *ought* to carry
out her written plan, found that Kohl gave her "permission" to be
flexible.

Of all the conclusions students drew about teaching, one stood
out: If they are to teach well and lead their students to real understanding, teachers need to know a great deal more about subject
matter than most TE-101 students had previously expected.

Knowledge of Subject Matter

Many students came to the moon project without illusions:
They had never given the moon much thought and were aware that
they knew very little about it. The few who had taken astronomy
courses in college felt that they already understood the moon's
phases and its path very well. Most of these students could not
produce satisfactory explanations for the phenomena that they and
their classmates had observed.

The astronomy course graduates, like their classmates, soon
concluded that they needed to know more than they had anticipated
in order to teach well. Linda discovered that she was all right as
long as she was lecturing and demonstrating, but that she could not
answer the questions her sister asked her about the moon's orbit
and position. Shaken and embarrassed by her ignorance, she found
herself retreating from the teaching:

> [The student] . . . started to become curious about the specif-
> ics of what side of the moon was lit and where in the sky the
> moon was, etc. I was at a loss. My heart sank. My confidence
> was shaken. I was honest, and I told her that I didn't know.
> From that point on I felt totally inadequate. The last part of
> my lesson was simply hurried through. I sensed that she felt
> uncomfortable about asking further questions because of my
> reaction. I really handled the situation poorly. . . . I am very
> afraid that I was more worried about myself in this challenge
> than my student . . .
>
> *Through this teaching episode I came to realize that, as Lampert*
> *suggests, teachers need to know a lot more than just one aspect of subject*
> *matter.*

Others discovered that, because they understood less than they thought they did, they were actually teaching things that were not true. Often their pupils' questions revealed inconsistencies in their explanations that they had not spotted in planning their lessons.

For most, however, lessons about teaching came in trying to make the patterns of the moon's cycle clear to their students. A verbal explanation produced puzzled looks; if they understood what they were teaching well enough, they turned to diagrams, or, eventually perhaps, to three-dimensional models. Those who succeeded in making their ideas clear through multiple representations knew that they had utilized all their knowledge and understanding to get to that point: They saw their own hard-won understanding as the critical ingredient of their success. Those who failed regretted that they did not know enough to be able to create the range of representations their students required.

Multiple representations, students concluded, were essential to real teaching of complex phenomena or ideas. If teachers couldn't explain and demonstrate in a variety of ways, many students would never understand the message.

Some students came to a less obvious but equally upsetting conclusion: If they had only a "surface" understanding of subject matter, they would be *boring* teachers. Warm memories of teachers who had made learning "fun" with cute projects and imaginative presentations of material draw many 19-year-olds to teaching. Being creative ranks high among their goals. As they studied and taught about the moon, these students began to see an unexpected connection between creativity and knowledge. For Dana this insight had direct implications for her own college program:

> What do teachers need to know in order to teach well? My thoughts on this have changed drastically. Most of the ideas we've talked about in class I never really had thought about before. This one is different, however, because I considered this quite thoroughly as I decided on my major as I entered college.
>
> This may make me look like a weasel looking for an easy way out, but a factor in my deciding to become a child development and teaching major is the fact that I don't have to take any math classes. I'll only be certified to teach preschool through fifth grade, therefore I thought I'll only need to know the basics: adding, subtracting, multiplying, and dividing, and I'll be fine. My ideas began to change when I read Lampert's

article on teaching and learning math. . . . But it was this moon project that showed me how important teacher knowledge really is . . .

. . . [I began my lesson by administering a quiz.] Chris got three wrong, but guessed at a couple of the answers and didn't know why they were correct. I used the opportunity to demonstrate answers using a pumpkin, a tennis ball, and a hanging lamp in our room. This worked great for about three questions. After that, all I could do was give the correct answers by telling, and I was afraid I'd be very boring, and I was. I couldn't think of another way to present the answers. Right then and there I realized how creative teachers need to be, but to be creative, they need to know the subject so well that they can twist it around 30 different ways if they need to. Does that mean I am destined to be a boring math teacher?

Dana has come a long way: Few teacher candidates see any connection between "creativity" and knowledge of subject matter. For most, creativity is more a matter of inserting songs, games, and the construction of dioramas into the necessary chore of learning facts, rules, and skills.

FUTURE DIRECTIONS

Learning and teaching about the moon convinced almost all students that in order to teach well they needed to understand subject matter deeply. In addition, the project either illustrated and made vivid some of the understandings that students had begun to develop from readings, group work, and class discussions, or it catalyzed new learning about themselves, teaching and learning, and the role of knowledge in teaching.

Still, the project taught some students far more than it taught others. Analysis of papers and in-class fastwrites suggests some ways to revise the project to increase the benefits to students who seemed to have been less intensely involved.

Getting Started

The moon assignment startled our students. Even though we explained that this project would provide them with an opportunity to study their own learning, most thought it an eccentric deviation from the usual college courses. (Even in astronomy courses, as Melissa noted, professors do not ask students to look up at the sky.) Those who had already taken astronomy seemed particularly skeptical; most reported that at the outset they had thought that they knew everything worth knowing about the moon.

Initial skepticism did not always impede learning: Most students, having heard that they would be writing a graded paper on the moon project, dutifully started their journals even before the project made much sense to them. However, since the moon was not visible at night during the first 2 weeks of the term, not all got deeply involved at the outset. Although some noted with astonishment that they had never before realized that you couldn't always see the moon on clear nights, and began to take a greater interest in figuring out when (and why) the moon *was* visible, others, feeling stupid or frustrated, simply stopped looking. Many reported that getting together in "moon groups" sparked their first real interest in the substantive focus: comparing journals, discovering that someone else had seen the moon during the afternoon or in the early morning on days when they themselves had given up on it, puzzling over other people's questions, and sharing what they had picked up from elementary school, summer camp, astronomy courses, and the Skywatch section of the daily paper, they began to formulate questions of their own.

This common observation suggests the wisdom of convening moon groups earlier in the term than we did. Because we wanted to use the first seven classes to help students to make sense of four key texts and because we thought students needed to collect data for at least a month before they would have hypotheses about the moon to discuss with one another, we did not convene our moon groups until the fourth week of the quarter. Although this schedule left students with plenty of time to consult outside resources, pool new knowledge, plan a lesson, teach it, report back, and write up their experiences, it gave many of them a rather frustrating and unproductive start. And, given the vagaries of Michigan weather, it did not give slow starters enough time to make more detailed, systematic, and curious observations. As a result, several groups brought little additional information about the moon and its behavior to the second meeting. These groups relied heavily on books for the substance of what they taught. Had they begun meeting earlier in the quarter, a number of students might have gotten more out of their personal observations, and they might have contributed more to their groups.

Groups

Groups affected their members very powerfully. Denise's interest in the moon and her enthusiasm for the project infected her whole group. She raised questions about seasonal variation in the moon's path; Melissa had heard something about this in her astronomy class, although she had never really understood the patterns. Their speculations piqued the interest of others in their group, and five of them decided to divide up the 24 hours of the day in such a way as to be sure that they would be able to track the moon's path across the sky for several weeks. Ultimately the group used these data as the basis for a discovery lesson in which their students derived some hypotheses about the path of the moon from the raw data they were given. Other groups used the questions and expertise of their members in a variety of ways.

Most students reported that they had learned a great deal from others in their group, but we were troubled by the few who did not. Rebecca reported:

> Group work helped many people in my moon group learn
> more material about the moon. On the other hand, I found
> that I didn't learn better, or much at all for that matter, in the
> group setting. I learn better in a one-on-one situation or on
> my own, if the material isn't too difficult. I probably get more
> done on my own because there is nothing to distract me. I
> don't like working in groups because there is always room for
> someone to slack off and not do their share of the work and yet
> still take credit for it.

Could we alter the project so that Rebecca could experience more satisfying learning or teaching, or expand her view of group work?

Perhaps part of Rebecca's problem lay in the composition of her group, none of whom knew much about the moon to begin with, and none of whom believed strongly in their own capacity to learn from this sort of inquiry. Surely her experience would have been different if she had had a Dana, a Melissa, a Linda, or a Rena to press the collective inquiry forward. (Interestingly, in her first fastwrite — see page 72 — Rebecca noted that the first group meeting stimulated her curiosity about the moon.)

With this thought in mind, we might have put moon groups together more craftily, distributing students with some background in astronomy, and those with energy, enthusiasm, and a disposition to inquiry, more evenly across groups.

The experience of those now teaching TE-101 suggests that there are real benefits to composing *permanent* groups very early in the term — at the first or second meeting of the class. Those who have tried this strategy report that when students meet repeatedly with the same small group they develop the trust and courage to ask questions and take controversial stands in the larger group much earlier in the term than they do when groups are composed anew at each meeting. If true, this constitutes a powerful argument for assigning students randomly to groups during the first or second class meeting — before the teacher knows the students well enough to do this on any other basis.

It might, however, be possible to make particular students' knowledge and enthusiasm visible to all by asking each group to make a brief presentation of their questions, hypotheses, and observations early on — perhaps during the third week of the term. These presentations might help groups by impelling them to focus their ideas and questions while they still have time to collect observational data, and by giving groups that were having trouble getting a grip on the project a glimpse of other possibilities. It is hard to know whether earlier group meetings and earlier sharing of ideas across groups would have convinced Rebecca of the merits of group learning (which, after all, she had experienced on many other occasions in Exploring Teaching), but they would, at least, have given her more opportunities to learn from others.

Learning from the Experience of Others

Like our students, we have had opportunities to learn from our colleagues about the teaching of TE-101 and, more specifically, about the use of moon watching to help students deepen their understanding of teaching and learning. At the same time that we were trying this version of the moon project for the first time, another colleague, trying it for the third time, was very discouraged: Whereas in previous terms students had written thoughtfully and enthusiastically about their learning and teaching, the shallow and insubstantial papers she received this fall convinced her that many students had not actually observed the moon.

Such reports remind us that luck plays an important role in

most educational experiments, that perhaps the missionary zeal of the novice and experimenter plays an important role in making something like this work, and that the chemistry of groups can spell the difference between success and failure. Our colleague's experience has strengthened our resolve to bring the moon groups together earlier next term so that students can share observations, questions, and, we hope, enthusiasm, and so that those who haven't managed to start a journal can rectify their error while they still have time. We would also collect and respond to moon journals at this time — perhaps 2 weeks into the term — so as to create some early accountability and help those who feel confused to begin to formulate some questions.

Conclusion

In his 1904 essay on the relation of theory to practice in education, John Dewey reminds us that the greatest asset of the beginning teacher — or, for purposes of this discussion, the beginning teacher education student — is "his own direct and personal experience" as a learner.

> There is every presumption (since the student is not an imbecile) that he has been learning all the days of his life, and that he is still learning from day to day. He must accordingly have in his own experience plenty of practical material by which to illustrate and vitalize theoretical principles and laws of mental growth in the process of learning. (p. 35)

In TE-101 we have always encouraged students to use their own experience as learners to understand and evaluate both the texts in the course and their own assumptions about teaching and learning. But because their experiences of *school* learning have often not extended much beyond the memorization and reproduction of facts, rules, and technical skills, they often have difficulty connecting to the points Apelman (1980), for example, makes about the gradual way in which true comprehension of complex new ideas evolves. For this reason TE-101 instructors often feel that they need to give students something new to learn *about*, and a new way of learning it.

On the last day of class, one of us asked students to write and talk about one reading that had seemed to connect to their experience teaching and learning about the moon. We discovered in the subsequent discussion that, taken as a group, the class had used more than three-quarters of the readings in making sense of their experience as learners and as teachers. We hope that this experience will make them more ready and able to look to their own experience as they try to understand and evaluate theories about teaching and learning.

5

Exploring Teaching
With Cases

Michelle B. Parker
Linda J. Tiezzi

A common strategy in business and legal education, case-based teaching has attracted teacher educators searching for powerful ways to link theory and practice. Despite the intuitive appeal of teaching with cases, we know very little about their use in teacher education. If case-based teacher education is to become more than a passing fad, we need to consider what counts as a case, and what teaching and learning with cases is and could be. This chapter contributes to that agenda by describing and analyzing the use of cases in an introductory education course.

Cases of teaching figure prominently in TE-101. One of their functions is to help students discover what they know and believe about teaching and learning in schools by eliciting reactions that contain clues about taken-for-granted beliefs. Cases also expand students' ideas about what teaching could be like by offering vivid portraits of unconventional practice. Finally, cases illustrate concepts and clarify key ideas in theoretical readings.

These purposes guide our selection of the cases that we draw from diverse sources, including teacher writing, case studies and videotapes made for research purposes, commercial documentaries and news reports, and cases that students construct based on field assignments. Because TE-101 does not focus on how to teach, we do not use decision-oriented cases in the course. Rather we use concrete instances of teaching (cases) in conjunction with essays about teaching to explore three main questions: What does it mean to teach? What are schools for? What do teachers need to know?

In this chapter, we describe and analyze how we work with three cases of teaching. The first case consists of excerpts from *Wally's Stories* by Vivian Paley (1981). The second case, a "60 Minutes" (CBS, 1983) episode about Marva Collins, and the third case, a documentary featuring Leslie Stein (Holmes, n.d.), offer contrasting videotapes of urban elementary classrooms. We use all these cases to elicit students' beliefs, broaden their thinking about teaching, and illuminate theoretical ideas.

THE CASE OF VIVIAN PALEY: LISTENING TO CHILDREN

Selections from *Wally's Stories* provide a springboard for helping TE-101 students think about what it means to teach, the first organizing question of the course. Paley, a kindergarten teacher at the University of Chicago Laboratory School, presents her pupils' actual conversations, painstakingly audiotaped and then transcribed for the book, to illuminate the multiple thoughts and actions of kindergarten children as they develop through one school year.

As a teacher, Paley does not tell her students what to do or think. Nor does she correct their errors, resolve their conflicts, or take responsibility for ensuring that the fairest solution carries the day. Rather, she creates opportunities for pupils to talk and solve problems together. As a teacher, Paley challenges what our students know and believe about teaching.

From the 30 episodes in Paley's book we ask students to read five, which illuminate her attention to both the academic and social agenda, and the way in which she embeds those concerns in an intellectual approach to teaching and learning. In class we usually analyze two of the five episodes that attend to the academic goals in Paley's kindergarten class.

"Rulers"

In the first episode, "Rulers," Paley's pupils are ready to act out "Jack and the Beanstalk" when they are stopped by a staging problem: They need to figure out which classroom rug is larger so that it can be used for the giant's castle. Although some of his friends think the rugs are the same size, Wally insists they are not. He walks around each rug, counting how many times he says "walk," and concludes that one rug is larger because he had to say "walk" ten times as opposed to five. Eddie suggests they get a ruler — "the long kind that gets curled up in a box"—to measure the rugs. Instead, Wally recommends arranging students on the rug end-to-end until it is covered. "That's a great idea," says Eddie, "I never even thought of that" (p. 14). They line up children until both rugs are covered.

The next day an unforeseen difficulty arises when the children try to measure the rug again. Whereas the day before the larger rug held four students, today four students fail to cover it. The problem, as they see it, is that Warren, a "longer" student, is absent. Various actors suggest rearranging the people or substituting different students. After several unsuccessful attempts, the children declare a rule: "Nobody bigger than Warren can measure the rug" (p. 15). Paley asks if there is a way to measure the rug without using people.

> Kenny: Use short people.
> Paley: And if short people aren't in school?
> Rose: Use big people.
> Eddie: Some people are too big.
> Paley: Maybe using people is a problem.
> Fred: Use three-year-olds.
> Paley: There aren't any three-year-olds in our class.
> Deanna: Use rulers. Get all the rulers in the room. I'll get the
>   box of rulers. (p. 15)

When they run out of rulers, Eddie suggests they can "put a short, short person after the rulers . . . " (p. 15). A student identified as "short short" isn't pleased, so Wally suggests using dolls. After they lay out ten rulers and two dolls, Paley demonstrates how to measure the rug with one ruler. Since Eddie was unhappy about the "empty space" left from picking up the ruler, Paley suggests using a tape measure. The class finds that the carpet is 156 inches long.

At this point, Paley thinks the lesson is over. The next morning, however, when Warren returns to school, Wally announces that now they *really* can measure the rug.

> Paley: Didn't we really measure the rug with the rulers
> Wally: Well, rulers aren't really real, are they? (pp. 13–17)

As Paley concludes this episode, she puzzles about her students' ideas about what is and is not "real."

Weighing Stones

In another episode, a question arises from the class reading of *Stone Soup* by Marcia Brown. In the book, three hungry soldiers trick some peasants into giving them food by pretending to make soup from three stones. One kindergartner, Rose, asks if stones melt. When Paley refers the question to the other children, they suggest that the stones would melt if cooked. If the stones get smaller, the children decide, they would know that they had melted.

After cooking the stones for 1 hour, some children are convinced the stones got smaller. Paley asks how they could prove it. Mickey suggests outlining the stones in pencil, recooking them, tracing them a second time, and comparing the pictures. "Thirty minutes later the stones do look smaller" (p. 17), writes Paley, and so she suggests that the children weigh the stones on a scale. Before and after cooking, the stones weigh 2 pounds. Eddie thinks that "they only got a *little* bit smaller" (p. 18), and Wally questions the validity of the scale — "the scale can't *see* the stones" (p. 18). Besides, he recalls, once he saw three stones melt away in a fire. Deanna speculates that perhaps the stones in the story are magic. "The endless contradictions did not offend them; the children did not demand consistency" (p. 18), concludes Paley.

Cases as a Way to Elicit Students' Beliefs

Most of our students enter TE-101 believing that teaching means "telling somebody something they didn't know." This belief colors the way they interpret the Paley case, which they encounter a week after the course begins. By posing the question, "Is Paley teaching?" we uncover two strong — and opposed — reactions: that Paley is indeed teaching, and that what she is doing cannot possibly be called teaching.

Some students argue that Paley is teaching because even though she is not telling her students anything, she is asking questions and allowing them to "discover things for themselves." These students point out that Paley lets students have fun and talk about what they wish. She reads stories and encourages students to act them out. Paley's actions conform with these students' beliefs that in kindergarten academics matter less than having fun, learning how to get along with others, and enjoying school. They reason that what Paley is doing can be called teaching, given that she is teaching in kindergarten.

Skeptics counter by asserting that Paley is not telling her students anything. They argue that the content in her classroom is not academic — "they just tell a lot of stories" — and that "Paley lets her students go away believing stones melt and rulers aren't useful." These students believe that all Paley is doing is asking questions, and that the questioning does not count as teaching because Paley is not *telling* her students anything. Although she might be learning what her students think, these students argue, Paley does not do anything with what she hears.

As instructors, however, we cannot always tell exactly what our students are thinking about teaching, for the conversations that reveal their assumptions may also raise questions and offer students new ways of looking at a vignette. Some hold firm to their entering assumptions about what teaching is and is not. Like Dana, they try to fit what they see in Paley into their initial beliefs.

> DANA: Well, she really should have just explained it [that stones cannot melt] at the end.
>
> BEVERLY: But she tried. I think she just couldn't think of another way to explain it.
>
> DANA: But you have to tell them what you know when you teach. Someday they'll realize it.
>
> BEVERLY: But the kindergartners were bound and determined to only believe what they could see. And they thought they saw smaller stones.
>
> INSTRUCTOR: What is Paley doing here?
>
> EMMA: She poses questions and challenges her students.
>
> DANA: But she [Paley] doesn't say much.
>
> DENISE: No, but she helps her students bring things out.
>
> BEVERLY: She makes the students reason things out and not wait for an adult.
>
> JUDY: The teacher makes students solve the problems.

As instructors we wonder whether, if after listening to her peers, Dana is beginning to believe that even though Paley does not say much, she is still teaching. We wonder if Beverly's comment that the kindergartners were determined to believe only what they saw is the beginning of a realization that Paley's actions are connected to what her students see and understand. Did the comments

Denise and Donna made reflect changing beliefs about what they just read, or were they still based on stereotyped views of what teachers do? Even after carefully analyzing such exchanges, we still struggle to get inside the heads of our students. We wonder whether we can uncover our students' thinking about teaching in the same way that Paley uncovers her kindergartners' thinking.

Cases as a Way to Broaden Students' Conceptions

Merely confronting students with an example of teaching different from that of their own experience will not alter long-standing beliefs. We need to structure activities in which they will test their assumptions about teaching and learning against the evidence from Paley's classroom. In so doing, we hope to alter students' beliefs that Paley is not teaching because she is not telling, or that her teaching works only because in kindergarten the content is nonacademic.

One way we challenge students' beliefs is to have them closely read the text as a way to see what actually is happening in Paley's classroom. To focus students' attention we usually read the text aloud in class. While reading we stop and point out, for example, that Paley does not agree with her students after the melting stones experiment. We read how Paley (1981) shows students (using the scale) that the stones weigh the same after boiling them—"two pounds before and two pounds now. That means they didn't lose weight" (p. 18). But we also read how Paley's pupils find ways to dispute the findings and how Paley continually encourages students to consider the results of their "experiments" and to draw conclusions.

We hope that evidence from the text, extracted through careful reading, will help students see the interactive dynamic that shapes the conversations Paley has with her students. We hope students will see that Paley's children learn when they are ready, and that Paley is doing what she can to challenge her pupils' thinking. Yet some of our students remain unconvinced, insisting that Paley "just needs to keep telling students until they finally see it" and that Paley is shirking her responsibilities by letting students believe stones melt.

Some TE-101 instructors try to challenge these students' beliefs by dividing the class, having one half argue that Paley *is* teaching and the other half that she is *not*. When we ask groups to list reasons for each position, the group proposing that Paley is not teaching usually has an easier time. They point to students' being left to believe incorrect things about measuring areas and to dismissing rulers as not real. They note that Paley cannot convince her pupils that stones do not melt.

The group arguing that Paley is teaching must work harder because most students actually believe that Paley is not teaching, or at least is not teaching anything academic. They note that Paley suggests students draw a picture of the stones before they are boiled and compare it with the picture they make after the experiment. This group concludes that Paley is helping students see that boiling the stones does not change them.

By setting up opposing groups, we force some students to advocate a position different from their own. To do this successfully, they have to support their group's findings with evidence from the text. Instead of seeing themselves as arguing with a fellow *student*, students see themselves as arguing for their team against an *opponent*. By casting students in these roles, we hope to free them from the discomfort that may arise when disagreeing with a peer. We also hope to frustrate their natural impulse to tell us what they think we want to hear (for they surely realize that we think Paley is teaching, even if they do not).

As instructors we want to teach students ways to analyze the case and to question opposing viewpoints. We work to set up and maintain dissonance between what they as individuals believe, what their peers believe, and what they begin seeing in the text. At times, we play the devil's advocate and provoke students to say what they believe and what they question. "Maybe Paley let an incorrect conception go unquestioned," we say when reading about how her students believed stones could melt. "Is that good teaching?"

We also challenge and broaden students' conceptions by giving feedback to their writing. Sometimes we show students a claim Paley (1986) makes in an essay entitled "Listening to Children" — that she cannot teach her students "that which they already don't know" (p. 126). In response to Paley's claim, Jessie wrote

> Paley and her students see the world in different ways. Being an adult and teacher, Paley can use concepts such as numbers that her children simply cannot grasp at this stage of life. Children are instead logical in their own view of the world. . . . Children's logic is what makes dealing with them ever changing and interesting.

Jessie appreciates that students make sense of the world in a certain way. She seems to be struggling to understand Paley's teaching, pointing out that some things children just cannot "grasp" at a particular developmental phase. Because her use of "grasp" and "children's logic" are vague, we ask her to question her own language and to think about the teacher's role in situations where students "simply cannot grasp" something.

After two to three class sessions during which we discuss the Paley case materials, some students start seeing Paley and her pupils as individuals who bring their own beliefs, knowledge, and ways of making sense of the world to each experience. Some students begin to realize that Paley's actions and comments emerge from careful observation of her students. Some students can see how what Paley does helps students develop from where they are.

Other students remain convinced that teaching is telling, at least after kindergarten. The challenge for us as teachers is to provide other ways to examine this idea.

The Paley Case as an Illustration of Theoretical Ideas

Shortly after we introduce Paley we usually read an essay ("I, Thou, and It") in which David Hawkins (1967/1974) considers the place of teacher, student, and content in teaching and learning. Hawkins argues that teachers must create and sustain environments in which they can elicit students' "interests and talents" and deepen through active involvement their engagement with the subject matter.

Using the Paley case, we highlight two ideas central to Hawkins's argument: that respect is part of a teacher's attitude, and that the teacher's respect for the student and the content shape the teacher's role as provider of an "external feedback loop." Hawkins distinguishes between the parental attitude toward a child, characterized by love, and the teacher's attitude, which he characterized by respect. Though he does not deny that affection is an integral aspect of the teacher/student relationship, Hawkins argues that the essence of the relationship comes from the ways that content, the "it" in Hawkins's terms, "enters into the pattern of mutual interest and exchange between the teacher and the child" (p. 50).

"Now let's use Paley to understand Hawkins's argument," we suggest to our TE-101 students. Because we know many of our TE-101 students feel that a teacher must, above all, love her students, we ask, "What does Paley like about her pupils?" We want our students to see that by watching her pupils act out "Jack and the Beanstalk," Paley is hearing how they think about a problem (finding the largest rug) and seeing what they do to investigate and solve it. She develops an attitude of respect as she hears and sees students think about and act on solving a problem.

We also discuss Hawkins's (1967/1974) contention that the teacher functions as "a kind of external loop, to provide selective feedback from the child's own choice and action" (p. 53), that his job is to respond "diagnostically and helpfully to a child's behavior, to make . . . a response which the child needs to complete the process he's engaged in at a given moment" (p. 53). Paley is responding in a diagnostic fashion when she watches her students solve the carpet problem, when she suggests using rulers, and when she wonders what students mean by "real"—"Does 'real' mean that which can be imagined and acted out?" (Paley, 1981, p. 16). We want students to notice the sorts of "feedback" Paley provides, the way in which this feedback helps Wally "to complete the process he's engaged in at a given moment."

Students' comments often reveal a growing understanding. Betsy, Latasha, and DeeDee, a group of students working together to illustrate Hawkins's idea of the teacher as provider of an external feedback loop, had this conversation:

> BETSY: Paley uses their words. She gave students a chance to talk to each other and be part of the feedback loop.
>
> LATASHA: And Paley's ideas and comments come from what she hears. She starts with her students' ideas. I think that will help them remember it more.
>
> DEEDEE: Also, Paley's pupils wouldn't have been as involved if she'd just told them what to do to measure the carpet.

Applying Hawkins's framework to the Paley case helps students actually see what Paley is doing and what its effects are on students. After this exchange we might redirect other students' attention back to Paley's comment: "Maybe using people is a problem" (p. 15) to further illustrate Paley's work as an external loop, and how what she does arises from her students' thoughts and actions.

Teaching with the Hawkins and Paley texts enables us to help TE-101 students realize the interrelated nature of theory and practice. Hawkins's theoretical ideas about the relationships between and among student, teacher, and subject matter inform students' understanding of Paley's actions and goals. In turn their understandings of Paley inform their broader interpretation of Hawkins.

Comparing and contrasting the texts also leads us to analyze our own teaching. What is *our* "it" — the Paley case, the theoretical ideas in Hawkins, our students' initial conceptions and beliefs? What are we doing as instructors to connect our students with the content? We wonder if students will provoke each other enough when working in small groups to look analytically at Paley's teaching and her students' learning. Should we tackle the texts as a large group and risk losing some students who might rely on others to do the analysis? In what ways are we constructing an activity that capitalizes on our students' prior beliefs and new understandings?

By referring to the Paley case throughout the course, we continue confronting students with the discrepancy between their old ideas and real practice; by maintaining the dissonance between what they believe and what they begin to see in Paley, we work to broaden their conceptions of teaching. As students talk and write about this case, they develop intellectual skills, such as making arguments and supporting claims, necessary for studying teaching.

Yet despite our efforts, at the end of the course some students still miss the complexity of Paley's teaching. On final exams we ask them to think about major purposes of Paley's teaching. Often students continue to see only the social aspects of her work, as Justina states: "Paley gets children to relate to each other . . . and to get along with others even if someone's ideas are different from theirs. She helped children iron out differences in a civil manner." These students either cannot see or cannot express the relationship between Paley's questions, her students' actions, and the opportunities for talk and activity that Paley creates to support further inquiry.

But other responses give us faith that students are on a path toward understanding. Many students recognize the important role of inquiry in Paley's classroom. Molly, for example, sees the connections Paley makes between the child's thinking and actions and the content. She writes

> Paley lets students reveal what they do know as opposed to
> what we may think they know. She lets this happen frequently
> by letting students act out stories and plays. When the group
> of students prepared to act out *Stone Soup*, they talked about the
> stones. Most of them agreed the stones would melt. Paley
> didn't say they were wrong but asked how they could measure
> if this were true. The group decided to boil the stones, then
> weigh them to see if they were smaller. She let students make
> the decisions and watch the consequences.

As instructors we have learned about the strength of students' initial beliefs and conceptions, and the difficulty of helping students to alter and to broaden their ideas. We want students to see that teachers do more than act as tellers, directors, and bankers of correct answers. We want them to see that Paley's intentions and decisions come from her students' actions, from her understandings, and from her judgments. We want them to see that her teaching has academic as well as social and moral aspects.

THE CASES OF MARVA COLLINS AND LESLIE STEIN

The cases of Marva and Leslie are critical in helping students confront and expand their notions of what it means to teach and learn. Explored in tandem, they also help students investigate issues related to the multiple and often conflicting purposes of schooling and how those purposes influence teaching practice. Students meet Marva and Leslie, two very different teachers, through videotape recordings: Marva, in a "60 Minutes" (CBS, 1983) episode, and Leslie, in a documentary film, *We All Know Why We're Here* (Holmes, n.d.). Using videotape recordings instead of written text offers students an opportunity to "see" and "hear" how differing viewpoints on "what schools are for" manifest themselves in classroom learning environments, curricula, and teacher–student interactions. The videos also provide entry into the real world of teaching at a safe distance, a distance that allows for reflection and analysis.

Although both Marva and Leslie teach in alternative urban schools, the subject matter, teaching methods, learning environments, and educational goals of each teacher look unfamiliar to TE-101 students. In these two cases, our students encounter surprises and puzzles that offer rich opportunities to explore connections between the framing questions of the course, the particulars of these two contrasting cases, and their own past schooling experiences.

Marva Collins

A "60 Minutes" episode introduces students to Marva Collins, founder of and teacher at Westside Prep, a private elementary school in Chicago for poor minority children. Marva's frustrations with public schools that have failed to educate city children become clear as she insists that *all* children can learn. According to Collins, schools should provide a basic, yet exemplary, education so that students can compete in the job market and escape the poverty in which most live. Economic survival is a consistent theme. She constantly tells her students: "If you don't work, you don't eat!"

Marva tells us schools should provide the structure that inner-city children want and need. She takes a "no frills" approach to education: no recess, no art, no gym, no music, no audiovisual aides, no leisurely lunch, and therefore no chaos. Her students proudly proclaim that this school makes their "brains big" as they read literature written by Chaucer, Dante, Emerson, Thoreau, and Dostoevski. The film shows students sitting at their desks, answering factual questions about those literary classics, performing vocabulary and spelling tasks at the chalkboard, and reading aloud their daily essays. Marva is on her feet, questioning, pushing, cajoling, praising, and insisting that students use the King's English.

Leslie Stein

The film *We All Know Why We're Here* (Holmes, n.d.) introduces students to Leslie Stein who, with a group of other teachers, participated in the establishment of Central Park East, an alternative public elementary school in New York City. Leslie and her students interact with one another in an open-classroom environment rich with materials and opportunities for exploration and discovery. Here, the purpose of schooling is to help students discover themselves as learners within a learning community.

Leslie does not believe that oppressed city children need traditional classroom structures in order to succeed. Instead, she thinks children learn best when they have opportunities to participate actively in a learning environment that encourages them to construct their own ideas, interact with their classmates, and manipulate materials. Leslie organizes her curriculum around common themes. In this film, the teaching–learning activities focus on the Tutankhamen exhibit at the Metropolitan Museum of Art. Throughout the film, we observe the interactions between Leslie and her students as they read to each other, tell stories, write journals and speeches, construct newspapers, create games and ceremonies, design artwork, and solve academic, organizational, and social problems at various learning centers throughout the classroom. Leslie moves from group to group, asking questions, nurturing individual responsibility within the larger community, and monitoring student engagement in purposeful activities.

Cases as a Way to Elicit Students' Beliefs

While students view the video cases of Marva and Leslie, they take notes on what they see and hear. Afterwards, we often ask our students to describe incidents that they find intriguing. Students pool their recollections in order to construct rich descriptions of events in both classrooms. Listening to the ways in which students report particular classroom events facilitates TE-101 instructors' understanding of their students' initial intellectual and emotional responses. Later, as we become more concerned with uncovering students' conceptions of teaching and learning and their views about the purposes of schooling, we may ask students what they think was being taught or learned in each classroom and eventually use that conversation as a basis for exploring the purposes of schooling. Regardless of which question is asked, students use their field notes and recollections to substantiate their claims.

In their initial reflections, TE-101 students are amazed at the smart children and the challenging curricula in each classroom. They are surprised and puzzled that students at Westside Prep can read classical literature that they themselves did not encounter until high school or college. Having heard that inner-city children are difficult to teach and often fail in schools, TE-101 students are often surprised to discover that Marva's students are so "book smart." Marva's focus on the classics both amazes and inspires the students. However, not everyone agrees that elementary children should read Dostoevski. "How can they understand the messages in these literary classics?" "Why aren't they reading children's literature"? "Wouldn't they rather be reading *Charlotte's Web?*"

Students are surprised and puzzled by the ways in which reading and writing are integrated throughout the curriculum at Central Park East. They do not expect urban students to be so articulate about what they are learning in school and why they are learning it. Although most TE-101 students are captivated by the ways in which Leslie nurtures curiosity and creativity, they also ask, "Why would a teacher allow students to spend so much time exploring their own interests?" "Do they just get to read whatever they want?" They also wonder how Leslie's students will learn things like math, which they themselves would never have chosen to study.

TE-101 students are struck by the contrasting teacher–student and student–student interactions in the two rooms. They note that in Leslie's class, interaction among all participants is both promoted and constant. Some students think, "Leslie's class is too noisy. Kids wouldn't be able to concentrate." Some wonder if Leslie is teaching if she's not up in front of the room explicitly directing her students learning. They ask, "If she doesn't hear what each child says, how does she know how far her students have progressed?" A few students argue that Leslie's students are "on the subject" and working diligently. "Leslie's teaching is like Paley's," they assert, "because both pay a lot of attention to setting up a stimulating learning environment." Still, many remain puzzled by the kinds of interactions in Leslie's classroom and wonder whether these interactions represent actual teaching.

The interactions in Marva's classroom seem to be more familiar for some TE-101 students, who note that "Marva talks in literal questions and her students talk in answers." They point to a particular episode during one lesson when Marva asks her students: "Who wrote *Canterbury Tales*? How many pilgrims were there? Where were they going? Who was Thomas à Becket?" Other students agree with her focus on the "basics." Hardly any student questions whether Marva is teaching and her students are learning, though some students feel that "she hovers over each of her students, telling them exactly what is expected of them every step of the way."

The structures of the two classrooms also present unsettling issues. Most students report that they have observed structure in Marva's classroom. They cite Marva's traditional seating arrangements, predetermined classical curriculum, and rigid daily schedule as evidence of this structure. They disagree, however, about the need for such structures. Some confidently state that "this structure is just what most students need," but others argue that Marva's structure is rigid and stifling.

Many TE-101 students are confused by the structure of Leslie's classroom. Leslie's "open-classroom" arrangements of space and time and her involvement of children in making decisions about their learning are inconsistent with the classroom structures most of our students have experienced. Students disagree about whether there is any structure in her room *and* whether its presence or absence has merit. Some students claim that there is no structure in Leslie's class. They say that "Leslie's classroom is chaotic. Leslie's students learn on their own and make all their own decisions. They don't even have their own desks." Some students argue that the environment Leslie has established "is creative and allows students to follow their own interests," but many of these continue to wonder whether the established structures will help students learn everything they need to know.

Cases as a Way to Broaden Students' Conceptions

Faced with such opposing views, confusions, and unexamined reactions to the cases of Marva and Leslie, we puzzle about how to help students reconsider their initial reactions, reflect on the assumptions behind their judgments, and speculate on the reasons Marva and Leslie may have for their decisions and actions.

As a springboard into this discussion, we sometimes ask students which classroom they would like to teach in. Once again, the responses vary. Some students say they would rather be a teacher in a room like Marva's because "I need structure and order." Or, "It's what I like; it's what I'm used to." Some say, "I'd like to teach in Leslie's room but I personally couldn't function in this kind of situation." For a few, teaching Leslie's way represents an opportunity to right the wrongs they have suffered in their own schooling experience. They like the idea of teaching in a room where "kids have more choice in what they learn" or where "the teacher can meet individual needs, . . . but maybe it would be more like a combination of both their rooms."

As we compare and contrast Marva's and Leslie's classrooms, students begin to reveal their own preferences for particular classroom structures. We ask them to describe how their own schooling experiences were structured, and their revelations lead naturally into a consideration of the role of prior schooling in learning to teach. Although most TE-101 students have little trouble understanding how past experiences influence their present ways of thinking, it is still a difficult task for them to build upon their initial responses, or put them aside, in order to reexamine Leslie's classroom structure.

Hoping to push students beyond their initial judgments regarding the lack of structure in Leslie's room, we revisit the scene where Leslie calls a class meeting when she senses that her students have strayed from their tasks. She is especially concerned about one student, Rhonda, who seems to be wandering around the room. After asking students to say what they are doing, Leslie invites the class to make suggestions to Rhonda about what she can do. Rhonda makes her decision, and the class resumes.

Exploring why Leslie stops the class and how her action reflects the structures or expectations in her classroom poses pedagogical challenges for the TE-101 instructor. This excerpt from a colleague's journal captures some of the complex issues raised and the dilemmas we face when we try to help students move beyond their prior conceptions of classroom structures.

I wanted them to see that she was monitoring what was going on . . . and that, indeed, she has some pretty clear expectations about what her students should be doing . . . which is that they should be doing something purposeful . . . that they are accountable to themselves as well as to a larger learning community. So when things got off track, it was time to do an accounting and help Rhonda get back on track. I wanted to challenge their claim that the kids [in Leslie's room] were doing whatever they wanted and the teacher wasn't doing anything. I asked them, "So why does she stop the class and do that?" And one student said " . . . because Rhonda wasn't working with somebody. And since in this classroom you have to always be working with somebody, she stopped class to let Rhonda find somebody to work with."

When I asked "What did you see in the film that makes you say that?" she said that she had noticed that everyone worked together. So then I asked, "Why didn't she just go and tell Rhonda and work it out with Rhonda? Why was it important for everybody to participate in this?" And then, since nobody seemed to have remembered that scene very fully, I described what was going on. I kept working and asking, "What was Leslie doing? What was she saying? Why did she ask others?" With more prodding, the students finally began to focus on the substance of Leslie's talk, which reflected her expectations. But then fewer and fewer students were participating in our discussion. At this point I'm still not sure how many see that Leslie has expectations, but I'm afraid that if I push them any harder, they will feel less and less sure about saying anything about the films.

The tensions between pushing students to look carefully and think critically and encouraging students to participate and say what they think are omnipresent as we work to help our students delve into all there is to see and hear in Marva and Leslie. We often ease that tension as we continue to investigate the cases of Marva and Leslie through another perspective: the course readings.

The Marva and Leslie Cases as a Way to Illustrate and Illuminate Theoretical Ideas

We use the cases of Marva and Leslie to illuminate various concepts from many of the course readings. These include Jackson's (1986) notions of knowledge reproduction and knowledge transformation, Apelman's (1980) contrasts between the teacher as in-structor and teacher as facilitator, Goodlad's (1984) ideas about the purposes of schooling, and Jackson's (1968) concept of the hidden curriculum. Although the cases help clarify these theoretical con-cepts, the relationship between the cases and readings is reciprocal. As cases illuminate ideas from the readings, the concepts in the readings provide new frameworks or illustrations that help students "see" more clearly and intricately the events in each case.

The video cases of Marva and Leslie are especially effective in helping students continue to unpack Hawkins's (1967/1974) essay. Analyzing the teacher–student relationships and how those relation-ships are built around certain kinds of subject matter in Marva's and Leslie's classrooms not only provide concrete examples of the "I, Thou, and It" model but also initiate conversations about the purposes of schooling. To launch the inquiry, students analyze how the teacher's role (the "I"), the student's role (the "thou"), and subject-matter knowledge (the "it") are manifested in each class-room, and what those ideas suggest about the teacher's purposes.

Students generally report that their conception of the "I" and "thou" in Marva's case is that of a teacher ("I") who instructs by choosing the subject matter, telling students what they are to learn, setting a consistent work regimen, and establishing high academic and personal standards. The student's role ("thou") is to absorb knowledge, morality, and a work ethic from the teacher. Students claim that the ("it") in Marva's room is a traditional curriculum with classical overtones, an "it" designed to provide students with a firm grasp of basic skills and the knowledge needed to get a good job.

We revisit this issue in the final exam when we ask students to draw a diagram that depicts the I-Thou-It relationship in each classroom and then write a brief paragraph describing the illustra-tion. Sam offered these insights as she wrote:

> This diagram (Figure 5.1) is how I envision the I–Thou–It tri-angle for Marva Collins. Her "It" consists of the basic skills and the students' growing perfection of those skills. She does not have students interacting with her or other students. She talks to her students and they answer her. Students in Marva's classroom are really losing out because of the lack of teacher-student and student–student interaction. The students are only learning what they read from books and what Marva tells them and we all know that teachers don't know everything.

Figure 5.1   **Figure 5.2**

Students offer a contrasting portrait of the I-Thou-It relationships in Leslie's case, observing that the I–Thou relationship is interactive: The teacher and students learn from each other (Figure 5.2). They describe Leslie as a facilitator who establishes an open-classroom environment where individuals and groups actively engage in learning while she supports them by answering their questions with more questions, by encouraging students to pursue their own interests, and by providing materials and problems that are interesting and challenging. Students report that the "it" in Leslie's room is a curriculum strongly influenced by real-life events and problems that students would encounter in their daily lives and community. Although there is a strong emphasis on language arts, it is treated as a tool to help students understand the world around them.

Taken from a final exam, this quote illustrates Sandy's reflections on Leslie's classroom:

> I see Leslie's room as being open to student and teacher interactions. I think this characteristic is important in all classrooms because these types of interaction increase a student's understanding of subject matter. Another important part of this triangle is Leslie's "it" — knowledge relating to the real world. Students are learning their basic skills (reading, writing, mathematics) as ways to help them function independently in the real world. They know why they are learning those skills.

The cases of Marva and Leslie, in tandem, provide numerous substantive occasions for students to explore school learning and teaching. Although the videotapes provide only a brief view of classroom life, the field notes students take and subsequent discussions enable us to revisit these cases on multiple occasions and for multiple purposes. And, these cases continue to be valuable for comparative analysis when we reach the part of the course that centers on what teachers need to know in order to teach.

REFLECTIONS ON TEACHING WITH CASES

The current discussion of using cases in teacher preparation emphasizes the analysis of decision-oriented cases (Merseth, 1991). This chapter describes a different use for cases, emerging from a different conception of case-based teacher education. We use cases as stimuli for eliciting and broadening students' beliefs about teaching and learning in schools. By presenting instances of teaching our beginning teacher education students may not have experienced as students, we challenge and broaden their conceptions of teaching.

Like decision-oriented cases, cases we use have some qualities of good stories: action, humor, good characterizations, and lots of interaction. Lively and compelling, the cases stimulate discussion about issues ranging from teachers' practical decision making to facing and managing moral dilemmas. Our analyses of the cases nurture our students' skills of inquiry and their reflection on practice.

At times the purposes and outcomes we set in our case-based instruction lead to uncertainties and dilemmas, yielding problems for students and teachers. Since our cases introduce students to unfamiliar approaches to teaching and learning, students' questions sometimes evolve into confusion and rejection. Some students suspend their inquiry, believing the case is simply a peculiar example of teaching that cannot and perhaps should not be reported. Other students discount the cases as unrealistic or idealistic accounts of teaching, believing, as Wally did about the rulers, that they simply are not real. Probably some of these students conceal their thinking, resolving to accept without question what they perceive as an unrealistic scenario or idealistic rhetoric.

As instructors we feel overwhelmed by the variety of students' responses and uncertain how to manage them. We work hard to understand our students' prior experiences, and how those experiences influence the "formulas" for teaching that they believe they have discovered or created from reading the cases. We wonder how best to validate what students see while at the same time encouraging them to question the grounds for their thinking.

Finally, we have learned that success in teaching with cases depends on our purposes as well as on the ways we connect the case analysis with the larger framework of the course. Teachers like Marva, Leslie, and Vivian provide vivid insights into teaching, yet their stories also become touchstones with which we move back and forth between the particulars of the cases, our students' entering and evolving conceptions, theoretical concepts in the readings, and course goals. Just when we think we understand the ways the pieces fit together and set out to write a chapter on using cases in an introductory teaching course, we find ourselves puzzling once again over the specific cases and concepts and how they fit with what we want students to learn.

6

Teaching Through Conversation: Making the Hidden Curriculum Part of the Overt Curriculum

Margery D. Osborne

I began teaching TE-101 without prior experience teaching courses in an interactive, conversational manner. My teaching in university-level science classes (graduate and undergraduate) had been almost exclusively teacher dominated. Although I wanted my science students to understand the fragility and "man-made" nature of scientific knowledge, my method of teaching was to tell the students things. *I* told them and *I* did the thinking; *I* integrated the ideas, concepts, facts that I hoped would lead to understand.

The deficiencies in this style of teaching become apparent in the laboratory, where I asked my students to develop strategies for pursuing scientific knowledge and making sense of ideas. I wanted them to think for themselves and develop strategies for developing scientific knowledge as well as frameworks for making sense of scientific ideas by *doing* science — solving problems and pursuing questions. Teaching in the laboratory involves facilitating this integration and demanding that students reflect upon the understandings that they construct. I tried to do this primarily by modeling scientific inquiry and by asking questions. Students seemed, however, to see a fundamental divergence between the two pedagogical philosophies of the courses: the transmission of knowledge through exhortation in lecture and the construction of understanding by the students in lab. Worse, the first form of pedagogy appeared to impede students' engagement in the second.

The curriculum of TE-101 does not communicate "right an-swers" or prescriptive messages and methods. Students construct their own understandings, both in interaction with others in class and at home, during study. They reexamine and justify the ideas they are constructing by comparing them with the ideas contained in the readings and those shared in class. My role is to supply raw material for and to facilitate this process, to build a classroom environment that nourishes the discourse upon which this learning depends, enabling students to construct individual understandings.

I wanted my TE-101 students to reflect on and question their preconceptions about their future role. To this end, I consciously offered alternative visions and images of effective teaching—written descriptions of thoughtful teaching (e.g., Paley, 1981; Kohl, 1984), videotapes of alternative pedagogies, and visits to observe innova-tive mathematics teaching in a third-grade classroom (see Chapter 3). I also tried to model many of the values illustrated in the readings and videotapes so students would experience this alternative style of teaching and learning firsthand. Recognizing that the discussion-oriented environment of the TE-101 classroom differed from most of my students' previous experiences, I asked them to reflect upon their perceptions of this environment and discourse. I wished to use the discourse of the class and their reflections on this discourse to encourage students to question the models of teaching and learning they had brought with them. This had three stages: demonstrating and participating in different models; producing dissatisfaction with preconceptions and fostering a need for a different model; and re-flecting upon the model. In this chapter I am going to concentrate on the first and the third stages of this process (see Chapter 3 for a discussion of the second stage). In the first stage we develop an alternative model for the role of teacher and learner. The final stage involves recognizing and thinking about the roles that we have been playing.

AN ALTERNATIVE MODEL OF TEACHING AND LEARNING

Students who have never participated in a discussion course have to learn to value both their own processes of thinking and the construction of knowledge through interaction with others. They have to learn to value the thinking of others and its potential contri-bution to their own thinking. The traditional processes of schooling neglect, avoid, or actively discourage this social construction of meaning. The reconstruction of these values imparted by previous school experiences is slow and at times frustrating. In order to demand that students think hard and value this process, I have to demonstrate that I respect and value others' questioning and evaluation. The first few meetings of the class are, for me, filled with the tension between creating a place where ideas can be safely aired and questioned and creating a place where we can push, confront, and challenge one another's ideas.

Conversation in which people interact and share ideas, in which the roles of hearer and speaker are equally valued, allows participants to broaden their conceptions of teaching and learning by listening to the ideas of others as well as by speaking about and critically examining their own (Buchmann, 1985; Grumet, 1988). Students present their conclusions and feel the uncertainty and ambiguity generated by comparing these conclusions with those of others. In this situation, the instructor's role is to mediate potentially divergent conversational directions, keeping the goals of the curriculum in focus. Deciding the direction of the conversation creates tension.

The overt curriculum of TE-101 is to question and reflect on teaching and teachers, learning and learners. The hidden curriculum supports those processes as the students and I construct together a setting for good conversation. For me the hidden and overt curricula intertwine, serving complimentary and supporting roles. The students and I must construct this environment together because in a class where the discourse is the focus, creating and perpetuating an environment that nurtures conversation must be mutual. Such a conversation is symmetric, requiring two (or more) parties to participate willingly and freely.

In a class where students are teachers as well as learners, the most critical decisions for the instructor come in the moments when questions are asked and opinions shared. These moments can nurture conversation as opposed to argument or lecture, despite the tension arising from challenge and confrontation. When I teach in classes oriented around conversation, however, I feel torn between my role as facilitator and my role as participant, between manipulating the conversation and being a part of it.

Discourse in my classroom follows a pattern. First, students in small groups of four or five work together on a broad question about the readings. For example, when discussing "crowds, praise and power" (Jackson, 1968) as features of a hidden curriculum, I asked the students to define those terms in relation to Suina's (1985)

" . . . And then I went to school," Kohl's (1984) *Growing Minds*, and Paley's (1979) *White Teacher*. I asked, "How did the teacher in each reading define those terms?" During the whole group discussion that follows, I write the opinions expressed by these small groups on the blackboard, sometimes transcribing students' words verbatim, sometimes paraphrasing their ideas as a way of challenging, with my own ideas or with the ideas of others, the student's rationale, sometimes confronting the student's ideas outright. Over the term, students gradually begin directly interacting with each other.

EVOLUTION OF THE DISCOURSE
CLASSROOM DISCUSSION DURING THE FIRST WEEK

During my first TE-101 class, I asked students for their views of good teaching. Below is an excerpt from that discussion:

> BOBBI: You should respect your teacher . . . if the teacher is constantly putting the kids down, the kids aren't going to have any respect for the teacher and they're not going to want to pay attention or learn . . .
>
> INSTRUCTOR: Are you saying respect of teachers for students or students for teachers?
>
> BOBBI: Well, both, actually.

My question asks the student to clarify for others what she was saying but also suggests that she is saying both that students should respect teachers and that teachers should respect students. It suggests that the two are linked, which is not, I think, what she actually meant to say. My initial, framing question, "What does good teaching look like?" centers on the teacher. Here and throughout this conversation I repeatedly try to move the students' ideas from a focus on what a teacher does and thinks to what a student does and thinks. I want them to see the two as linked, not as isolated spheres. Subsequent readings and assignments address this linkage directly, and I wish to start building an awareness that I can draw on later.

> INSTRUCTOR: How do you think teachers gain the respect of students?
>
> LAURA: One way would be for the teacher to have prepared beforehand . . . be prepared and

organized and . . . to have a plan and idea of what needs to be done . . .

INSTRUCTOR: And anything else?

LAURA: It seems that from the very beginning, when the student first meets the professor, with the introductions, start off right and once the teacher can gain the respect of the students they will listen and mutually keep up on things. It seems that if things start off right, then the respect would be on both sides.

INSTRUCTOR: [repeats, and writes on board]

KATHY: [talking about teacher making the mistake of getting "buddy-buddy"] It's fun to get on the floor in reading groups, but I think if they start to think you are too much of a buddy, they won't respect your authority; so I think you have to try to find a point where you're warm and kind, and they know that they can come to you . . . especially small children.

INSTRUCTOR: Do you think children, especially small children, come to the classroom and assume respect for you?

I want them to separate the meanings of the words *respect* and *authority*. I would like them to examine the sources of both sets of feelings about the role of teacher. How is respect generated? What is authority? I want them to think about the latter as linked to a definition of role, whereas respect is something they create, they earn.

BOBBI: It depends on the child and how authoritative the parents are at home and if they have respect for someone like that.

INSTRUCTOR: Then there is a continuity between the home and the school . . .

SUSAN: I don't think it's always from the home, I think that if kids start out young enough . . . like, my brother is younger than me. I've talked to him a lot about this . . . and they've never disciplined him because he's the baby. He's always getting in trouble. This year he's got a teacher in school that demands perfec-

> tion and my brother gives it to him . . .
> maybe if you demand perfection, if you de-
> mand respect, you're going to get it.
> INSTRUCTOR: Are respect and authority equivalent?
> SUSAN: I guess you have to respect authority, because
> if you don't respect it, then you're not going
> to abide by it.
> INSTRUCTOR: But if the teacher is respecting the students
> . . . the students are not authority figures
> . . . are the students authority figures?

I turn around a previous statement that they have made with this question — that respect should be reciprocal — in the hopes that this new cut on their assumed respect/authority relationship will generate a sense of dissonance with the definitions that they have been articulating.

> SUSAN: Oh, I was talking about students to teachers.
> INSTRUCTOR: What about the other way around?
> SUSAN: I don't think the students should have au-
> thority.
> INSTRUCTOR: But you should still respect them?
> SUSAN: Respect their feelings . . .
> INSTRUCTOR: And you think that love comes into this? Do
> you think that respect and love and authority
> are all intertwined?

I use the word *love* here because the students' make a connection between authority and the home. I was thinking of love as another place where assumptions are made about role relationships. Again I wanted another example of how we assume certain preexisting role relationships, but there is actually a dynamic construction of those relationships.

> TORY: If you don't know a person for who they are,
> then you can't really respect them.
> INSTRUCTOR: So do you think that the subject of authority,
> the student, loves the teacher? Is there that
> kind of relationship?
> SUSAN: If they respect them — not in the sense of a
> mother for a child, but love in that they are
> going to respect how they feel . . .

TORY: You can say that you love them for the fact of what they are trying to do.

INSTRUCTOR: The goal.

TORY: Yes, the world that they are trying to portray as long as you love the fact that they are doing it and they are trying . . .

I allow the students to go on about love and relationships defined by that love because it anticipates some of the ideas in two later readings by Kohl (1984) and Hawkins (1967/1974).

NELLIE: I've respected a teacher before but I very much disliked the person — the way he presented material that was interesting and I wanted to learn, but when he wasn't up there teaching and in the staffroom, he was just awful . . .

INSTRUCTOR: It's possible to respect somebody and not love them?

NELLIE: Yeah.

INSTRUCTOR: Is it possible to respect someone who has no authority over you?

STUDENTS: [yeah's]

INSTRUCTOR: So maybe they're not so equivalent, or sometimes they're equivalent and sometimes not equivalent?

BOBBI: O.K.

INSTRUCTOR: O.K., so if they're not equivalent, can you generate respect for yourself in someone . . . without showing authority?

BOBBI: Um hum.

INSTRUCTOR: How would you do that?

BOBBI: It seems that if you give respect, then you might get respect back from people.

INSTRUCTOR: Yeah?

BOBBI: We've been talking in a general way, but every person's different, and I think that for a teacher, if you have some kind of structure in your classroom and consistency combined with respecting your students, getting to know them, hopefully, that will set up the right tone for your class.

The questions that I used during these interactions progress from simple mirroring and asking for amplification to confrontation—for example, questions that ask the students to differentiate professional and private roles, using the word love. My questions reflect my uneasiness with the students' tendency to equate the teacher as authority figure with the teacher as object of respect. I also demonstrate my interest in the students' words and thought processes through mirroring, probing, and questioning the students' statements. I participate in the conversation—many of my thoughts are spontaneous reactions. My questions reflect a conscious decision not to challenge their value judgments but rather to push their justifications of these statements in the hope that they will ultimately challenge these themselves. My role in this conversation involves modeling the quality of conversation that I want, facilitating the progress of this conversation, and, finally, participating in the conversation. The first activity becomes less and less prominent as the classroom discourse develops over the semester. Facilitating and participating in the classroom discussion dominate in later classes and the tension between my role as facilitator and my role as participant increases; I become more involved in the content of the conversation and less preoccupied with developing the discourse.

This evolution of my role is illustrated by another theme of the course—the concept of common sense. The concept of commonsense knowledge and commonsense beliefs about teaching and learning is focal to TE-101. Many of the readings implicitly discuss "folk" concepts about the teacher's role (Jackson, 1986; Lampert, 1985a; Feiman-Nemser & Buchmann, 1986b), and it is a conceptual thread that runs through many of our discussions. For example, here is an exchange from the first class:

MARY: [The excellent teacher would be] able to think on her feet, be prepared for things that come up that aren't in the plan, like emergencies.

INSTRUCTOR: How do you think you would get to be able to do that?

MARY: I think it's experience . . .

INSTRUCTOR: What do the rest of you think, do you do that by experience? Any other way?

JUSTINE: Having been in lots of situations.

INSTRUCTOR: Uh huh.

JUSTINE: Knowing how to act, being organized, by saying this could happen or that could happen or . . .

INSTRUCTOR: So you're saying something different, the first
               thing was essentially depth of experience and
               you're saying that it is in your nature.

Six weeks later, during a discussion of the paper "Pitfalls of
Experience in Teacher Preparation" (Feiman-Nemser & Buchmann,
1986b), the students again introduced the concept of common sense.
This time, however, I pressed them to redefine the phrase and to
explore its role in learning and teaching. In the exchange below,
my role is primarily confrontational. In paraphrasing students' statements, I distort them to force the students to confront the meanings
and logical implications of their own words. I hope to get them to
reevaluate those justifications. I also play the part of participant to
a larger extent. I enjoyed this conversation because the students'
thoughts helped me to rethink my own ideas. My roles as participant
and facilitator did not conflict dramatically here; the tension results
from pushing people and their ideas.

DISCOURSE AT THE TWO-THIRDS POINT OF THE COURSE

After discussing in small groups the questions; "Where do
teachers learn to teach?" and "Can teachers learn to teach just by
teaching? Is teaching just common sense?" we have come back together for the whole group discussion. Nellie has started listing her
group's ideas. I am writing these on the board as she talks.

NELLIE: The things you need to know in order to
               teach are common sense — knowing how to
               deal with problems and kids and just getting
               your knowledge, of a certain subject.
INSTRUCTOR: Wait a second . . . dealing with problems
               [writing on the board]. Problems that what?
               Common sense is dealing with problems as a
               child?
NELLIE: Anything that you encounter in your life-
               time. Just how to move about in the world,
               how to . . .
INSTRUCTOR: [reading what I am writing on the board]
               . . . dealing with problems . . .
NELLIE: Not necessarily problems, just learning how

	to survive and cope with, move along in the world.
INSTRUCTOR:	Yes, but how is that common sense? What do you mean by common sense?
NELLIE:	It's just something everyone learned to do, how to survive.
INSTRUCTOR:	Let's do something on common sense, . . . [it's] something everyone learns to do? Is that what you just said? How does it become something that everyone has learned to do? How do you learn to do something, in a way that's common sense?

I make a decision to pursue definitions of common sense. I realize that she is talking about what people learn, how they learn, and subsequently act, as all arising through common sense. I want them to sort these things out.

JUDE:	You just watch other people.
INSTRUCTOR:	And what do you get by watching other people?
JUDE:	Knowledge.
INSTRUCTOR:	How do you get knowledge by watching other people?
JUSTINE:	You just watch what they do and imitate.
INSTRUCTOR:	Watch what they do and imitate?
JUSTINE:	Yes.
INSTRUCTOR:	How do you know what to imitate?
JUSTINE:	Oh, Lord . . .
JUDE:	Their own judgment.
INSTRUCTOR:	Their own judgment? Did you say that, Jude? Watch what they do and imitate?
JUDE:	Yes. Watch what they do and imitate.
INSTRUCTOR:	. . . How do you learn judgment?
JUDE:	When you're a child.
INSTRUCTOR:	But how do you learn it? That's *when* you learn it.
JUDE:	Your parents, school, neighbors, and then you decide what's right and wrong, you know what I mean, based on what you think your parents would think was right or wrong and should be . . .

INSTRUCTOR: Is that what you just said? Learn judgment
              from other people's values? [checking what I
              wrote on the board]
      JUDE: And then compare them to what your parents
              would think you should do.
INSTRUCTOR: Does it have to be just comparison to your
              parents?
      JUDE: No.
INSTRUCTOR: So you learn judgment from observing other
              people's values and by comparison, so there's
              an element of assessment in there? You're
              saying some things . . . Well, there's not an
              element of assessment necessarily in that.
              You're just comparing, but how do you know
              which ones you want to do?

This is another decision point: I decide to push the conversation to
discuss the ways that we come to critique our ideas and how we
arrive at our subsequent choices of actions and values—when and
how values are examined and justified.

      JUDE: It's different for each person.
    NELLIE: Most people want to do what's right.
INSTRUCTOR: How do you know what's right?
    NELLIE: By what other people . . .
   JUSTINE: Watch what other people are getting praised
              for.
      JUDE: Yeah, watch their actions and then decide.
   JUSTINE: Kids know if they're going to get in trouble
              for something, then it is probably wrong.
INSTRUCTOR: Choosing on moral grounds, base your [ac-
              tions] on concepts of praise and punishment?
              Is this what you are saying?
   JUSTINE: Yes.
INSTRUCTOR: So you know what's right and wrong because
              of threatened punishment? [This is a confron-
              tational paraphrase]
[Several people answering at once]
   JUSTINE: More praise . . .
INSTRUCTOR: O.K., upon understanding the conse-
              quences? O.K., so we learn judgment from
              other people, other people's values, by com-

parison. We do that by choosing on moral grounds, choosing the values on moral grounds. And this is based upon understanding of consequences? I guess not choosing values, choosing a course of action. Is that what you're saying?

JUSTINE: Yeah [she doesn't like this and makes a face].

INSTRUCTOR: O.K. [laughing]. You see what I wanted to get out of this was whether or not your concept of common sense involved learning things and examining them or it was learning without self-examination.

I let the students see my ideas about why I was pushing the conversation in a particular direction rather than continuing to manipulate the conversation toward hidden goals. My questions from now on, at least from my vantage point, are as a participant because I'm interested in the students' ideas on this subject and do not really have a preconceived opinion.

NELLIE: Well, it's common sense that you don't go with a gun and shoot someone. That you don't even really think about [it]. You just know. You just learn it from parents, watching other people.

INSTRUCTOR: Yes, if you know not to go and shoot somebody because you thought about the consequences of not shooting somebody or just do it because that's the way society is.

NELLIE: I think when you're young you just do it because that's the way society is. You don't think, "Well, if I do that, I'm going to sit in prison. Prison is awful." You just know not to do it . . .

INSTRUCTOR: [. . . C]ommon sense involves self-examination, examination of the underlying principles of that knowledge? Or do the underlying principles of that knowledge come later? And they aren't part of the common-sense understanding.

SUSAN: Well, I think common sense has to do with logic.

INSTRUCTOR: Do you? Why?
SUSAN: Well, my mom always says common sense is not so common. Well, it's not, if you really think about it. I don't think it just has to do with knowledge, because there's lots of examples where you don't really apply so-called knowledge, but it's just that would be the best way to do it. Like if you were studying, you wouldn't go just randomly throughout your notes. You'd probably work from one end to the other just because that's logical. Or if you had 25 questions you had to answer with a book and notes, you'd probably not go through and totally answer all 25 just by the notes and then go through and answer all 25 by the book. You'd probably get in depth on each question as you go along with the book and the notes because that's just . . . common sense.

INSTRUCTOR: Some procedure on how you do [things].
SUSAN: It would be common sense for a teacher not to totally snap at a kid and make them feel totally worthless, because then that kid is not going to respect the teacher, not like them. Or if you're watching a class and they're totally struggling and you have to make the decision of whether to go on or not. Well, if they're still struggling, then it's pretty much common sense that you don't go on if they don't have the principles. It would be stupid.

INSTRUCTOR: Uh huh. So you're saying that understanding by common sense is really logic?
SUSAN: Right. But I don't think it has a lot to do with moral judgment. I guess moral judgment could play a part of it, but I don't think that's what common sense is based on.

INSTRUCTOR: So you're saying it's practical knowledge.
SUSAN: Right.

This conversation went on to juxtapose the definitions of common sense involving practical procedural knowledge and moral socialization. As it progressed and the conversation became more a sharing of equally valid ideas, the quality of my participation altered. I no longer asked questions except for clarification, and the things that I said got lengthier. Finally, we began to consider when moral and practical values might become conscious and justified decisions. Is it through a process of self-examination? Why does that process happen? Because it provides an important conceptual link to the final third of the course, when we examine the sources and effects of the hidden curriculum, I leave this question open here:

KATHY: Maybe it's the same thing as saying first people have to know certain things. I'm talking about the math again [they have been observing a third-grade mathematics class]. I had such a problem with that. There's certain things that you just have to accept and you have to know. And then you get a base and then later on you go back and kind of use that and examine what you think about that and expand on it . . . like when you say that you know the Ten Commandments, you just know them and that's what happens when you're younger. Later on you begin to think about it.

INSTRUCTOR: Yes, but if I think about the way we were working with that math, I would say that thinking about why you were doing such and such is almost optional. You learn how to deal with the world using these common-sense principles, and later on as you get to go back and assess them, and justify them and think about them, that's real nice, but maybe it's not necessary for living in the real world.

KATHY: I don't know. I was just thinking about what [the math class] is doing. They already had the basics, if you want to call it that, down; they know a little bit about numbers and everything. And now since they've got that, they're going through and examining it. I'm not really arguing anything. It just reminded me of it.

INSTRUCTOR:	Yes. I think that's good. But I'm just wondering whether the self-examination part which comes later is necessary. . . . Do you consider it necessary? A luxury?
NELLIE:	I wouldn't call it a luxury.
KATE:	I guess I don't know what you mean by self-examination.
INSTRUCTOR:	Well, all the justifying that we've done in this class. Asking "why?" when people say, "Teachers should be friendly with their kids." I turn around and I say, "Why?"
KATE:	So you're saying question your morals and values. Figure out why you have them?
INSTRUCTOR:	Yes, or with Kathy's idea with math, you can get through in the world knowing the rules for math but you don't really necessarily need to know why those rules exist or how they are created. Is that what you were saying?
KATHY:	No. I'm not really arguing anything. I think it's just like the idea that now kids are going back and learning why because I never learned that. And I can see where I'm reading all this stuff about how teachers should be knowledgeable, and I can see that I'm going to have to go back and work on some of the things that I've learned and figure out why I learned them. I can do, basically, a simple math problem, but it's hard for me to explain it.
INSTRUCTOR:	So are you saying that common sense isn't enough to teach?
KATHY:	Yes, we know that teaching's common sense. . . . Well, part of it is. It's knowing what's working with the students and what's not. That's just common sense. You can see if they're confused. You can see what's working, but also you needed to have learned knowledge of subjects so you could explain them in different ways. It's kind of two parts. Teaching isn't just all common sense. You have to know what you're talking about.

This conversation progresses from a question concerning how a person becomes a teacher, through a philosophical exploration of the students' and my own concepts of common sense — what the term means, how commonsense knowledge is acquired, used, and justified — and then back to issues of teaching and learning. The students and I jointly create the topic of conversation. As facilitator, I determine the path of the conversation, but as a participant I must allow the students to decide where to terminate the exploration of common sense. By defining my role in this way, I create equality between the students and myself. It is problematic, however, to say that at this point I'm participant rather than facilitator; that I fill one role rather than the other. Rather, I move back and forth between the two roles. When I ask students to continue pursuing the meaning of the term *common sense*, I am facilitating. Their ideas about what constitutes common sense are as valid as mine, and I am interested in hearing them because they help me to develop my own ideas as a participant.

I let this exploration go until one of the students repeatedly signals to me that she wants to change the subject. I consciously allow her to share in the decision making because of an incident that occurred during a previous class meeting. Her insistence that she "isn't making an argument" comes from the central role she played in generating a previous "argument." I let her take control in part because I don't want to always be pushing her and making her feel defensive. I feel that we need to recenter on what we are supposed to be talking about — where prospective teachers learn to teach. Also, the atmosphere in the room makes me think that people are feeling restive with the conversation.

Perhaps in allowing the students to change the topic of conversation, I resume the role of facilitator. Probably they always see me as facilitator and I periodically resist the role they've cast me in and then allow them to reimpose it. In the end, however, the students and the teacher determine the direction of the conversation together.

DISCOURSE AT THE END OF THE QUARTER

A conversation at the end of the semester deals with students' unexamined values. We begin with two articles by Philip Jackson (1968) and Joseph Suina (1985) and the concept of the "hidden curriculum" and "socialization" in the classroom. After a time we move to individual students' examples of their acceptance of particular values and the conflicts they cause when dilemmas arise. I facilitate the introduction of personal examples by sharing a personal incident of my own. I do this for two reasons. First, I believe that these ideas will become real for students only when they connect them with experiences that they have had with them. Second, I can bring home the problematic character of school socialization—the fact that it acts to erase the individual—by creating a space for students to recognize their own personal frustrations with being treated as a member of an imposed category. This understanding of the removal of freedom of choice is essential before the class moves on to Oakes (1986a, 1986b) and Anyon (1981). This is the last place in which I try to get my students to reexamine their previous beliefs about teaching: They assume the role of the teacher to be both central and authoritarian, one that legitimates making decisions, both implicit and explicit, about and for another person.

Again I act as facilitator and as participant, but this time the roles are connected as I confront my students.

INSTRUCTOR: O.K., are there any other ways in school that you are taught to be part of the group rather than an individual?

KATE: Well, we were talking to [a previous student] about how you forget your heritage and conform to social norms. Another thing was that . . . on report cards you had little sections for citizenship and conduct. You were never taught those things. You were just expected to know how to behave and know what they were.

INSTRUCTOR: Like my little daughter, her report card comes home . . . reading excellent, math excellent, getting along with the group terrible. So grades work two ways, positively and negatively, as punishment.

KATE: I think definitely they do. I guess I believe that if your grades are overemphasized . . . If you give the child a grade that is poor and suppose that child has really tried hard. What does it mean? Then the kid looks at all the hard work he's done, and it doesn't help, according to him. So then his attitude is probably going to be, "Why should I try hard? It doesn't matter anyway." My boyfriend just applied for an internship and he had an interview, and the guy, the only negative thing he had to say about him was his grades. And he's kind of had to make himself look better because of his grades, you know. He's a residence hall assistant and there's a lot of other things that he does. He says, "I probably get more valuable an education from that than I do from the classes that I have." People are so used to placing an importance on grades.

INSTRUCTOR: What I'm seeing here, . . . isn't that working both ways, as far as teaching you to be part of a group? Isn't it also making you into an individual? Isn't it on the basis of comparison and how you compare to other people? Doesn't it both make you conform and set you apart?

TRACY: It takes you as how you are individually as compared to the group.

KATE: O.K., . . . So in other words it's on *their* grading scale.

INSTRUCTOR: O.K., so what else, other than grades, makes a child want to be part of the group?

TRACY: I think if in elementary school, even high school, the kids are put into groups . . . we were always put into groups to decide about and discuss the problems . . . and each student — you know, like what we're doing right now — it's different if we had to think about it by ourselves and then we were checked one by one, but if we are in groups we can kind of [share].

INSTRUCTOR: [I am putting things on the board and checking them back with her]

KATE: Not only that, everything that you do when you are in school is a group activity. Think about it. The classroom that you're in is based on a group. Usually to begin with, your age group and then if you fall behind, it's based on the group's learning abilities. You go to lunch as a group. You go to recess

as a group. You see what I'm saying? And
then at times, the girls are separated from the
boys as groups. And if you fall out of that
anywhere, it's looked down upon. I guess that
kind of goes with the crowd part.

INSTRUCTOR: Everything you do is done as a group, and
when the different groups are selected out
. . .

KATE: Groups and subgroups, I guess.

INSTRUCTOR: So, you've got to identify with those groups
. . .

KATE: Yes, you have a place within each group, and
if you step out of that place, then . . .

INSTRUCTOR: So you generate an identification with that
group, within that group, and when you start
to separate from the group, you feel out of
place. It's not just that other people are dis-
couraging you . . . you, yourself, also feel
bad about not being part of the group?

KATE: Does your little girl feel bad because she
doesn't get along with the group?

INSTRUCTOR: Sometimes.

KATE: It's important to kids at that age to fit in, so I
think when they're not, yes, I think it bothers
them. It may not bother us as much now, but
when you're young like that, usually it does.
Unless you have a child that's withdrawn,
or whatever, and does not want to — like at
recess plays with himself instead of other
kids.

INSTRUCTOR: Yeah, when you go to the school, when you
visit schools and whatnot, you see kids playing on the playground . . . and you see one
little kid playing off by herself. How do you
feel?

KATE: I feel bad for them . . .

INSTRUCTOR: . . . or you wonder what's the matter with
them.

KATE: Right. So, see, look at that right there. The
fact that you automatically feel bad for someone that is alone. Not taking into consideration that they may want to be or they like

that. It's just that you're taught that that's bad to be alone. You should be with a group.

INSTRUCTOR: So, we're talking about how the child starts to absorb values . . . they're graded . . . and the basis of the grading is whether or not we absorb these values that aren't defined by ourselves, and we start to absorb these because everything we do in school is done this way, all the rewards are generated by the people who belong to the group and anything negative in the school will probably cause you to get bad grades . . . feel bad about yourself if you are not playing with all the other little children, and if you do something deviant in the classroom, you get punished.

SUSAN: I think you need to teach kids just to have a level head and really think through their actions and take responsibility for their actions. When I was in high school, I didn't drink and my whole high school was centered around drinking. And I wasn't in the "in" group. I was a cheerleader. I was in every activity and everything, but I wasn't . . . If somebody said, "Name somebody popular who's in a lot of activities at school, they wouldn't name me first because I wasn't in the "in" group because I didn't drink. And that was just a personal thing that I didn't like. My mom used to be an alcoholic and I just never did.

This discussion continued to examine the conflicts between students' beliefs and the values they adopted without reflection and rationalization. Susan's anecdote about her high school experiences was the beginning of a phase in the conversation in which students told stories about coming to recognize previously unexamined values and mores. In each of these tales, recognition was triggered by a confrontation of values. The stories ranged from a student telling of her family's experiences with the Ku Klux Klan to a deaf student's anecdote about her confrontation with her mother when she broke the news that she was about to marry another deaf person. The conversation climaxed as students shared their opinions and personal experiences of interracial relationships.

The students and I began to think that values rarely are examined or justified until challenged. We achieved this understanding by drawing personal connections during the public sharing of private experiences. This conversation illustrates the value of grounding a discussion in personal experience; the intensity and depth of potential understanding reached around issues of unexamined value judgments and conflict would not occur without such sharing.

This conversation was again under the shared control of teacher and students. As the confrontational quality of the interactions escalated—during the discussion of interracial marriage—I became more of a facilitator than a participant. I could not allow the conversation to degenerate into argument, with its implication that one person or idea was more "correct" by virtue of features other than the intrinsic rationality of the argument (Buchmann, 1985). My own ambivalence about this choice of role increased as my emotional reaction to the subject matter intensified.

I ended this class by trying to recenter on schools and how we might use a recognition of the hidden curriculum and its effects — how teachers needed to examine and justify their own value judgments and choose to create a particular environment in their classrooms. I wanted the students to see this as an active personal choice rather than a passive inheritance. I also wanted to move the conversation back from a discussion of choices in their personal lives to personal choices in public roles—in their future role as teachers. This topic, which had its roots in previous class conversations, became the central issue during the remainder of the course. As the teacher, I was the one who chose to pursue it, but my choice reflected the shared ideas and needs of all the people in my class. The directions and pathways of this class were communally constructed but mediated by myself and my maintenance of the initial goals and values generated at the beginning of the semester.

The increased value that the students have placed on their own thinking and the thinking of others is apparent both in the interactions illustrated in the previous discussion and in the subject matter of that discussion. The students are no longer resisting my probing questions and are actually asking the same sort of questions of each other. There is a merging of the overt curriculum and the quality and form of the discourse in the classroom. We were modeling within the class the alternative visions of learning and teaching that we were studying. In effect, I wanted the overt curriculum of my version of TE-101 to contain the hidden curriculum of the classroom. The conversations that we engaged in during the semester are, in reality, the intersection between these two spheres.

CONCLUSION

In order for the students to recognize as real the alternative images of teaching and learning presented in the overt curriculum — in order to reflect on and understand what they are and that they are possible to enact — they have to experience them. Making these visions of education real to the students through personal experience is an important step in giving them other ways to recognize and examine their assumptions about the role of teacher. This link between experience, reflection, and choice is apparent in the students' own descriptions of personal incidents in their lives brought out during classroom conversation. The students are saying that reflection on values, rationalization, and conscious choice comes through a lived experience in which these choices appear problematic, comparisons are made, and differences between choices are articulated.

The students' unexamined beliefs about teaching and learning and about the roles of teachers and students in classrooms can only be challenged by exposing these students to alternative images of pedagogy. The most powerful of these "exposures" is one in which the students experience a profoundly different form of teaching and learning. For this reason, I have designed my classroom discourse to mirror the images of teaching that I am simultaneously presenting to the students in the overt curriculum. I finally ask my students to reflect upon what has been happening in our class. I feel that in order for experience and reflection to be educational, the students need to feel both uncomfortable and comfortable in the classroom. They must feel uncomfortable enough to recognize that this classroom is different from classrooms that they have experienced before. At the same time, they must feel comfortable enough so that, first, they can express their discomfort with the classroom discourse and, second, they will introduce personal experiences that serve as touchstones during our explorations of fundamental assumptions about roles and beliefs.

In order to create and maintain the classroom environment, I must play multiple, and at times conflicting, roles. The tension between my roles as participant and facilitator is in one sense resolved during the quarter; the discourse does evolve in such a way that the two roles can both be accommodated. In another sense the tension and conflict between the two roles increases as the classroom discourse becomes the focus and medium of the curriculum.

On the one hand, it becomes increasingly important to maintain my role as facilitator, so that the conversations remain open to multiple viewpoints. Simultaneously, because of the personal quality of the conversations, the ideas and beliefs exposed during the later stages of the course become more and more compelling to me as a participant. However, the responsibilities of my role as the course instructor complicate my role as participant. As teacher, I must ask students not only to recognize their incoming values and assumptions about education and the role of the teacher but also to reexamine and alter them. To enable this I must be both participant and facilitator: I cannot afford to be merely a facilitator who makes no judgments and recognizes no responsibilities for the curriculum and purposes of the course, and I am not a participant who is sharing equally weighted opinions about the subject matter. Rather, as instructor I use both roles in the service of the curriculum and the purposes of the course.

7

Thinking About Teaching, Teaching About Teaching

Suzanne M. Wilson

> It was the sweetest, most mysterious-looking place any one
> could imagine. The high walls which shut it in were covered
> with the leafless stems of climbing roses which were so thick
> that they were matted together. . . . It was this hazy tangle
> from tree to tree that made it all look so mysterious. Mary had
> thought it must be different from other gardens which had not
> been left all by themselves so long; and indeed it was different
> from any other place she had ever seen in her life. (Burnett,
> 1962, pp. 71–72)

I think I know how Mary felt when she discovered her secret
garden at the manor, at once overwhelmed with its dormant beauty
and its rampant disrepair. As each new term begins and I face
another set of prospective teachers, simultaneously I am excited by
their promise and distressed about their ignorance. I can see roses
and lilacs and lilies in my classroom — buds that could blossom into
beautiful and vibrant teachers. But I also see weeds and vines —
selected beliefs about teaching and learning, planted and watered
throughout years in classrooms, that could choke a promise. Each
teacher in my class is but a piece of the garden I tend as a teacher
educator, a plot of land populated with both flowers and vines,
needing watering and weeding.

In order to teach my students well, I must take seriously that
which they believe, and incorporate their knowledge and beliefs into
my instructional choices. It is not sufficient to tell them that they
are wrong about some things: that teaching does not have to be

telling, that students do not have to be silent, that teachers don't always have to have the answer. Instead, I must find ways to help them see what they believe and sometimes question those beliefs. This takes deep thinking about my purposes, the content of the course, the context in which I work, and the characteristics of the students that I encounter. The purpose of this chapter is to illustrate what that thinking looks like. I begin by reviewing some of the beliefs my students enter TE-101 with. I then describe two examples of the ways in which I try to construct classroom events that accommodate their beliefs and follow this with a discussion of how I help them begin rethinking their assumptions. I close the chapter with a few observations about why the work of teacher education is both important and difficult.

BEGINNING THE WALK: EXPLORING TEACHING

Many students who enroll in TE-101 want to waive the course. They've all met and worked with lots of teachers, helped friends with assignments, taught Sunday school. Many have parents who have been teachers. A course intended to introduce them to teaching? How ridiculous! They already know a lot about teaching and teachers. They're advanced beginners in this field, well beyond any bunny slope course labeled TE-101. And they're right. As students and parents and babysitters and friends, they have learned a lot about teaching. But my intention is to make them reconsider what they *know* and what they have come to *believe* about the nature of classroom work.

We start with the question: What is teaching? Some students respond by claiming that a teacher is a person with a key to the faculty lounge, a briefcase, a credential. Others say that teachers are information dispensers. Still others aver that teachers help people learn things. Often, the same student will hold multiple, sometimes conflicting, beliefs about teaching and teachers. My job is to help students scrutinize those beliefs, look at themselves as learners and potential teachers, discard detrimental beliefs, and polish those that will facilitate their development.

We read a lot, essays like Philip Jackson's (1986) "Real Teaching" and David Hawkins's (1967/1974) "I, Thou, and It." My students find Jackson's discussion of multiple definitions of teaching troubling, circuitous, confusing, belabored. "Why doesn't he just answer the question?" they cry. When Hawkins claims that teaching means more than caring for children, that it is both about respect and about teaching people something, students are taken aback. They puzzle over what he means when he writes, "love can blind and bind." Many of them want to be teachers because they love children and their love is a warm, fuzzy, comfortable affection. The idea that a teacher's respect for the minds of her pupils might drive her to push them, causing them intellectual discomfort, is foreign to my budding teachers.

My pedagogy varies. Many days involve small-group activities in which students share ideas and answer questions that they have generated. We watch videotapes of teachers like Marva Collins, Magdalene Lampert, and Deborah Ball, discussing their pedagogy and purposes. We meet in large groups, in pairs; at times we work in solitude. Sometimes I do a lot of talking, sometimes I am but one voice among many, sometimes I say nothing at all. To give you a flavor for the content and texture of my teaching, I illustrate with two example lessons.

TWO LESSONS

The Voyage of the *Mimi*

I adapted this lesson from one that was developed by other TE-101 instructors. The purpose is to help students think about the nature of intellectual engagement, as well as the pleasure and excitement of real learning. Many of my students believe teaching means packaging boring content in pretty boxes, adding bells and whistles to make it more attractive. I want my students to understand that learning can be intrinsically motivating and motivated.

I also want students to consider the interactions of pedagogy and content. I want them to see that the learning opportunities we craft for students may have an impact on how interested, animated, or concerned they are as learners *and* on what they learn. I want them to think about pedagogy as a powerful mediator in learning.

One of the problems I face is that many of my students have never experienced genuine intellectual engagement. For those students, TE-101 is one of the first times when they've been treated with intellectual respect, when someone has suggested that they can construct their own understanding, when they have been asked to be active participants in the process of learning. Being a student for my prospective teachers has meant taking notes and tests; it has not involved passion, excitement, action. Hence, I cannot refer to their past experiences as impassioned learners; instead, I have to *create* this opportunity for them before we can reflect on the nature of learning. The first part of the lesson involves creating such an experience.

I use one episode from a videotape series developed by Bank Street College called *The Voyage of the* Mimi. The purpose of the series is to demonstrate applications of mathematics and science in real-world settings. The series does this by creating an engaging story about a diverse group of scientists and assistants who are tracking whales on a sailboat captained by an old salt who has brought along his grandson. As class begins, I provide vague instructions, "Watch the film carefully. Take notes."

We watch the film. Some students grumble as they meet the crew and passengers on board the *Mimi*, a research ship. In this episode, the scientists have sighted the whales and are studying their feeding behavior, in particular their use of bubble clouds. At one point, a young woman scientist invites the captain's grandson to help her measure the temperature of the water using an XBT, a disposable sensor that charts the temperature of the ocean at various depth. As the XBT drops to the floor of the ocean, it sends signals to the ship's computer, which displays the data in the form of a graph. During the episode, two readings are taken. As the camera goes below deck, we see graphs being produced on the *Mimi*'s computer. The first graph looks like the one shown in Figure 7.1. The second reading, taken closer to the whales, looks like the one in Figure 7.2.

After the film, I ask students to get into small groups and to generate as many reasons for the change in the XBT graphs as possible—ranging from serious to silly. Five minutes later, we regroup and I list all the reasons on the board: The whale peed. The whale swallowed the XBT. The whale warmed up the water with his body heat. They hit a nuclear waste dump. There was a current. The whale batted the XBT back up toward the surface.

We laugh at how ridiculous some of the answers are. My students are confused. The grumblers are still frowning. What do whales and XBTs have to do with teaching? Why did I make them watch a videotape? This sure is a strange class.

I then ask students to return to their groups. The assignment this time: Come up with the right answer and a rationale for it, including evidence. Fifteen minutes later, we regroup for the final time and discuss their answers. I have never had every group agree.

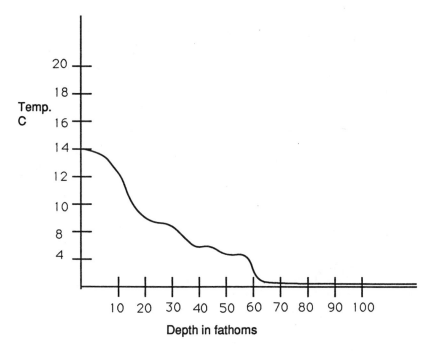

Figure 7.1   XBT Graph #1

There are always at least two explanations proposed: (1) The whale
was feeding and the bubble cloud heated the water so that the temperature rose and (2) they were approaching St. George's Bank
and there were water currents that changed the temperature of the
water.*

I never tell the students what the right answer is. I don't have
time. Already an hour has passed and we haven't even begun to
talk about learning, and how the decisions teachers make about
instructional strategies might motivate it. Besides, telling them
would contradict one of the points of the lesson. My students believe
that teachers should tell students the answers to all of their questions. I believe that, in so doing, teachers often teach their students
to be passive consumers of knowledge rather than active explorers

---

*Bubble clouds are a technique used by humpback whales to catch food. They
blow a cloud of bubbles that stuns small fish, which they then swallow.

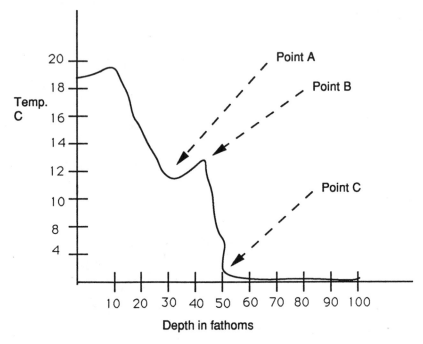

Figure 7.2   XBT Graph #2

or constructors of that same knowledge. I resist telling them "the answer," knowing full well this will frustrate them. But I'm hoping to use that frustration to my advantage and ask them a series of questions that will lead them to some insights about the consequences that certain teachers' actions have on students' learning and thinking.

So I ignore their pleas and ask them, "What was this all about?" We talk. Sooner or later, someone says that she didn't really care about whale feeding or XBTs or bubble clouds before today, but now she's dying to know why the second graph is different. They're surprised how much they care about the "answer" when the search for it was handed over to them. We talk about how I created an opportunity for them to be intellectually engaged. We think through why it was fun, how the challenge of explaining something took them into territory few had ever had the opportunity to explore, how they had to draw on knowledge they didn't realize they had.

Sometimes I note how few words I contributed as teacher in the lesson. I ask them to think about how they would have felt, what they would have learned, had I lectured for an hour on whale feeding and XBTs. They consider the effects that my pedagogical choices had on what they learned.

The lesson is a powerful one. My end-of-the-course evaluations inevitably include a few comments like, "I wish she had told us why the XBT graph changed." The discussion we have always contains seeds for further conversations about learning, about motivation, about teaching, about pedagogical reasoning. Typically, I teach this class early in the term, for I need little knowledge of my students to do this well, and they need not have highly refined skills of debate or argumentation to participate. I save other lessons, like those on tracking, until later in the term when my students have learned to disagree with one another and have substantive arguments.

Tracking

Tracking is a difficult topic to teach for a plethora of reasons. For one, it's a much more blatantly political topic than some of the others we explore. I also find it difficult to define tracking. There are some obvious cases: The honors track at a local high school, the college prep classes at another. But the boundaries for me are fuzzy. When I was a bluebird in third-grade reading, was I being tracked? Is Calculus a tracked course because only the select few manage to get there? When does tracking start? Where does it end? How intentional does it have to be to qualify as tracking?

To complicate matters, I respect Jeannie Oakes's (1985, 1986a, 1986b) research, but as a scholar I know where the holes are. It's persuasive, not definitive. There are still a lot of unanswered questions: What about the quality of instruction? How much do we really know about the experience of low achievers in untracked high schools? What do teachers need to know to teach heterogeneous classes well? What supports do they need? How do teachers and schools respond to other pressures, most notably accountability, with respect to heterogeneous and homogeneous classes?

I'm also concerned about my students' entering beliefs. Most of them have succeeded academically and many of them have been in tracked classes. Most of them also come from homogeneous environments in which concerns for diverse populations were not as relevant or significant as they could or should have been. They come to me as nonquestioners, believing that tracking works. They also come with no historical knowledge, and when we read David Cohen's (1984) essay on the history of the purposes of education, it surprises them that schools have political and social agendas that can be traced back in time.

I think about my purposes. I'm preparing teachers for the classrooms of the future, classes in which we can predict there will be much more variability, much more diversity than these youngsters from Michigan have ever seen. I'm concerned about their assumption that their own experiences as students are a sound source of information about how to teach. My students are very different from some of the students they will teach in the future. I worry that the teachers I prepare will think that "what worked" for them will work for others. I want them to see that traditional methods haven't worked for large portions of the American population. I want them to understand that those methods probably didn't even work for them. I want them to learn to think beyond their own experiences in classrooms and consider practical experience and empirical and theoretical scholarship as powerful sources for ideas about how to teach.

I wrestle with my own political agenda. I'm worried about letting students believe that tracking is a good idea. I want them to question that assumption. On the other hand, I don't believe that I should use my power as a teacher to persuade others of the value of my own beliefs. Instead, I want to empower students with knowledge and skill that will help them make their own wise decisions. Because it's their first teacher education course, I don't want them to draw any conclusions about these issues. All I really want them to do is think hard about tracking — its history, its purposes, its effects, the assumptions upon which it is based.

What to do? Late in the term, I have them read Oakes's research. We have a schoolboard meeting in which I assign sides. Half of the students become parents and teachers and children who support tracking, the other half oppose it. Five students become school board members who moderate the discussion, listen to the arguments, consider the evidence, and eventually decide whether tracking will continue in their district. I use the roles of parents and children because I want to acknowledge and confront the emotional aspects of tracking. Students who consider tracking harmful often change their minds when they play the role of a parent whose child is gifted. Likewise, students who extol tracking question their assumptions when they are assigned the role of a child who has been labeled as less able and whose options are being limited by that judgment.

On the day of the school board meeting, I sit in the back of the classroom and listen to their thinking. Because it's late in the term, the class has developed into a discourse community where people think hard about their ideas and offer justification for their beliefs. But on this day we enter a new arena where emotion is added to the stew. This is not just a scholarly debate, for they take their roles as real children and parents and teachers seriously. Important ideas surface. Once, Bruce, a tall, healthy, athletic wrestler full of the confidence of experience, stood and explained, "Tracking is good. After all, in a race, the tall, thin kid with the long legs deserves to win. The fat, short kid just runs slower. You can't drag the taller kid down just because the shorter kid's less able." Gloria, a quiet black woman who had never said anything all quarter, stood. "What you don't understand, Bruce, is that the other kid's not fat or short or less able. It's just that someone put weights on his ankles to drag him down." In the debriefing that followed the debate, we talked about what that meant and why Bruce and Gloria felt differently about the value of tracking and the role of competition in schools.

No matter how hard I try, though, all of my students aren't going to understand Gloria's comment. Nor are they going to be able to see beyond their past experiences as students or their future concerns as parents to seriously question the validity of tracking. It's just too messy. But I'm compelled to make them think. So I close the unit on tracking with a heavy hand, constantly asking, "But where is your evidence? How can you justify believing in it? On what grounds are you making these claims?"

I do this anxiously, uneasily, uncomfortably. I rely more than I would like on thoughtful research that is nevertheless problematic. I come close to preaching instead of teaching. But it's late in the quarter. I'm hoping that my students have already begun to under- stand that they are thinkers and that they have the right and the responsibility to reflect on what I say, weigh the evidence them- selves, draw their own conclusions. Sometimes I worry because I have a strong, articulate voice, and my students are just learning to speak up, to disagree, to be critical of their teachers. On the other hand, I question how powerful any one teacher can be in the face of deeply rooted beliefs. They might adopt the rhetoric but never change their beliefs. The best I can hope for is engraving a big question mark next to the idea of tracking in their hearts and minds.

DID SUZANNE TEACH TODAY?

Whatever the lesson, however I teach, uppermost in my mind is making students think hard about teaching: how and why and when it works, what it means, who is in control. One of the ways that I try to get inside those ideas is to sometimes end class with a question, "Did Suzanne teach today?"

They know it's a trick. On days when I have the strongest voice, like when I lecture on the results of research on tracking, the answer is clear. Of course I taught. On days when we see videotapes and answer questions in small groups like with *The Voyage of the Mimi*, I probably taught because I provided the videotapes and the questions. But sometimes they argue: "You didn't teach us, we taught each other." On the days I am mute — when the school board convenes, for example — there's even less agreement. They confront a paradox created by their disparate beliefs. They know I'm the official instructor of the course, the university says so. Does that make me the teacher? They know I didn't tell them anything, but sometimes they think they've learned something. Did teaching go on because there was learning? What if everyone learned something different? What about their empty notebooks? What exactly did they learn?

Beliefs About Teaching and Learning

What I am trying to do with my not-so-simple question is to push students to locate beliefs they have about teaching that are so deeply rooted, they take them entirely for granted. For one, most students believe that teaching is telling. The work of teaching, they assume, involves explaining things to students. Learning involves absorbing that information. Differences in good and bad teaching are defined by how well that story is told. This doesn't mean that they think lecturing should be the mainstay of their work, for many of my students will tell you that they believe in active learning — using manipulatives, writing stories, conducting science experiments, going on field trips. However, when I examine their talk closely, I learn that my students see these activities as methods to make the business of learning more palatable. They do not see these methods as expressions of different assumptions about how and why learning takes place, about what is to be learned, and about the respective roles of teachers and students in that enterprise. No matter what goes on in between, teaching ultimately means that students learn something specific that teachers provide.

This becomes most apparent around midterm when we watch several videotapes of teachers who encourage students to set, explore, and solve their own problems. Problem defining and solving are not efficient processes and the classes we watch are brimming with false starts, tangential conversations, seemingly endless arguments. Fifteen minutes of kids arguing over the meaning of one graph seems an eternity to my students. "She let them go on too long," they proclaim. "She should have given them 5 minutes to discuss. After that, she should have given them the answer so that they could move on. There's not enough time for all that talk." They don't seem to notice that, if the teacher stopped the discussion, she would have taken the responsibility for learning and constructing understanding away from the students. She would have changed what they were learning. She would have been relying on different assumptions about how they learn.

They have the same reaction to many of my lessons. The school board meeting was fun, but it should have ended with some wise words from me about its significance. The small-group activity about XBTs was nice, but I should have made sure that they all left class with the same understanding. Instruction can be participatory and active, but learning—real learning—depends on teachers' identifying and providing the bottom line. "Did Suzanne teach today?" "No, because we didn't all learn the same things." "No, because she didn't tell us what the point of the XBT lesson was."

It's strange. We read many an account that portrays learning as ineffable, hard to measure, something that takes time. In rational, polite discussions about such matters, students agree that learners twist and turn the information they encounter in classrooms, constructing personal meanings. They agree that an array of learning styles and modes exists. When I push them to critique an instance of teaching, however, or ask them to plan a lesson, or teach something in class, they assume that if only teachers would tell their students something in clear, concise prose, then every learner who is motivated and listens will leave the class with the same understanding. Embedded by years of classroom experience, the beliefs my students hold about teaching as telling and learning as absorption are deeply rooted and insidious.

Beliefs About Knowledge

My students' beliefs about teaching and learning are tethered to another set of beliefs, beliefs about what knowledge is of most worth. On the days when they leave the class more confused than when they entered, did they learn anything? "Probably not," they tell me. After all, learning results in propositional knowledge, nice sentences to be written on a page, not clouds of uncertainty and questions. On the days when they worked in small groups or led their own class discussions, they didn't take notes because other students might say interesting things but nothing worth noting. Only teachers say things you have to remember. "Did they learn anything?" I ask. "Maybe from each other, but not about class."

Joe made his assumptions clear one day in his journal:

> It is my opinion that to teach is to impart knowledge or skills. Today in class, two videos were shown and we were asked to take notes so that we would be able to answer specific questions. It was not an exercise in the transmission of knowledge. . . . To answer the question, no, you did not teach today. You provided an exercise but no knowledge was imparted and no skills were passed on to us.

My students envision knowledge about teaching as lists of methods concerning discipline, management, evaluation, and instruction that, once committed to heart and mind, will ensure success. For them, knowledge is static and true, not dynamic and interpretive. No one has ever suggested to them, for example, that history is not a parade of facts but rather a field in which people interpret the past, use evidence, construct arguments. Or that these interpretations and arguments are refuted by other scholars and sometimes change. Similarly, no one has ever suggested that teaching might also involve a similar learning community in which scholars hold different theories of how to teach and what to teach in which there is much disagreement, argument, refutation, reinterpretation, and change. It is not surprising that my students want answers. School has taught them that knowledge about teaching or history or mathematics or biology is conclusive, final, concrete. They have never been exposed to the exciting aspects of knowing: refutation, argument, construction, interpretation. No wonder learning is boring to them—even distasteful at times. On the way to the classroom, the very characteristics that make knowledge worth knowing got lost.

Did Suzanne teach? If they arrive expecting to learn a set of recipes that will make them good teachers, the answer is "Never." I don't believe that knowledge of teaching exists in such forms. Rather, I believe that knowledge of teaching takes the form of stories and experiences, parables and principles, tentative claims about what works sometimes in some contexts. There is knowledge that informs teaching, but I want them to understand how it has been constructed and what forms it takes so that they can be critical consumers of it.

Manifested Beliefs

The beliefs students have about learning and teaching and knowing reveal themselves in more than their answers to my question. They also surface in behavior. Polite and dependable, hardworking and sincere, concerned and obedient, my learners are model students.* They raise their hands when they want to speak, they read the assignments and take copious notes on what the authors "said," they come to class prepared. Given their assumptions about knowledge, it's not surprising that my students treat texts as authorities whose contents should be memorized, not human constructions about which we might converse, argue, disagree. The difficulty I face with my students is that they believe school is about obedience and politeness and respect for the teacher, the one with the goods. Arguments are not nice, nor do they belong in classrooms for they waste precious time.

I find the politeness, passivity, and silence in my classroom oppressive. They do not facilitate learning and discussion; they strangle it. If I ask a question about one of the readings at the beginning of the term, the discussion is stifled and short. Students cannot explain their answers or express their own opinions, and they don't know how to disagree with one another. I ask lots of questions. Blank stares greet me in return.

My students want to answer my questions, but they have never been asked to justify their answers, explain their reasons, define their terms. When I ask them, "Why do you believe that?" they're taken aback. They speak of the "W" word (why) with trepidation. When I push them to support their answers, I violate the classroom

---

*As is the case at many large, public universities, the number of students who currently want to enter teaching far exceeds the resources available to teach them at Michigan State. Consequently, our college has capped admissions using proxies of academic achievement like grade-point averages for admittance to the programs. Hence, entrance to the College of Education is now very competitive. My students are not just well behaved, they also have a history of scholastic achievement and success. They are serious students.

code. In fact, I'm being rude. I'm making them think about what they say. I'm making their brains hurt. I'm making them feel anxious, uncomfortable, insecure. This kind of classroom discourse is unfamiliar to them. They're not used to being pushed intellectually; they're not used to being asked to defend their ideas; they're not used to a teacher demanding that they find and contribute a voice in class.

I talk to them about their passivity and the expectations they have developed of appropriate school behavior. I ask them if they want their students to feel like they do: afraid to answer questions for fear of being wrong, afraid to change assignments to suit their own needs, afraid to ask the teacher or a classmate to clarify something that was said for fear of appearing stupid. "Of course not," they say in slightly exasperated tones. I push again, asking how they plan to teach. "Like my favorite teachers," someone explains. Befuddled, I ask, "But did those teachers teach you to answer my questions, to speak up in class, to have a voice here?"

Eventually, the paradox becomes obvious to them. My students have good intentions. They want their pupils to be empowered. Yet they themselves are disenfranchised learners. They can't depend on their memories of good teachers to guide them in their own teaching. Confronting this dilemma can be painful, for it requires that my students acknowledge their own weaknesses and question their pasts as learners. They feel sad, guilty. I feel bad and try to dispel their despair. It's not their fault they are passive. They learned to act that way in classrooms. We taught them to behave in school, but we forgot to teach them how to learn.

I am not doing my students or my work justice by treating these issues so superficially. My students are not wrong in what they believe about teaching: Teaching does and should involve some telling. Teachers are often the source of information. Learning can involve memorizing lists of numbers and words. Some of my students do occasionally stand up, speak out, take a stand. But most don't. And most believe that telling and absorption and obedience and silence are the hallmarks of teaching.

SHAKING THE ROOTS: THE PEDAGOGY OF TEACHER EDUCATION

I want to teach my students that teaching is hard work—not only because teachers have to manage 30 students at a time and teach a range of subjects, but also because it requires reflection on one's own knowledge and belief, considering one's actions and their consequences. I want them to learn how to look at themselves, for much of the learning we do as teachers is done in isolation and depends on one's ability to critically evaluate and reflect on one's own thinking and action. Perhaps I shouldn't have started this essay with the image of prospective teachers as garden plots. Instead, I might have portrayed them as apprentice gardeners, learning from me how to nurture and weed their own teaching garden, how to get rid of the dandelions but look after the roses.

In 10 weeks, I cannot hope to pull out of my students the deeply rooted beliefs about learning, teaching, knowledge, tracking, nor can I teach them to do the same. Those beliefs and behaviors run too deep to uproot them the first time; as teacher educators, our weeding must be vigilant. But in one term I can shake them up a little and help them understand that the weeding is necessary, helpful. I can do this by providing a safe environment in which they can begin to act like real learners — challenging and justifying themselves and each other and me, hypothesizing and experimenting with ideas, experiencing (some of them for the first time) the kind of learning that they dream of providing for their pupils.

Lest you think I have muddied the waters enough already, I will add one more twist. Teacher educators teach prospective teachers these things on at least two levels. If I am the type of teacher I want them to become, I can't *tell* them these things about teaching and learning and knowing, I have to *teach* them those things. My students learn as much from how I act as a teacher as they do from the content of the course. That's why I make them answer the question, "Did Suzanne teach?" for this question helps us examine the implicit lessons they may take away from my teaching. As I respond to their comments about my pedagogy, I tell them why I do things. I am modeling for them what it means to reason through pedagogical problems. I look in a mirror at my own beliefs about teaching and learning to teach, in addition to my beliefs about my students' knowledge and beliefs about teaching and learning to teach. And so I let them watch me watch myself.

It is easy to get lost in mazes of concerns, and sometimes I lack the dexterity and facility to manage the multiple concerns and agendas. My success is sporadic. It takes me the entire term just to get students feeling comfortable enough to really talk to me and each other. They are fragile learners and it is hard for me to know when and how hard to push them to think about their assumptions. I do not have time for them to voice glib opinions. I want them to construct defensible positions.

I also care about how they feel and I don't want to scare them away. When do I know whether I've crossed the fine line between teacher and bully? It is scary for them to have a teacher who requires that they voice half-bake notions, that they challenge their own and each other's thinking, that they take control of their own learning. I know they feel frustrated leaving class with an empty notebook, especially around exams. Sometimes I wonder if I do more harm than good. Maybe all I do is confuse them.

Every quarter, though, I think I get a little better at it. I really am learning how to shake some roots a little loose for some students. For example, we spend some time thinking about a common assumption that practical experience in classrooms will teach them what they need to know as teachers. I want them to question that belief for, to paraphrase T. S. Eliot, we can have the experience but miss its meaning. A difficult idea to grasp, some students like Rosemary leave class reevaluating that belief:

> When I was 13, I had to memorize the 23rd psalm. Up until that point I had watched 13-year-olds in the years before me recite the psalm for the congregation in order to receive their Bibles. When it finally came to be my turn to memorize it, I had heard the sounds of the words so many times before that I was comfortable with them and it was easy for me to commit them to memory. I got up in front of the church, recited my verse, and received my Bible. What I realize now, 6 years later, is that I still don't know the meaning or importance of that verse.
>
> In other words, I had the experience with the verse, but still missed the meaning. This is not such a hard thing to do. And when training to teach it is especially easy. Having grown up in classrooms observing teachers all our lives, of course we will have preconceptions of what teaching should look like. But hidden behind those spelling lists and lesson plans is where the essence of teaching lies. This familiarity of classrooms will make us comfortable. . . . But we are only going through the motions without knowing why.

I find Rosemary's reflections heartening, for she is beginning to think about herself and her beliefs in ways that may liberate her from teaching the way she was taught. She may also be learning how to evaluate critically her apprenticeship in those classrooms.

CONCLUSION

But it is only a beginning. Sometimes I get depressed realizing that I am moving on to another group, another overgrown garden to prune and weed and water in 10 weeks. Who is going to continue to help my Joes and Rosemarys think about their assumptions? Our term is little time in comparison to a lifetime of pedestrian teaching and a future in schools that leave little room for the creative and critical thinking that good teaching requires. I'm worried too about the liberal arts and science classes (as well as the teacher education courses) that my students will take in which instructors model again teaching that reaffirms the very assumptions I have been trying to uproot.

Students leave my class drawing one of three conclusions: (1) Teaching is too hard, so I'm going to switch my major; (2) Suzanne is a quirky, although pleasant enough, person who should be tolerated but largely ignored; (3) teaching is hard work and I can't think of a better way to spend my life. I've made the same decision as that third group: Educating educators is hard work, but the mysterious tangle of violets and vines is a challenge well worth wrestling.

I began this essay by promising you a window into the thinking involved in teaching TE-101. I've purposefully stayed away from listing what someone needs to know, think about, listen to, consider in teaching this class. I think a lot about my purposes and goals, my students and their beliefs, the ideas of the course and the readings, the context in which I work, my instructional options and their limitations and strengths. All are important and none takes priority over another. Just as there are no rules for me to teach my teachers, there are no rules for teacher educators when teaching this course. But there are better and worse decisions based on more and less valid grounds. Just as I push my students to examine their beliefs about teaching and learning, we too must push ourselves to examine critically our own beliefs about what teachers need to know, how they learn, what we have to know in order to teach them well, and what our role in their learning is and should be. The assumptions we all make about teaching and learning — as prospective and practicing teachers and teacher educators — are like that garden at Misselthwaite Manor, for they have gone untended much too long.

8

Exploring My Teaching of TE-101

Susan McMahon

When I began teaching TE-101, I had 15 years of experience teaching English in secondary schools under my belt. In 5 years of teaching middle school language arts in a laboratory school, I modeled teaching for preservice and in-service teachers. Though I had assumed I could always learn more about teaching, I imagined that any modifications in my teaching would be minor; I was sure that my beliefs would remain essentially the same. Little did I know that my ideas would change radically.

Before doctoral students teach TE-101, they spend a term observing an experienced instructor. When I observed Suzanne Wilson (see Chapter 7) for my apprenticeship, I kept a journal of thoughts during class and reflections afterwards. I met frequently with Suzanne to discuss some of my questions and ideas. In this chapter, I examine these questions and the changes in my teaching and thinking that resulted. The initial section focuses on issues surrounding the content of the course; the final section, on general pedagogical issues.

COURSE CONTENT

Before I actually began teaching my own section of TE-101, I examined syllabi from various other course instructors. All of them organized the readings around three questions:

146

(1) What do teachers need to know in order to teach?
(2) How do the purposes of schooling affect teaching and learning?
(3) What does it mean to teach and learn?

What Do Teachers Need to Know in Order to Teach?

My experience had taught me that teachers need subject-matter knowledge as well as knowledge of teaching, of students, and of learning. Many preservice students believe that because they already know more than elementary students, they don't have to worry about subject-matter knowledge. I realized that I had to help my students confront this belief and come to the realization that elementary teachers need a great deal of subject-matter knowledge. I knew that many preservice teachers believe that because they know more than the children, they need not worry about their own subject-matter knowledge, and the students in TE-101 confirmed this impression. As I watched Suzanne teach, I discovered that changing beliefs is not as easy as I had initially thought. As a result, I found myself uncertain about how to create a context that facilitated such change.

In one class session, Suzanne organized a lesson around an elementary math problem. First, she asked her students to divide $1\frac{3}{4}$ by $\frac{1}{2}$. After students had worked on the problem, she told them to get into small groups to discuss the process they had followed. They were not allowed to say, "You just invert and multiply." They had to demonstrate that they understood mathematically what they were doing. Working together for 20 minutes, each group prepared to explain its solution to the entire class the way a teacher might to a class of elementary students. Sitting among the students, I watched group after group try unsuccessfully to explain how they divided fractions. I wondered, "Why is this so difficult?"

As I observed this lesson, I confronted my own limited knowledge of mathematics. Like many of Suzanne's students, I could get the right answer. I know that $1\frac{3}{4}$ divided by $\frac{1}{2}$ equals $3\frac{1}{2}$, but could I explain the process without resorting to a formulated rule?

The next term, responsible for my own section of TE-101, I decided to try this lesson even though I was not sure I could do what I was asking my students to do. I watched students wrestle with the issue like the previous class; as their teacher, however, I was even more aware of their confusion and feelings of inadequacy.

Members of one group became extremely frustrated as they taught their lesson. This group decided to explain its problem by dividing a pizza. They drew one and three-quarters pizza on the board. They then proceeded to divide it by 2. This is, each section of pizza was cut into two to create half-pieces. They did not divide the total pizza by ½. *They divided it by 2 to create halves.* As other class members and I questioned them on this procedure, they became more and more confused. Finally, they asked if we could just go on to another group. They knew they were wrong, but they did not know why. Many students remained after class to discuss their frustration; a few even called me at home. They wondered why they were not prepared to explain such an elementary math problem, how best to prepare themselves, and whether it really was so important to be able to explain concepts instead of simply stating rules.

As a result of my conversations with these students, I decided to try to explain the solution myself. I had two reasons. First, I have always believed I should never ask students to attempt anything I myself have not attempted. As a teacher who has always stressed effort, problem solving, and fairness, my success or lack of it was less important than what I could model for students and what I could learn about the activity myself. Second, I mistakenly thought I could help them to see how really close some of the groups were to an understanding of the process and a sound explanation. However, I was not much better prepared to teach math conceptually than they were. This lack of subject-matter knowledge clearly emerged as I prepared for and taught my lesson.

Although I thought I understood the mathematical basis for the algorithm, I could explain the problem only one way. If my students did not understand the first time, I knew I had no alternate representations. I became more anxious and uncertain. I explained as I wrote and drew on the board while asking them to work the problem with pieces of paper I brought in. Each student group had two circles and several half-circles. I asked them to find out how many half-circles went into one whole one. Each group proudly responded with the correct answer, "Two." I then handed them a series of ¼-circles and asked how many times ¼ went into 1. Again each group proudly responded correctly. I then asked the total class if anyone could explain how the pizza example differed from the ones we just completed. Group pride diminished somewhat as students wrestled with this new problem. One group volunteered to explain, but the students soon became confused and class morale sank further. No group could apply my example using circles and fractions of circles to their problem. Perhaps their previous experiences of resorting to rules prevented them from transferring this example to a new problem. I am not sure. Whatever the reason, they could not explain the same procedure with the pizza problem.

Did I understand what I was doing when I divided by a fraction? I think so. Did I understand it well enough to teach? No! My lack of subject-matter understanding kept me from being able to figure out other ways to represent the same concept. Was my lesson a mistake? I do not think so. What I clearly conveyed was that I needed more knowledge to teach math, just as they did. As I observe other students wrestling with this math problem each term, I realize I am no closer to understanding division of mixed numbers than I was before. However, I wonder whether I need to know more math to teach the concept related to teacher education. I ask myself the course question, "What do I need to know to teach this class?" My answer: *Teachers need to know the domain they are teaching.* My students leave class understanding the importance of teacher knowledge even if they do not understand division of fractions.

How Do the Purposes of Schooling Affect Teaching and Learning?

This question focuses on many issues, two of which I recently confronted as a doctoral student — tracking and equity. As a classroom teacher, I had supported tracking, thinking it most equitably served the needs of all students. I assumed that some students would best benefit from a focus on job-related skills whereas others needed preparation for college. In my doctoral proseminar my views changed; we discussed Jeannie Oakes's (1985) research and her conclusions that, despite good intentions, tracking does not work. She demonstrates that students whose ethnic or economic backgrounds do not match the school's middle-class values quickly fall behind. Instead of fulfilling the American dream, tracking perpetuates existing class distinctions. When I began teaching TE-101, I was still revising my thinking about these matters and wondering how undergraduates would respond to the issues of tracking and equity. Observing Suzanne, I saw that many undergraduates resisted accepting evidence that tracking perpetuates the current social status of certain groups. Of course, they all professed a belief in equality and none would say anything someone could interpret as biased against any population of students; however, they held firmly to two apparently contradictory beliefs: (1) Tests measure competencies but (2) students who work hard succeed. They were confident that ability was static and measurable on standardized tests yet convinced that anyone, regardless of ability, could succeed with hard work. Clearly, years and years of schooling had convinced many of them that teachers formed ability groups to help students, not to separate them. Could one 10-week course, in which only one 3-week section addressed the ills of such grouping, significantly change student thinking?

In previous class sessions, Suzanne had remained open to all ideas and comments. She never told students they were wrong nor that one answer was better than another. In the first session addressing the issue of tracking, she took the most vocal and obvious stand she had taken all term (see Chapter 7). She stated that she opposed all tracking and that no evidence proved that it served the best interest of students. Skeptical, I privately wondered how she could take such a strong position. First, I questioned her pedagogy. Throughout the term she had maintained that telling students what she wanted them to believe would not work; they had to learn through the readings, discussions, and their own reflections. Second, I questioned her certainty that tracking was always negative. Certainly it could work. As a cornerstone of most classes and schools in America, it had to serve some beneficial purpose in building learning environments. I resolved to teach the issue of tracking differently.

With my first section, I did just that. I tried to remain open to any ideas students voiced about grouping students. I hoped that as they listened to one another and worked through the readings, they would begin to question the beliefs they brought with them into class. However, I discovered that many of their experiences with tracking were so positive that they could not see any problems. Further, ability grouping was so much a part of their schooling that they could not imagine any other approaches. For balance, I began stating stronger and stronger positions by citing Oakes's (1986a, 1986b) articles and referring to Suina's (1985) selection about his own experiences as an Indian child in a white school. Although some students verbally acknowledged the problems noted within these texts, I still wondered whether they had really begun to see the problems associated with tracking.

When I taught my second section, I approached the topic differently. Without indicating my own position, I encouraged students to take whatever stand they wanted, as long as they found evidence for it. Because the course readings provided arguments against tracking, students needed to look elsewhere for support. Instead of taking a clear stand that they could dismiss as the "teacher's preferred response," I asked students to seek out other sources.

The evidence students most commonly provided was their own experience. For example, some argued that they had done very well even though they were not good students themselves. Some reported that they had been poor readers in the early elementary grades or that they had not been serious about school until college. One student related being placed in special education classes for a short time until being reinstated into the regular curriculum by his regular classroom teacher. His story supported his belief that mistakes are made, but they are rectified by the system. The room was filled with white, middle-class females, but this did not conflict with student belief that anyone can rise above difficult schooling experiences. When the occasional male or minority student would describe the pain of being placed into lower-tracked or special education classes despite a goal of a college education, such testimony evoked mixed reactions. Some questioned the system. Others interpreted the stories as affirmations that the system worked: Here was a student who really *did* try hard and succeed.

Students assigned to seek evidence for their beliefs were challenged to confront the established tradition. Because these students generally benefited from tracking, their belief in its value is firmly established. This course asked them to begin to question this practice.

What Does It Mean to Teach and Learn?

A third question, "What does it mean to teach and learn?" initially left me struggling. As a teacher, I did not remember worrying very much about this issue. What I did in front of my class each day was teach; what the students did was learn. I had never thought about how interdependent these activities were. As I observed Suzanne, I began to see the boundaries between teaching and learning as less distinct. As she and I discussed lessons, I would see that she was learning from her TE-101 students. Their responses in class and in journals made her think of course issues in new ways, and I saw evidence of their thinking in her own explanations of ideas. At the same time, she clearly was preparing class discussions designed to facilitate their learning.

As I wrestled with this third course question, my observations confused me even more. On days when we watched videotapes or worked primarily in groups, Suzanne asked, "Did I teach today?" I was frequently glad they had to respond and I did not. Did she teach? I thought some students seemed to have learned because of the lesson she created, but how could I know for sure? Did they really learn or just seem to learn? If they did learn, was teaching just the creation and implementation of a lesson? The question seemed to be grounded in the relationship between teaching and learning. I believed I understood the issues at some conceptual level, but could I identify teaching and learning in a classroom on any given day?

In my own TE-101 sections, I still wonder, "Did I teach today?" I, too, frequently ask students to respond to this question in writing, and I thoroughly enjoy reading what they have written. They sometimes learn more than I think I taught. At other times, they learn things I did not know. Occasionally, I wonder whether they learned anything at all. I find myself reading Jackson's (1986) "Uncertainties of Teaching" over again. A teacher may never know whether students have learned. Teaching and learning are not only related but seem to be recursive — the teacher is sometimes the learner and the learner, the teacher. When I teach, preparing and conducting the lesson help me to learn the material better. Does this guarantee student learning? No, not necessarily; much depends on the student. However, it does create a better context for learning. Further, because my lessons include a significant amount of interaction, I learn more about how students are making sense of the issues so that I can tailor future instruction around their meaning-making.

GENERAL PEDAGOGICAL ISSUES

The questions organizing the course gave me the first inklings that my teaching would change. They compelled me to peel back old beliefs in order to examine their assumptions. I found that I was learning more and more from my students. Old assumptions that guided my general pedagogy also underwent revisions.

Every new or experienced teacher confronting a new context needs to consider how to build a classroom environment that fosters the best learning. The environment I observed in Suzanne's class was very different in some ways from the one I had established in middle school. Three aspects of her teaching significantly influenced my general pedagogy:

(1) her use of journals,
(2) her use of oral questioning and synthesis, and
(3) her use of modeling.

Journals

Perhaps the first clear difference between how I would have managed a middle school classroom and how Suzanne managed her college classroom emerged in her use of journals. I had used journals occasionally with middle school students, but I had always asked open-ended questions, encouraging students to choose the topics on which they wrote. Suzanne's journal assignments focused on a set of questions about the course readings. Although she added a few questions attempting to get at what students were actually thinking about course issues, the journals in Suzanne's section of TE-101 resembled what I considered homework notebooks. I wondered how well such restricted journals could get at student thoughts about the readings. On the surface, these questions probed recall of information from the text more than they elicited student ideas about the readings. When I began teaching my own section, I realized how invaluable this version of student journals could be if I probed student responses.

TE-101 aims to confront the students' assumptions about teaching and learning. In any class of 25 no teacher can get at every individual's assumptions. However, journals give the teacher an opportunity to see a student's interpretation of key readings and the rationale for that interpretation. As I responded to journals, I began questioning the assumptions behind students' reasoning. I could challenge such assumptions in an individual, somewhat less-threatening manner in this private forum.

I found that very simple questions written in the margins could push students to write more and, I hoped, think more about what they wrote. My first journal assignment asked students to explain in one page why they wanted to become teachers. Many students responded with, "I love children"; others with, "I want to make a difference"; still others stated, "I know I'll be good at it." I wanted them to explore these answers, so I tried to advance their thinking through additional questions. Responding to "I love children," I would write, "Do you love all children? Why or why not?" or "Is loving children important to teaching? Why or why not?" or "Can a teacher be effective and not love children? Why or why not?" I would then ask them to respond to my questions in the subsequent journal entry. After students became used to my style of questioning, I began to respond with a simple, "Why do you believe this?" Instead of providing cryptic answers, students began sharing their reasoning in journals, in small groups, and in total class discussions. In journals they soon wrote, "I know, you're going to ask me 'Why?'" They would then respond to the "why" question I had not yet asked. In small-group discussions, students probed one another with "Why?" or, "You know, she's going to ask us 'Why?' so we better think about it." My written responses in journals initiated student exploration of their own thinking about the readings and their future teaching. I do not know how I could have encouraged this so quickly and with so many students without the journals.

Initially, I had questioned Suzanne's open-ended due dates for journal assignments. Although Suzanne accepted all journals until the last class session, my middle school teacher mentality revolted against such laxity. I believed that to maintain standards, students needed deadlines with consequences. If I were open to any due dates, I believed I would convey to students a lack of concern for promptness and fail to reinforce their need to keep up with the readings.

Therefore, in teaching my own section, I began by insisting that all students turn journals in to me by specific dates. Soon, however, I allowed more flexibility. College sophomores were generally more mature than my middle school students and often had good reasons for not staying on my schedule. More important though, I found myself questioning the reasoning behind such a schedule. Which was more essential to students' learning—turning in the assignment "on time" or completing the work and the thinking I had hoped would evolve as a part of the assignment? When answers were incomplete or hastily written, I encouraged students to write more about the same question the next time. I did not allow anyone to bypass a difficult question by skipping the response and taking a lower grade, nor could any student plead there was not enough time during the week to complete one response. I sympathized with each student's problems, but insisted that they use the journals as one way to think and write about all the issues. The emphasis was not on completing a task within a specified time period but on taking time to think about difficult ideas and putting that thinking in writing.

The act of writing forced students to probe issues more thoroughly. If they tried to avoid this, my questions pushed them further. In initial journal entries all students had several "Why?" questions as described above. Although I did not expect them to answer all of my questions, I did ask each of them to select five of my questions to respond to the following week. After a few weeks, I could tailor my assignments more to the needs of individual students. I asked students whose entries demonstrated thoughtful consideration of difficult issues to respond to fewer of my questions the following week. Those who seemed to be writing shallow answers just to complete the assignment I asked more probing questions and assigned them for the subsequent week. I found myself abandoning the last vestige of the work ethic model of efficiency in education. We were not on an assembly line. Students needed different amounts of time and encouragement to learn. It was part of my role as instructor to provide that flexibility.

Students think and write more if they see this is so important that I will not just grade what they have finished. I do encourage them to keep up and require a conference if they fall behind. I did the same as a middle school teacher, but now my reasons are very different. I now see the importance of stressing to students the need to think about these issues. My message is not that I have established a time frame for their learning. If I had continued to enforce due dates rigidly, I would have been telling students that performing tasks on time was more important than learning.

Oral Questioning and Synthesis

Watching Suzanne prompted me to think about my role as I asked questions and tried to pull together student ideas. In my middle school classes, I had asked factual recall as well as synthesis and evaluation questions. I frequently challenged students with, "Why do you think so?" However, at the end of class sessions, I always tried to pull their contributions together into some answer. Although I did not always have a "right answer" in my mind initially, as students discussed an issue I would organize their comments in my mind, then review this organization with them.

Suzanne never did this. Many times I would leave class wondering why she never synthesized the discussion. As the term wore on, I noticed that, like me, the students were becoming more and more frustrated. Although I never assumed there was one right answer, I wanted the class to arrive at its own best one. This never occurred.

Reflecting on my viewpoint, I see that I believed student learning required a structure, and, as the teacher, I felt responsible for

providing this framework. I questioned the students' ability to create
such structures on their own. After I had gained experience teaching
TE-101, my view changed. Although I began teaching TE-101 by
summarizing daily content, I later started having students synthe-
size our discussions on their own or in groups and write about this
in their journals. I realized I do not know the "best" answer for
many of the issues we discuss. Furthermore, I do not want to provide students with my answers. I want to challenge their thinking
and the assumptions that drive it. Asking them to pull together the
major aspects of any given class facilitates their own meaning-
making.

One issue that is not easily resolved through class discussion is
the role of the teacher when children are confused. We read a selection from Vivian Paley's (1981) *Wally's Stories* in which she describes
kindergartners' confusion after hearing "Stone Soup." In this story,
men trick peasants into feeding them by saying they are making
soup from stones. The peasants bring vegetables to add to the soup.
Paley's kindergartners think that the stones melt in the boiling water. Paley tries to demonstrate to her students that boiling the stones
does not cause them to melt. Despite the evidence to the contrary,
the children still believe the stones do indeed get smaller. Paley's
account implies that the children are not yet ready to accept what
the evidence shows. Because they are not ready, any efforts she
makes to convince them will fail.

TE-101 students have mixed reactions to this reading. Some
agree with Paley; others say that, although they support experimentation, they think Paley had a responsibility to tell the children "the
truth" so they would not leave school believing in a fallacy. These
students miss Paley's point about student readiness to believe. Class
discussion is lively as TE-101 students align themselves with one
side or the other: Yes, she should explicitly tell them that stones do
not melt, or no, she should not. As class ends, students sometimes
seem confused because I do not tell them the "right" answer to the
dilemma Paley's vignette creates in our class.

Later, when they write their synthesis in their journals, they
ask me what is best. Although I have a preferred response, is it the
"right" answer? Is there a right answer? I could provide my best
answer based on what I believe or on what the class has discussed,
but it would probably not change anyone's thinking. Some might
repeat my answer on the final exam but leave the course with their
preconceived notions firmly in place. Only by continually pushing
students to examine why they believe as they do can I hope to get

them to question their own assumptions about teaching and learning. My synthesis is just that — my synthesis. Each individual must create her or his "best" answer for the day. We discuss what Paley means, why she might think this, and what they think, but do they believe as Paley does when we have ended our discussion? I doubt it. They must form their own ideas.

Modeling

The third challenge to my existing ideas about the learning environment was in the area of modeling. As a classroom teacher, I realized the importance of being a role model. I could not stress promptness if I were consistently late. As a writing teacher, I was aware of the process writing approach and modeled my thinking when composing with the class. I knew I needed to demonstrate what I valued in the learning process.

During my mentoring period with Suzanne, I conducted class twice while Suzanne was out of town. At this time, I became aware that modeling takes on even greater importance when one is instructing future teachers. In one session, students viewed videotapes of two classroom teachers with very different approaches. One teacher more closely exemplifies the orientation of many of the authors we read and discussed in the class. That is, she fosters student problem solving and encourages student interaction. During our discussion of these teachers, a dilemma arose. As with the issue of tracking, students' prior experiences and beliefs influenced their viewing of the tape. To them, the teacher exhibiting the more traditional approach was the most successful. The other, who encouraged student participation and problem solving, they liked less, and they questioned how students could learn in an environment so different from the one they had experienced as students. Because I wanted them to see the value of the less traditional approach, I was frustrated in their overwhelming rejection of it and felt caught in a dilemma.

On one hand, I was tempted to praise the efforts of the teacher whose approaches more closely matched those of the authors we studied and to criticize those of the other teacher. However, in doing this, I would convey a subtle message that there is one "right" way to teach. On the other hand, I knew that modeling the approach I had supported all term would include questioning them about the methods each teacher adopted. Through this, I could push their thinking and help them see value in the less traditional teacher's approach. The solution resided in my consistency as the course instructor. If I believed in less traditional approaches to teaching and learning, then I had to model them. I could not adopt traditional methods without realizing that my students would follow my example when teaching their own classes.

I wanted my TE-101 students to understand that good teaching takes different forms. Thus, I was pulled in many directions. I wanted to point out that a less traditional approach to teaching could work and is often better. I could tell them this or model it. I found modeling more compelling. Modeling required me to analyze my own teaching methods each day because they convey subtle messages.

As I teach my own section, I spend many hours thinking about how I want to conduct class. My actions and words convey much more than I had ever imagined in my previous teaching experiences. My high school and middle school students could dismiss what I did as "Ms McMahon's way," but those students were studying English, not teaching. By contrast, in TE-101, not only what I say but what I do "teaches" the undergraduates about teaching.

I find myself doing more and more thinking aloud about the basic issues of planning and management. For example, because I believe students benefit from trying to articulate their thoughts and from encountering their peers' interpretations of readings, I frequently suggest they form small groups, stating aloud why I think this is a good teaching/learning strategy. I also am explicit about my purposes in making an assignment and why it best meets my goals. I openly discuss the problems of timing, stating how much class time I have planned for an activity and why; when we go beyond our time frame, as we frequently do, we discuss why that happened. Are my students always conscious of this? Some mention it in discussions or journals; a few probably dismiss it as a quirk of my class; I imagine others take it for granted.

CONCLUSION

Teaching TE-101 revolutionized my thinking about teaching and learning, for it challenged my assumptions every day. Is my approach totally different? I doubt it. Someone who saw me teach 5 years ago would still recognize me in a classroom. The differences are often in my reasons for what I am doing, in the responsibility I place on students to think, and in my perceptions of how students learn. No one can teach future teachers effectively without thoughtful reflection on her own practice.

9

After You. No, After You: A Collision Between Two Programs

Tom Bird

As the beginning course for the teacher education program at Michigan State University, TE-101 is intended to address prospective teachers' experience as students, which Lortie has called their "apprenticeship of observation" (Lortie, 1975). The central dialogue in TE-101 involves conceptions of teaching and learning as "knowledge reproduction" or as "knowledge transformation" (Jackson, 1986). The students tend to bring the former conceptions with them; the instructors tend to promote the latter. The resulting dialogue runs throughout the course and ties in one way or another to much of its substance. In this chapter I describe my attempt to open the dialogue by inviting students to study the beliefs that they brought with them.*

I also discuss some trouble I had in that effort: Four weeks into the quarter, the students complained vociferously about the course activities thus far. I speculated that TE-101 students and instructors were *acting* on their beliefs about teaching and learning, so that the

*When I volunteered to teach TE-101, I was delighted to discover that I had also joined a group that cultivates the course and its instructors, so that being a novice is not only a challenging state of affairs but also an interesting and rewarding standing among one's colleagues. For that, I wish to thank Sharon Feiman-Nemser, Helen Featherstone, Michelle Parker, Gem Reid, Paul Ongtooguk, Joyce Cain, and Suzanne Wilson.

encounter between students' and instructors' preferred *conceptions* of teaching and learning was accompanied and complicated by a corresponding encounter — or collision — between their *programs* for getting through the course.

In the conception of teaching and learning as knowledge reproduction, knowledge is put forth, taken in, and given back; the learner somehow takes possession of the knowledge that is offered but does not change it. Students entering TE-101 tend to hold this conception. To the extent that they also act on that conception, they are likely to invite the instructors to tell them the right answers about teaching and the right ways in which to express those answers, so that they can give those answers back in correct form, ace the course, and get on with their lives.

The conception of teaching and learning as knowledge transformation holds that learners have relevant prior experience, that they will employ their prior experience in the attempt to make sense of knowledge they encounter, and that they will transform that knowledge as they reconstruct their experience in the course of learning. Holding this conception, TE-101 instructors tend to employ tactics to match. Notably, their tactics do *not* include the immediate or obvious telling of right answers about teaching. Rather, instructors invite students to consider, discuss, and write about concrete instances of teaching, about arguments expressed in the course readings, and about connections among the instances and the readings. If the students accept those invitations, then instructors can begin providing feedback to the students about the implications of their talk and writing, and so help them to reconstruct their experience.

In various ways, both the students and instructors in TE-101 try to *get the other to go first*, so that they then can carry out their own programs for getting through the course. In the preliminary stages of that transaction, the students and instructors tend to resemble two extremely polite people who arrive simultaneously at a door. "After you." "No, after you." "Please, after you." "I insist, after you." Then the parties collide as they move through the door at the same time. Their respective programs clash, producing trouble for both parties. From the instructor's side of the transaction, one sort of trouble is that students tend to treat course readings as collections of potential answers to multiple-choice questions, whereas the instructor tries to help them reconstruct that same reading as a coherent argument that applies to cases of teaching. From the students' side of the transaction, the clash between programs means that they get no right answers to give back. They may wonder what the game is.

By a combination of intention, invention, inadvertence, and ineptitude — all accompanied by rationalizations regarding knowledge transformation — I made my spring 1990 section of TE-101 a strange place for my students. I stymied my students' knowledge reproduction tactics and, at the same time, required them to employ skills with which many of them had little practice. The resulting collision of programs provoked a strong outburst of student complaints about 4 weeks into the course. I responded to those complaints by reviewing with students the preceding 3 weeks of the course, thus shifting our attention to our immediate experience as teacher and learners in TE-101. Afterward, I felt that the review had not been a digression from the aims of the course but had helped to achieve them.

My story lacks some important evidence. I retained my lesson notes, which help me to reconstruct my tactics for teaching the course. I kept copies of work by 10 students, which helps me to retrace the transaction in ideas about teaching and learning. However, I collected no parallel data on students' perceptions and intentions. I was trying to teach a class, not conduct a study. As a result, the principal exhibit regarding my students' feelings about the class is their outburst of complaints about my conduct of the course. Those complaints are subject to alternative interpretations.

With that warning, I will proceed. First, I will describe my plans and activities in the first 3 weeks of class, along with the students' activities, reports, and complaints. While presenting an approach to the students' apprenticeship of observation, my description may serve to show what the students were complaining about. Next, I will describe my review of the class for students and suggest what the students may have gained from it. Finally, I will revise the speculation given above and suggest how I am revising my approach to the course.

THURSDAY, MARCH 30: FIRST MEETING

In the previous quarter, my first attempt to teach TE-101, I had taken the students' prior experience with teaching as my problem. By the end of that quarter, I had begun to think that the students' prior experience and conceptions were also their problem and needed to be treated as such. I would struggle with their past experience as pupils for 10 weeks, but they would struggle with it much longer. I wanted to invite the students to join me in attending to their apprenticeship of observation, but I faced a problem of tone and presentation: how to diplomatically call their attention to its influence without claiming that their heads were full of stuff and nonsense.

At our first meeting, I began a survey of the course. I started by describing how we all serve a long apprenticeship of observation in teaching, from which we acquire a variety of images, ideas, beliefs, and preferences about teaching. If we are human, I said, some of our accumulated ideas are wrong or misleading. Sound or not, they are likely to influence what we do as teachers. I suggested that we will probably teach as we have been taught, reproduce what we have experienced, when we would prefer to teach deliberately, to do what we do for good reasons. With those comments as background, I said that the purpose of TE-101 is to provide students with opportunities to take stock of their current views and to see if they agree with them.

Outlining the Course

I proposed to divide the course into three stages. In the first stage, students would examine their current beliefs by reporting and studying their reactions to videotapes of three school lessons. This activity would help them to make their beliefs explicit, facilitating the testing of their beliefs against arguments they would encounter in their reading. In the second stage, we would study some articles and essays, selected to address certain general problems in teaching and to provide the students with different vocabularies for thinking and talking about teaching. Students would apply these new vocabularies to the three videotaped lessons that we had studied in the first part of the course. This activity would give students a chance to test their current views against arguments encountered in readings and thereby judge the validity of these earlier views.

In the third stage of the course, we would again view, discuss, and write about the same three videotaped lessons, but this time we would attempt to provide an eclectic interpretation, employing several of the arguments that we had studied in the course. This activity would serve to consolidate the students' growing repertoire of interpretations.[1]

I said that I would try to be evasive about school teaching, because the focus of the course is not what I think about school teaching, but what the students think and what the authors of their readings think. I also said I would be clear about form and procedure, because the students needed ways to do the work.

Forming Groups

The next order of business was to organize small working groups. I thought of preparing teachers as a matter of intellectualizing teaching and of socializing teachers — preparing them for a career of conversation about their work. I said that one aspect of life as a teacher is being assigned to a school where you meet various people you don't know (and perhaps might not like), but with whom you must work, for example, in a department or a grade-level team. I proposed to provide students with some experience along that line.

I formed groups of four by asking students to raise their hands and counting off. The main issue was to distribute experience that might come with age and with time in the university. I asked the groups to convene, get acquainted, share telephone numbers and schedules, review the syllabus, and so get organized to work together.

Students Study Their Own Ideas

The final activity of the day was to begin the first phase of the course: the students' study of their own thoughts about school teaching. We began with a videotape of a second-grade lesson using small-group procedures similar to those described by Elizabeth Cohen (1986). As the tape began, the teacher had just finished reading a story (*Bedtime for Frances*) to her pupils. She reviewed group-work procedures including the assigned roles of "facilitator," "recorder," and "materials person" in each group. She said that, in groups, the students would share and record their answers to a set of questions, including "How are you like Frances?" and "How are you different from Frances?" Before sending students to their groups, the teacher reviewed the questions, asking and suggesting what facilitators and recorders might do to carry out and record the discussion. Then she assigned groups and roles and monitored the work with occasional intervention. After about 20 minutes of group activity, the teacher brought the students back together to hear and comment on the reporters' accounts of their groups' discussions and to give her reactions to the groups' activities and products. Her reactions included lavish and descriptive praise for some groups (and their facilitators) as well as a direct and disapproving description of how one group did not attend to its business, did not cooperate, and so did not complete the assignment.

I showed the videotape in 5-minute segments, allowing 2 or 3 minutes between segments for students to record their observations and reactions. I had provided a form for this work, and students took notes as they viewed the segment. When the segment ended, students wrote four sentences: a description of what happened in the segment, a reaction to it, a question about it, and a prediction of what would happen next. Some students said that they were uncertain about how to proceed, so I stopped after the first and second segments of the lesson to hear some of the students' reactions to the tape and to suggest how they could express their thoughts on paper.

The students wanted to know my relationship with the teacher in the videotape; was she my friend or acquaintance? I assured them that, although I knew some of the teachers, I had chosen the tapes because they gave us something to talk about; the students could not offend me by criticizing the lessons. The point of the course, I said, was to recognize and examine their beliefs about teaching, and we could not do that if they worried about my relationship to the teachers on the tapes.

What's My Thought?

After viewing the tape in segments, I asked the groups to play "What's my thought?" I introduced this activity by saying that it might be difficult for a person working alone to recognize his or her own assumptions and beliefs; others might help. Members of each group then took turns reading their four sentences for given segments of the tape, and other members of the group tried to guess, from those sentences, what the author believed about teaching. I had anticipated that students might be uncertain how to proceed, so I took the first turn as guesser, then asked the students to try a round of the game so that we could talk about what went on. Although the students seemed uncertain about what to do, I suggested that things were going well enough to proceed.

For the following class, the students were assigned to type up their notes from the day's exercise and to write a more detailed "commentary" on one segment of the lesson they had viewed. They were asked to report what that commentary revealed to them about their own beliefs. I gave the students a guide for writing their reports.

Students' Reactions

Rereading these reports, I am again struck by the certainty and emphasis with which most of the students offered their reactions to the taped lesson. They tended to make firm inferences about the videotaped pupils' actions and states of mind.

I saw some trends in my students' responses to the group-work lesson. Many commented that the group activity was too complicated for the second graders on the tape. Words like *facilitator* are too big for second graders to understand and group procedures are too involved for them to carry out. Young children cannot understand the teachers' feedback about their performance in groups. Their attention spans are too short for some of these activities. When the videotaped second graders went to work in their groups and the noise level rose, my students tended to see chaos, disorganization, and lack of discipline. Many worried about the teacher's control. Others described pupils working on their own as being off the subject; they get back on when the teacher reassembles the whole class for a debriefing of the group work. If an activity goes on too long, then the videotaped students get restless. Most of my students approved of the second-grade teacher's description and praise of some groups' work (a couple of students thought it was overdone). Her description and criticism of one group's work, however, was evaluated as not in order, capable of harming the students, and better given privately. Although all reports made some reference to the story and to the group discussion of questions about it, none of the reports directly probed the subject matter.

Later in the course, we would be viewing the group-work tape again and reading some of Elizabeth Cohen's (1986) *Designing Groupwork*. I anticipated that the reading and discussion might complicate the students' thinking about the joint pursuit of intellectual and social aims in the classroom.

TUESDAY, APRIL 2: REACTIONS TO DIRECT INSTRUCTION

We followed the same procedure with the second videotape, viewing it in segments with intervals for recording descriptions, reactions, questions, and predictions, and then playing "What's my thought?" Because the students seemed uncertain about the game, I repeated the rationale and reviewed the procedure.

The second videotape showed an English lesson on complex

sentences for eighth graders; in many respects, this lesson resembled direct instruction (Rosenshine & Stevens, 1986). The lesson started with what seemed to be a daily routine of studying two vocabulary words; the teacher said that the students should use the words in complex sentences. After announcing objectives for the day, the teacher reviewed the definition and parts of a complex sentence, then wrote a student's complex sentence on the board and showed how the sentence could be improved by selecting or changing adjectives and verb. The eighth graders were seated at round tables in groups of three or four. The teacher distributed a worksheet, showed the students two pictures, and told them to write complex sentences about the pictures. Next, they handed their papers to the students to their left, who edited the adjectives in their sentences. The paper was passed again, and a second student worked on the verb in the main clause. When their sentences had gone around the group, the students were asked to draw on others' efforts in order to write an improved complex sentence. Throughout this lesson, the teacher issued instructions for each small step of the work, moved about the classroom, looked at students' work, and made many suggestions and corrections.

Judging by their reports, my students far preferred this lesson to the group-work lesson. They remarked on the quiet atmosphere and the good organization (a few thought that the teacher might have been rushing a bit). They thought that the teacher's discussion and demonstration would help the students to understand complex sentences and that the teacher was quick to attend to students' questions and problems. Some reported that the lesson was practical and that the teacher had made the learning fun; a couple of students worried, not quite disapprovingly, that she might be spoonfeeding her students. A few complained that the teacher's questions were largely rhetorical, because she often answered them herself, and that she was directing the students' work too closely, not giving them time to work things out for themselves. Most of my students approved of the ending activity, in which the eighth graders passed their sentences around their small group for revision; they judged that the eighth graders could learn from and help each other. As before, my students were quite definite in their opinions of the teaching and confident in their inferences about students' attitudes and learning. As before, they paid little attention to the subject matter, commenting more often on the videotaped teacher's treatment of complex students than on her treatment of complex sentences.

Later in the course, we would be reading David Hawkins's (1967/

1974) "I, Thou, and It" and Magdalene Lampert's (1985b) "Mathematics Learning in Context." I anticipated that these writings might stir my students' interest in subject matter and its role in the relationship between teachers and their students. Also, those readings might lead them to reevaluate the decontextualized and technical treatment of complex sentences that they had just witnessed.

THURSDAY, APRIL 5: REACTIONS TO A MATHEMATICAL DISCUSSION

The third tape was a mathematics lesson for fifth graders, taught by Magdalene Lampert. In various ways, this lesson resembled "mathematics learning in context" as described by Lampert (1985b). Lampert had shown her students an episode from *The Voyage of the* Mimi, a 13-part series about a research expedition to observe whale behavior. In the episode, the scientists dropped an XBT probe over the side of their vessel. As the probe fell through the water, it reported the water's temperature and depth to a computer onboard, which displayed the data in a graph. The scientists dropped a second probe and produced a second graph. I showed the *Mimi* episode to my students, and then played the tape of Lampert's lesson.

Lampert distributed copies of the two XBT graphs and asked her pupils what they could tell from the graphs. Some reported immediately that the water temperature declined with depth; Lampert probed their reasoning about the details of the graph. This sort of questioning and argumentation continued for about 45 minutes, with Lampert calling pupils' attention to various features of the graphs, asking their views, summarizing their arguments and reasons, asking what other pupils thought about those arguments, and eliciting their interpretation of the information in front of them. Some pupils in Lampert's class interpreted the line on the graph to represent related points of data (temperature and depth), whereas others thought that the line on the graph represented the path of the XBT probe as it fell through the water.

Pressed for time, I did not show my students all of Lampert's lesson. I showed them two 5-minute segments at the beginning, another in the middle, and a final segment from the end of the lesson. I told them the total length of the lesson. The students played "What's my thought?" as before; for homework they wrote their third report.

Students' reports indicated that many of them initially admired Lampert's lesson: Lampert had put a question to her students and had worked with their answers. My students reported, favorably, that she made her pupils think for themselves. A few of my students stuck to that opinion, even as Lampert's lesson stretched to 45 minutes. Others had disliked the lesson from the outset; they judged it pointless and complained that the students had questions, but that Lampert wasn't answering them. As the lesson progressed, more and more of my students began asking why the discussion was dragging on so long, why Lampert kept on asking questions and summarizing fifth graders' arguments, why she didn't step in and get them back on the right track. None of my students discussed the different student interpretations of the graphs.

When we finished with the third tape, I suggested that the students had demonstrated in their first two reports that they had many thoughts about teaching, some of which were quite definite opinions. I asked them whether people going into accounting, engineering, or medicine had so many thoughts, or such definite opinions, about their future work. Joking, I asked them whether new medical students, on their first tour of a teaching hospital, would take a seat in the operating theater and say things like, "That's a good way to do a heart bypass operation."

I again raised the problem of the knowledgeable novice. I referred to evidence that people entering teacher education programs tend to think they don't have a lot to learn, and that they sometimes go away thinking they didn't learn much (Lanier & Little, 1986). One possibility, I suggested, is that teacher education programs don't teach much. Another possibility is that people with many well-formed and stable views about something tend not to change their ideas readily.

I said, "I'm inviting you to consider how your prior knowledge about teaching will affect your ability to learn whatever the university has to offer you that might help you to teach." I used myself as an example. "I know that I like to find out that I was right about something. Because I feel that way, 'success' means that I go through an activity that involves something I know about and end up finding out that I was right in the first place. I might pick up a few details or a little evidence to support my views, but I would basically stay the same. Complete success — feeling very good — would be *learning nothing at all — not changing my mind.*"

I noted that the students now had generated three reports of their thoughts about school teaching; they should hold these reports for later use. In the second part of the course, I said, they would compare those thoughts with arguments in the readings and figure out if they still agreed with themselves. Each of the next 7 weeks would follow the same routine: The students would read an article or essay about school teaching; they would consider a case of teaching described in writing or on videotape; they would write a report outlining the main argument of the reading, using that argument to interpret the case. I would grade their reports and return them at the beginning of the following week.

My lesson notes contain a script for a little speech about the readings. "The issue, at first, is not whether you agree with them; you have the rest of your lives to disagree with them. Rather, it's a question of gaining options for thinking. So, our aim will be to understand the readings well enough to use them to analyze the cases." Throughout the middle part of the course, I said, we would be practicing for the final exercise, in which they would use several of the readings to interpret the same videotaped lessons that they had viewed in the first phase of the course. Their assignment for the following meeting was to read and start outlining David Hawkins's (1967/1974) "I, Thou, and It" (the theoretical reading) and to read some vignettes from Vivian Paley's (1981) book *Wally's Stories* (the cases).

TUESDAY, APRIL 10: THE READING GAME

In the preceding term, I had formed the impression that many students are passive readers; although their participation in class suggested that most read the assignments, it also seemed that they had done little to get the readings organized in their minds before class discussion. If they were following a knowledge reproduction strategy, as I am speculating here, then I would suspect that they were reading to get through a multiple-choice test but not to get through the class discussions or writing assignments. For this term, I constructed a reading game, which I hoped the students could use in groups to make sense of the readings.*

By way of introduction, I asked the students to think again about the problem of the knowledgeable novice, for whom complete success—a triumph, really—would be to go all the way through a

---

*I had constructed the game from materials close at hand (Brown & Palincsar, 1990; Duffy & Roehler, 1987; Duffy, Roehler, & Herrman, 1988). Gerry Duffy reviewed the game and my plans for using it, and encouraged me to go ahead. He attended my class to assist in the launching.

teacher education program without learning anything — because he/
she already knew everything it had to teach. At some length, I tried
to describe how the students could do just that. They could fail to
overcome the inherent problems of figuring out what an argument
means. They could ignore arguments at odds with their own prior
beliefs. They could reconstruct arguments they did find acceptable
to accord with their own conceptions.

I offered an example concerning David Hawkins's (1967/1974)
essay, which the students were assigned to read for this day. Clearly,
"respect" is an important idea in that essay. After several readings
and discussions with others, I would hold that Hawkins is talking
first and mainly about the attitude of the teacher toward the students. Second, that attitude is admiration or esteem. Third, that
attitude is *conditional*; that is, it is possible to give or show respect
under some conditions but not others. In the preceding quarter,
students' papers showed reconstructions. They referred to Hawkins
when they wrote, but they had changed the usage of "respect." Most
common was that they had shifted from his concern with the teacher's attitude toward the student and were talking more about the
students' attitude toward the teacher. The attitude was something
like good regard, but it had become unconditional, that is, you
always respect other people. A couple of students also referred to
Hawkins when they used the word *respect*, but it was clear from what
they wrote that they were concerned mainly about the students'
attitude toward the teacher. Moreover, that attitude was not good
regard so much as caution or even fear.

Those students were successful in the peculiar way that I was
trying to describe — in their view, their prior belief was confirmed
by their reading. They could feel good that they had been right all
along. But they went away without the option that Hawkins had to
offer them.

In order to acquire the options available in the texts, I suggested, we should take on the reader's responsibility of trying to
overcome the problem of communication. We should try to notice
and assess how we reconstruct what we read. We should attempt to
give each text a first, friendly reading that would help the author to
make his/her case.

Launching the Reading Game

I then said that I had constructed a reading game, which we
would use in groups but would start practicing together. The game
divides the task of reading among the members of the group, so

that each member has a distinct role; the roles would rotate among the members over time.

I reviewed the five roles — Reader, Reader's Helper, Reader's Monitor, Writer's Advocate, and Anchor — which were described on a handout. The Reader was to read a passage aloud, interrupting herself along the way to report what she was thinking. When finished, she would compose a question that would make the members of her group tell her the main point of the passage. As the members gave their answers, she would try to clarify points of difficulty and to summarize the passage concisely. Finally, she would ask the other players to comment on the process of the reading. Then the roles would rotate and the group would proceed to the next passage. I thought that we might work on a few crucial paragraphs of each text in this way.

Other members of the group would follow the Reader's lead but also would have tasks of their own. The Reader's Helper would observe the Reader's work, help out as seemed necessary, and participate in the discussion. The Reader's Monitor would listen to the Reader's running comments and try to figure out what the Reader was doing to make sense of the text. The Writer's Advocate was to assure the first friendly reading by countering the reaction that "this *doesn't* make sense" with the question, "How *does* this make sense?" The Anchor's job was to draw the group back to the text when it wandered. She might ask, at her discretion: "Is this helping us to make sense of the text in front of us?"

I supposed that it would take some time for students to learn to play the reading game, so I planned to practice first with the class as a whole, coaching the students in their parts and gradually shifting the reading task from the whole class to the groups. In this first try, I didn't know whether that transition would take hours or weeks.

To begin reading some passages from Hawkins's (1967/1974) essay, I took the role of Reader and assigned the other roles to students. We pretended to be a small group reading together. I read the first passage, interrupting myself to describe what I was thinking as I read. Having read this essay several times, I found it a somewhat artificial undertaking, but I tried to stick to what I thought might stand out even to someone reading the text for the first time.

Coaching the Discussion

I asked my Reader's Helper if I had done my job. She stammered awhile. Gerry Duffy was present to help launch the reading game. He asked the students, "What's Tom trying to do?" After a bit, he wormed out of the students that the aim was to become more active readers, to interpret as we read. He gave another demonstration of reading the passage, so that the students wouldn't get the idea that every reading would or should be the same as mine. He read, reported some of his thinking, and described to the students what he was doing as he tried to figure out the passage and connect it to his experience in teaching. He proceeded considerably less formally than I did and, I think, with a much better sense of what the students might understand: "What's this guy trying to say about love and respect, and what does that have to do with teaching school? We are trying to pick out a theme, trying to get to his meaning."

I continued with the Reader's job, trying to ask questions leading the students to tell me the gist of the passage, trying to clear up confusions, trying to summarize the passage. The business felt very awkward and the students seemed hesitant to speak out. I felt I was not so much coaching the students in their roles as coaxing them to participate. I checked with my Helper frequently to see if I was carrying out the game as sketched in the handout; she and a few other students grew somewhat more active as the discussion proceeded.

Considering the difficulties we had encountered in the first round, it seemed rash to ask groups to carry on with the game by themselves. We tried again with the next passage, retaining our same roles. We negotiated the length of the three-paragraph passage. Having read the passage aloud, interrupting myself to report my thoughts as I went along, I then posed a question about the central meaning of the passage: "What's wrong with comparing the relationship between a teacher and a child with the relationship between a parent and a child?" The response I had in mind was Hawkins's claim that the "It" — an engaging object, the subject matter, a common interest between adult and child — plays a more central part in the relation of the teacher and student than in the relationship of the parent and child. Sometimes when students responded to the question, I asked them how they got from the text to their responses. That seemed to unsettle them; some would ask me to repeat the question. On the whole, however, the students participated more readily, and apparently more freely, than they had before.

At the end of the second round, the Reader's Monitor noted several things about my tactics as a Reader. She said that I had noticed that "triangle" is a metaphor, and probably an important one from where it sits in the text; that I had related ideas in the text to prior experience of my own; and that, at one point in the text, I had asked myself what other words Hawkins might have used, and suggested that the choice was significant. I was very pleased with the Monitor's report and tried to describe to the class what she had done.

THURSDAY, APRIL 12: READING HAWKINS, CONTINUED

Because the students seemed to have difficulty with the reading game, I suggested that we should continue to read together as a whole class, planning to move to reading in small groups the following week. The students asked me to explain the game again. The Reader, who had last served as Reader's Helper, began reading the paragraph in which Hawkins describes the teacher as providing the student with an "external feedback loop" (Hawkins, 1967/1974, p. 53). In the course of reading this passage aloud, the Reader interrupted herself twice to share her thoughts. Otherwise she read straight through, passing readily over sentences including "The adult's function, in the child's learning, is to provide a kind of external loop, to provide a selective feedback from the child's own thought and action" and "The child is learning about himself through his joint effects on the non-human and the human world around him" (p. 53).

Then, the Reader was to ask a question that would make the group tell her the gist of the passage. She tried twice and seemed stymied. I told her to take her time. Eventually she asked what the role of the teacher is and why it is necessary. From my audiotape of this class, I can hear that the students were talking about her question, but I cannot hear what they were saying. I suspect that only a few students were participating.

I can hear my participation. At one point, I told a student not to refer to me but to the Reader, who was discussion leader. I played a part in the discussion from time to time, as a member of the reading group. I emphasized that Hawkins says that the teacher's feedback is carefully selected *from the child's own thought and action*. I commented, "Hard, huh?" several times. As I listen again to the audiotape, I think that the exercise was going reasonably well—the Reader was leading the discussion, other students were participating, and I was intervening little.

When we had completed the round of reading for that passage, we discussed whether the Reader's summary was a good one. I responded to a distortion of Hawkins's argument. Hawkins had first argued that the teacher should construct an environment of engaging objects in which a student can exercise some choice, and so set off on his own course of thought and action. That background gave essential meaning to Hawkins's idea that the teacher's feedback to the child is carefully selected from the child's course of thought and action, and that the teacher's feedback helps the child to complete that course. My students were employing "feedback" more in the sense of correcting students' action in a course of teacher-prescribed action, where the teacher is trying to move the student toward a right answer that was chosen in advance.

After the reading and discussion, I proposed to provide students a "key" that they could use to unlock all the main ideas in Hawkins's argument. It was the metaphor of the triangle — I, Thou, and It; student, teacher, and subject matter. I offered that all of Hawkins's central ideas — trapping students' interests, getting information about students, providing them feedback — were triangular. To work out the meaning of any of these ideas, you had to say something not only about the relationship between the student and the teacher but also about the relationship between the student and the subject matter and about the relationship between the teacher and the subject matter.

I reviewed "respect" as a triangular term, then asked the students to tell me about traps and trapping. One student tried. I coached that effort and then offered a summary: A teacher who appreciates the potential in an interaction between an object and a child places that object in the path of a child to engage his interest and to set him off on his own course of thought and action. When the student has been engaged with something other than the teacher, then the teacher can watch, gather information, and select feedback that might help the child to pursue or complete his own project.

Near the end of the class, I gave the students a few minutes to revise their reports on Hawkins, as applied to Vivian Paley's (1981) teaching in "Rulers." To keep class discussion, students' writing, and my feedback on their writing close together, I had asked the students to begin their outlines of Hawkins's essay and their commentaries on one of Paley's vignettes prior to discussing them. Now they had an opportunity in class to revise and add to their reports before turning them in.

TUESDAY, APRIL 17: AND THEN
THE STUDENTS COMPLAINED

I began class by returning the students' reports on Hawkins's essay and Paley's vignettes. For this set of papers, I had given marks ranging from C to A —. Although I thought that a few of the papers deserved less than a C, I had put a floor under the grades on the grounds that this was their first such report and it concerned a particularly difficult text. I explained my grading to the students and made some comments that I intended to help the students produce reports in a form I had requested. Regarding the substance of their reports, I commented on inconsistencies between Hawkins's argument, as I understood it, and their outlines and applications of that argument.

To help consolidate students' understanding of Hawkins's argument, I invited them to use his ideas to comment on the first 3 weeks of our class. Part of the lore of TE-101 is that issues of teaching addressed in the course often are embodied in its own operations; the course activity provides ready means to connect abstractions and arguments in the readings to the students' immediate experience. It seemed reasonable to think that at least some of the students would draw on Hawkins's essay to interpret my initial showing of videotapes of teaching as an attempt to "trap" their interest. Similarly, they might interpret the assignment to study their own views as an attempt to set them on their own course of thought and action and might interpret my comments on their reports as an attempt to provide "feedback" in the sense that Hawkins uses the term. Perhaps they would attribute to me an attitude of "respect" for their potentialities, or even propose that I had attempted to promote a course of activity in which I could respect their "learnings and doings."

Put so baldly, my invitation for them to comment sounds like a bid for flattery. Nevertheless, "trap," "feedback," "respect for students' potentialities," and "respect for students' learnings and doings" are important terms of Hawkins's essay, which I had endeavored to exemplify in my conduct of the course. If the students could connect the ideas in the essay with their recent experience in my class, we might consolidate and enliven their tentative understanding of Hawkins's argument.

My hopes — either of flattery or of consolidation — were dashed. What the students did was complain. Some students, accompanied by mild or vigorous head-nodding by others, said that they didn't know what I wanted and that they didn't know how to do what I said I wanted. Some said they liked the content of the class but thought that the activities and assignments were strange and time-consuming. A consistently active and seemingly forthright participant in the class said that she was afraid to say or write what she thought. The students expressed considerable frustration and uncertainty about the procedures of the course, the reports being asked for, and the time those reports were taking. Those who spoke said they were not used to the procedures I was using and so didn't know what to do. The reading game was mentioned several times as a source of awkwardness and frustration; the students wanted to know why they couldn't just read and discuss an article, why I was asking them to labor so.

In immediate response to their complaints, I talked about how to prepare an outline of a reading and how to write a commentary on a case. I reviewed with them my understanding of the meaning of A and B and C grades, and the characteristics of work to which I assigned those grades. I reviewed the purpose of the reading game, and some of its procedures. When it appeared that the energy for complaining had dissipated somewhat, and the main complaints had been discussed or acted on in some way, I limped through some of the activities I had planned for the day and then faced a problem. I would not be present for the next class meeting. I had planned to ask the class to meet in my absence and, in their small groups, to carry out an exercise related to the week's reading, Magdalene Lampert's (1985b) "Mathematics Learning in Context." Anticipating that the students would find that exercise as disconcerting as they apparently had some of the other activities, I canceled the next class and told the students to work on their reports and commentaries. We would pick things back up at the next meeting of the class.

THURSDAY, APRIL 19: CLASS CANCELED

In the interval, the students' complaints nagged at me. Although their outburst could be regarded as an attempt to negotiate their workload and grades, that conclusion seemed overly simple and cynical. The activities of the course had been unfamiliar to me as well as to them. It seemed that there remained something to be settled, or gotten right. I rewrote the syllabus and prepared for the next meeting of the class.

TUESDAY, APRIL 24: RECONSTRUCTING
THE COURSE FOR THE STUDENTS

When the class next met, I noted that the middle of the term called for a review of progress. I said that I was dissatisfied with what I had done the preceding week, and that I thought we had unfinished business. I invited the students to help me reconstruct the class to date. I suggested that what had happened in the class provided us some teaching to discuss. From my lesson notes I recounted our activities during the first 3 weeks of class. I offered my rationale for those activities, incorporating some of the arguments from course reading into my rationale. I invited students to comment at any point. They did so; for the most part, they repeated the frustrations that they had expressed previously.

As I proceeded through the reconstruction, the students asked, in one way or another, "Why didn't you say that in the first place?" I reported that my reconstruction had been a review of my lesson notes — that is, I pretty much *had* said that in the first place. To relieve tension, I suggested that human beings may find it difficult to receive unfamiliar messages. Also, that practice helps teachers say things more understandably.

At the end of the reconstruction, I gave students a revised syllabus for the remainder of the quarter. In order to make up the lost week and to concentrate on making sense of readings, I canceled a couple of readings and activities. Students remarked, favorably, that they had not often seen an instructor revise the syllabus in response to their problems and concerns.

AFTERMATH

For the remainder of the quarter, many students seemed to proceed willingly, or even enthusiastically. I suppose that other students were resigned. Perhaps some of them perceived that they had registered a few complaints and, as punishment, had to sit through a windy defense of the course arrangements. Perhaps many of them felt that they had negotiated a satisfactory contract that they were now willing to carry out.

They had reason to feel that way. Beyond canceling a project and a reading, I also abandoned the reading game, which had played a prominent part in the students' complaints. I resorted to more conventional discussions and started revising the game for a fresh try next term. Students submitted their weekly reports with few exceptions. They ceased complaining about the volume of work. They said "I don't know what you want" only occasionally, when they were getting C's or lower.

Later in the quarter, another instructor took the class on a day when I was away. Some students repeated their complaints to her and asked her whether she would teach the course the way I did.

She refused to answer, asking instead how the ideas of "knowledge reproduction" and "knowledge transformation" from Philip Jackson's (1986) essay on "The Uncertainties of Teaching," which they were reading that week, related to the class.

WHAT HAPPENED?

The events in my class might be explained easily. I am a novice; at the time of the outburst, I was teaching my second TE-101 class, which was my second class of undergraduates, ever. The students' discomfort may be attributed to my clumsiness. Indeed, their comments suggested that their other courses did not present the same problems as mine; that they knew how to be university students but that I did not know how to be a university professor. Moreover, the students had an immediate reason to complain; I had just handed back their first piece of *graded* work, their reports on Hawkins's essay. Some of their comments and pointed questions conveyed that they had expected better grades. By inviting them to talk about the class, I provided them an opportunity to deflect any actual or implied criticism back onto me.

However, students who received high grades on their reports seemed to be complaining as much as (and more articulately than) students who received lower ones. The one day's outburst of complaints seemed to be only a concentration of ongoing and more pervasive signals to the effect, "What do you want me to do?" Some experienced TE-101 instructors have said that the course tends to make students uncomfortable and that they offer similar complaints in other sections, if not so uniformly or vociferously. Allowing for my clumsiness and the immediate provocation of handing back graded work, I reckon that there is more to figure out.

In beginning this essay, I speculated that the negotiation of ideas in TE-101 is complicated by a parallel negotiation of tactics for getting through the course. I suggested that many students hold and act on conceptions of teaching and learning as knowledge reproduction, whereas most instructors hold and act on conceptions of teaching and learning as knowledge transformation; and that their *ideas* about teaching and learning and their *tactics* for getting through TE-101 tend to collide. I speculated that such a collision occurred in my spring section of TE-101.

After telling my story and hearing some other instructors' reactions to it, I think that there was a collision of programs, but I place less weight now on the conceptions that distinguish the instructor's and students' programs and more weight on the knowledge and skills needed to carry them out. Perhaps the activities in my class did challenge the students' prior conceptions of teaching and learning. More clearly, I think, those activities taxed the students' skills and tolerance for ambiguity. Provided the opportunity, they complained. TE-101 students are members of an established institution with knowledge and skills adapted to institutional routines for getting through courses. Their experiences in school and college have taught them to demonstrate learning as knowledge reproduction and have provided them instruction and practice in doing so. That is what they expect and know how to do. I might have something to teach them, but I certainly do stand in their path to school teaching. They expect me to declare my aims, specify the forms for work in the class, and lay out the content for which I will hold them accountable; then, they can display purpose, proficiency, and understanding in ways that I will be likely to credit.

My conduct of the course presented them problems on all three counts. To begin with, I declared that a central purpose of the course was to help the students to notice and study their own ideas about school teaching. Perhaps that emphasis on their prior experience did surprise or offend their conception of teaching and learning in the university. More clearly, it required them to think, talk, and write about their own thinking.

Although I described, demonstrated, and coached the work that students should do, the format tended to be unfamiliar, not only to them but also to me. Perhaps the class activities did confound the students' conception of study at the university. More clearly, the activities themselves demanded skills of the students and threatened their reputations of competence.

With regard to the content, I tried to help students make sense of Hawkins's essay by describing how other students' reconstructions had led them to miss his point or misuse his language. I supplied the device that each of Hawkins's key terms is "triangular"; its meaning cannot be adequately expressed without saying something about the relationship between the teacher and the child *and* about the relationship between the child and the subject matter *and* about the relationship between the teacher and the subject matter. I chose Paley's vignettes as the cases to analyze because I thought that they lent themselves readily to applications of Hawkins's language. However, I did not adequately consider that each of these intended aids would itself need some deciphering, or that the application of the reading to the case would exceed the students' current abilities.

I still harbor the idea that TE-101 bothers many students because its procedure violates their conception of teaching and learning as the transmission and reproduction of fixed knowledge in texts. I will continue my efforts to conduct the class in ways that tend to expose and challenge that conception. In doing so, however, I intend to be more careful about the demands that the course places on students' knowledge, skills, and tolerance for uncertainty.

NOTE

1. I did not tell the students that I regarded the course arrangements as a pragmatic formulation: "For the pragmatists, the pattern of all inquiry — scientific as well as moral — is deliberation concerning the relative attractions of various concrete alternatives" (Rorty, 1982, p. 164). We would be heeding John Dewey's admonition that "the beginning and the end are things of gross everyday experience," and that "generalized findings [our readings] are employed to enrich the meanings of individualized experiences [the videotaped cases], and to afford, within limits of probability, an increased control of them" (Dewey, 1929, pp. 173-174). We would be acting on Joseph Schwab's suggestions that no abstractive argument by itself is sufficient to guide action, so our practical deliberations must also be eclectic (Schwab, 1978). We would be starting from the students' prior conceptions of schoolteaching, and we would be working toward their participation in eclectic deliberations on schoolteaching practice.

10

Managing Dilemmas in TE-101

Helen Featherstone
Sharon Feiman-Nemser

Although many people assume that university educators can contribute to the improvement of school teaching, few expect that schoolteachers can help improve the quality of university-based instruction. Despite the rhetoric of school–university collaboration, most initiatives channel resources from the university to the schools where presumably the real changes in teaching practice need to occur. Few initiatives support the joint exploration of pedagogical problems, insights, and questions.

And yet, teaching is precisely what university- and school-based educators have in common. Even with the obvious differences in content and context, we are all teachers, facing some of the same basic questions. What knowledge is worth having? How can I represent new concepts in ways that support genuine understanding? How will I know whether my students are really learning? How should I respond to differences among learners? How can I organize groups of students so that they will make knowledge together?

Recognizing teaching as a common meeting ground between university- and school-based educators suggests the possibility of joint work on problems of practice. Such an agenda could lead to fruitful and mutually beneficial conversations about pedagogy.

One image of teaching that has stimulated our own thinking is Lampert's (1985a) notion of teachers as "managers of dilemmas" rather than "solvers of problems." Reflecting on her experience teaching elementary mathematics, Lampert argues that, in trying

181

to solve common pedagogical problems, "practical dilemmas" arise because teachers hold competing purposes.

> As the teacher considers alternative solutions to any particular problem, she cannot hope to arrive at the 'right' alternative . . . because she brings many contradictory aims to each instance of her work, and the resolution of their dissonance cannot be neat or simple. (p. 181)

Lampert prefers to think about a pedagogical dilemma as "an argument between two opposing tendencies within oneself in which neither side can come out the winner" (p. 182). This perspective highlights the teacher's internal deliberation about alternatives rather than her choice between them. It follows that teachers must be able to act with integrity while maintaining conflicting concerns.

The idea of teaching as "dilemma management" captures some important realities about teaching TE-101. Each time we teach the course we confront a set of dilemmas stemming from opposing but equally compelling aims. In talks with colleagues, we have tried to externalize our internal dialogue so that others can join the deliberation.

In this chapter, we examine three related dilemmas. The first concerns the competing demands of depth and breadth, the imperative of the teachable moment compared with the imperative of the deliberate plan. The second arises from the desire to help students examine their own ideas and, at the same time, consider ideas beyond their ken. The third dilemma grows out of the tension between trying to foster wide participation and trying to encourage critical thinking.

DILEMMA 1: TO COVER OR TO UNCOVER

As TE-101 instructors, we always seem to be "behind." On the first day of class, we pass out a course outline listing the dates for class meetings along with the assigned readings and projects. Although we do not expect to follow the syllabus exactly, it does tell us where we are headed and approximately how much time we want to spend on each of the three focal questions: What does it mean to teach? What is it like to teach in school? What do teachers need to know?

Each year in preparing the syllabus, we consider possible new

readings and assignments. If we add a new reading, we force ourselves to eliminate something in order to make room. And we always
talk about how to pare things down so that we have more time to
examine issues carefully and to help students connect the ideas they
encounter with their own experiences. It seems as though the better
we understand the course—how the readings relate, what students
find confusing, how to extend particular assignments, what questions tend to yield fruitful discussions—the harder it is to get
through the syllabus.

In a way, we have already opted to uncover rather than cover
the material. The course treats a small number of core concepts.
Generally students prepare one to two readings and a journal entry
or study questions each week. During the term, they write two
papers, one on an issue or question that has come up in the course
and that puzzles them and another on their experience in the moon
project. (See Chapter 4 for a description of this assignment.) We
also try to build in some synthesis exercise for each part of the course
to help students pull together their thinking about the organizing
question in light of the readings, in-class activities, and discussions.
And yet, the syllabus often tells us to move on before we feel that
students have reached a satisfactory level of understanding.

This presents us with a dilemma. On the one hand, the course
asks students to think through a number of difficult and, for them,
new ideas. We know that the kind of learning we seek is not a
singular event but rather a gradual and continuing process. Maja
Apelman (1980) makes this point in a first-person account of her
own learning where she describes how she moved from an initial
romance with the language of cosmology (e.g., "red-shifted by a
factor of a thousand") to a place where she could connect new ideas
to prior understandings and begin to ask her own questions about
the phenomena she was trying to understand. We read this essay in
TE-101 to help students appreciate the fact that they, too, must
move through different levels of understanding.

> Understanding does not happen all at once. You need time for
> ideas to sink in and you need a chance to go back to your teacher
> to ask questions which only arise as you begin to think about a
> new idea. You cannot cover a topic in one or even a series of
> lessons any more than you can *do* Europe in a summer. (p. 25)

On the other hand, we have designed TE-101 around core
issues that we want students to think about early in their undergrad-

uate careers. These issues reflect our assumptions about students'
entering beliefs and our familiarity with their preservice program.
We know, for example, that most students will not focus on issues
of equity and ability grouping until they take School and Society —
often after student teaching. We also know that our students rarely
see their arts and science courses as part of their preparation for
teaching. If we rush through the second question about the purposes
of schooling or skip the third question about the intellectual requirements of teaching, then students won't expand their ideas about
these matters. And that would be a real pity, because their naive
beliefs about what schools are for and about what teachers need to
know may limit what they set out to learn from their liberal and
professional education courses.

How important is it to "cover" all three questions, at least in
the sense of opening them up for consideration? Would it be more
valuable to concentrate on developing a deeper understanding of
what it means to teach or what teachers need to know without
getting into the multiple and often conflicting purposes of schooling
and their impact in teachers' practices? A recent experience in
Sharon Feiman-Nemser's section dramatized this dilemma.

With 2 weeks left in the term, it was time to wind up our
discussion of tracking and move to the third and final part of the
course. Students had just finished reporting on their experiences
trying to teach someone about the phases of the moon. On the basis
of these reports, we had generated a set of questions to guide our
inquiry about teachers' knowledge: Can you teach something you
yourself don't fully understand? What role does prior knowledge
play in learning? Can teachers afford to ignore what students already know and believe about a subject? How does the teacher's
own understanding affect her ability to teach? What makes for a
good instructional representation? Rooted in students' own experiences, these questions had the qualities of vividness, importance,
and personal meaning that fuel significant learning. Thus the reports provided a natural transition to the last question.

Typically our students have not thought much about the different kinds of knowledge teachers need. Like most elementary education students, they often assume that they already know enough to
teach young children or that they will find what they need in the
teacher's guide. In exploring the intellectual requirements of teaching, we consider the difference between knowing mathematical rules
and knowing why the rules work, between remembering historical facts and appreciating what it means to "do" history. We empha-

size that teachers need a special kind of subject-matter knowledge in order to help students get inside different forms of public knowledge.

Thus it was disconcerting to see how students responded to the synthesis activity designed to pull together current thinking about tracking and ability grouping, a major focus in the second part of the course. For the past 2 weeks, the class had been exploring the rationale and consequences of tracking through a combination of personal recollection and discussion of various readings. Some of the readings provided evidence about the negative effects of tracking (e.g., Oakes, 1986a, 1986b), whereas others described alternative practices such as cooperative grouping (Cohen, 1986). We also held a mock faculty meeting in which students assumed the role of teachers and deliberated about whether their school should maintain or abandon the practice of grouping students for reading on the basis of standardized test scores.

As instructor, Feiman-Nemser had asked students to respond to a letter endorsing tracking written by a mother in a small rural community to the editor of the *Harvard Education Letter*. After enduring years of dismal teaching in heterogeneous classrooms where ditto sheets substituted for enrichment, the mother wrote, her daughter was eagerly looking forward to junior high where classes were tracked. But now, influenced by the very research we had discussed in TE-101, the school board had decided to abolish tracking and Christy was again stuck in a mixed-ability classroom. Needless to say, the mother was not pleased:

> The abolishment of tracking has a nice democratic sound to it . . . but do all kids have to be stuck in heterogeneous groups? I believe that we don't have to dilute the quality of education of the top kids in the country out of the hope that heterogeneous classes will somehow help the average and lower groups. (Smith, 1988, p. 3)

None of the TE-101 students had challenged the mother. All seemed to be caught up in the individualism so prevalent in American culture. No one had raised questions about the quality of education for all children in the school. Although most had felt sorry for Christy who had to look forward to more boring classes, no one expressed concern about the fate of the other children in the same classroom. Nor were students making any connections to our earlier discussions about how teachers can engage students in genuine learning. Feiman-Nemser saw the synthesis exercise as an opportunity to revisit ideas from the first and second parts of the course in considering alternatives to ability grouping. We had encountered teachers who accommodated student diversity without resorting to such a practice. Perhaps speculating about how Vivian Paley and Leslie Stein might have responded to the situation would help students imagine other options and also give them another chance to reflect on their own beliefs and assumptions.

Thus, there were good arguments for moving on to the third question and good arguments for lingering on the second.

The time dilemma operates on two levels. First, there is the matter of access to knowledge. If we don't get to the third question, we deny students the opportunity to consider issues that could affect their stance toward liberal arts and education courses. On a more microlevel, there are the moment-to-moment decisions about how to manage the flow of discussion and whether or not to probe particular questions as they arise. These reflections-in-action (Schon, 1983) also have important consequences for what we do with our time.

Of course, our rendering of the dilemma may not mesh with students' lived experiences. They may be tired of talking about tracking and ready to move on. From their vantage point, revisiting "old" readings might simply be tedious. It is often difficult to know exactly what students get out of the lessons we orchestrate. Take the case of Hannah. She said nothing memorable, either in class or in writing, for the first 6 weeks of the course. When the class began to analyze a pedagogical dilemma of a first-year teacher concerning the placement of a particular child, she asked how much she could write about it "because obviously there is so much to say that we clearly can't say it all." Hannah produced an outstanding analysis of the case. After that, everything she said in class was first rate. She commented incisively on readings and in-class activities; she also wrote an excellent final paper and exam. Different issues spark interest in different groups and individuals. If we concentrate on one question, we may never awaken Hannah and her silent sisters.

Perhaps we manage the time dilemma most successfully when we think more about creating experiences that encourage questioning and exploration and less about what we can help students reexamine and understand. Such a formulation would push us toward a deeper and perhaps more satisfying exploration of one set of issues. But what about . . . ? The claims of depth against those of breadth just won't go away.

DILEMMA 2: STAND AND DELIVER OR WAIT AND HOPE?

As TE-101 teachers, we want to model a particular sort of teaching — one in which teachers help students to examine their preconceptions and work out some reasonable and defensible ideas about teaching for themselves, by reading thoughtfully, by listening carefully to fellow students, and by trying out ideas on paper, in small groups, and in class discussions. We want to challenge the notion that the teacher has all the answers and that her answers are the only right ones in the context of the course.

At the same time, we wonder whether our students really can "break with experience" without our active intervention, whether they will ever see beyond the limited vision of schooling that they have acquired in rather ordinary schools if we fail to take a stand on behalf of what we believe about teaching and learning. We often feel caught between our resolution to model the sort of teaching that empowers students to make and explore their own meanings and our determination to make sure that students think seriously about ideas that are outside their current experience.

This dilemma emerges clearly in chapters by Wilson (Chapter 7) and McMahon (Chapter 8). McMahon was disturbed when Wilson, breaking with her usual nonjudgmental stance, told her class that there was no evidence that tracking ever served students' best interests. Wilson had chosen to "stand and deliver"; McMahon vowed to "wait and hope." The next term, however, when McMahon tried to teach about grouping as she had taught other parts of the course — accepting all comments with a neutral expression and asking for responses from other class members — she found that students' experiences with tracking had been so uniformly positive that they could see neither problems nor alternatives. "For balance, I began stating stronger and stronger positions against it," writes McMahon.

Deborah Ball (1990) alluded to a similar dilemma in her teaching of third-grade math: On the last day of school the students were discussing the relationship between $\frac{5}{5}$ and $\frac{3}{3}$. All agreed that $\frac{5}{5}$ must be bigger. Ball tried to get them to see that this made no sense. ("It was the last day of class. Inquiry teaching was out the window. I didn't want them to go on to fourth grade believing this.") She was not entirely displeased, however, that they refused to accept her viewpoint simply on her authority; they had learned, perhaps too well, that answers had to make sense to *them*.

Like Ball, we do not want our students to leave TE-101 with

certain ideas unexamined. We want, to use Wilson's image, to get them to weed the garden of their ideas about schools and teaching — to see what they assume, examine it thoughtfully, and reject ideas that do not stand up under rational scrutiny. But unless students understand the ideas and alternatives that we present them with, their current thinking will remain unchallenged, and, hence, not fully visible. An incident, recorded in Featherstone's teaching journal, illustrates this dilemma.

It was late October. Featherstone had launched the second part of the course two days earlier by reading "The Daily Grind" (Jackson, 1968) and by showing two short films, one of Marva Collins's West Side Prep and the other of Leslie Stein's second-grade classroom at Central Park East Elementary School in Spanish Harlem.

> Students had met in groups during the first part of the class to identify the "hidden curriculum" [Jackson, 1968] and the "its" [Hawkins, 1967/1974] in the several classrooms we had encountered thus far. The first group had tackled Marva Collins's classroom; Fran Bridges, an older student who always seemed to read carefully and participate thoughtfully in discussions, reported their findings. The group had found several "its" in Collins's classroom: The first was "the structured situation." I was astonished: I thought we had, as a group, developed a fairly clear understanding of what Hawkins meant by the "it" in the "I-Thou-It" triangle and that even if some people remained confused, Fran was not one of them. I wondered — a little desperately — what to do: I rarely interrupt group reports either to comment or to solicit reactions, but this formulation seemed so far off the mark that I wanted to deal with it immediately. Because any interruption would violate students' expectations, I could see no way to get Fran and her classmates to question the group's formulation while maintaining my customary neutrality.
>
> And yet, I hated to let her statement pass: Hawkins's arguments about teaching, about respect, and about the relationships between teacher and student hang on an understanding of what it might be like for students to actively investigate something which interests them. Since few of my students have spent school time doing this, they do not associate such investigations with elementary school. For them, an engaging "it" is "asking a child how many apples they would have if they had two apples and their mother gave them two more, instead of just asking them what two plus two is." To me, identifying "the

structured situation" as an "it" is a way of avoiding Hawkins's argument, of muddying the waters so that Hawkins no longer challenges familiar practice.

Like all teachers, I had only a few seconds to deliberate. Because Fran was a confident student who might benefit from a direct challenge, and because I suspected that her opinions carried unusual weight with other students, I decided to interrupt her report and ask why the group had concluded that "the structured situation" was an "it." She replied that it was "something outside the teacher and the student that is a focus of interest to both of them." I sought reactions from others in the class. When no one disagreed with Fran's analysis, I asked the class to look back at the essay to try to find places where Hawkins defines what he means by the "it." We looked through our copies of the article and came up with various definitions and phrases, including "something in the outside world which is of interest both to the teacher and to the student." Fran argued that because Marva's "structure" was so foreign to the students' experience, it was an object of study, interest, and learning both to Marva and to the students. I did not agree. However much students may enjoy the sense of mastery and power they achieve in Marva's classroom, I see nothing engaging to kids about the structure itself. Believing that her interpretation fed into the tendency to see Hawkins's "it" as anything that an adult wanted kids to study, I felt frustrated. But Fran had argued her case reasonably well. I capitulated.

Experience convinces us that even if Featherstone had insisted that Hawkins means soap bubbles rather than structure, she would have made few converts. We really do believe that we need to engage students in the inquiry, and have them see, from their shared investigations of text and from thinking about their own experiences, what each author means. If another student proposes an idea, students feel more able to debate it. Does that mean that unless a student proposes a "correct" reading, the teacher is stuck?*

---

*The parallel between this bind and the binds that arise in teaching math for understanding are striking (Heaton, 1991; Ball, 1990). Both Ball and Heaton report on class discussions in which elementary students convince one another of things that are not true, or confuse classmates who actually began by solving a problem correctly. Heaton's experience suggests to her that discussions tend to be most animated, and most useful to participants, around an engaging problem that is neither too hard nor too easy.

Another discussion earlier in the same term provides a sugges-
tive contrast. The class had been considering several excerpts from
Wally's Stories (Paley, 1981). Most approved of Paley's teaching
style—the ubiquitous questions, and the nonjudgmental interest this
teacher takes in her students' ideas. However, when Sarah proposed, with visible emotion, that Paley had shirked her duty in her
handling of one discussion, her classmates considered her suggestion
seriously and debated it with thoughtful attention. The discussion
that troubled Sarah focused on *Tico and the Golden Wings*, a children's
book about a wingless bird who, granted a wish by the wishing bird,
receives a full complement of golden feathers. The black-feathered
birds who had befriended him when he was wingless desert him
angrily when they see his splendid new plumage. Tico eventually
restores peace and love by trading his golden feathers for black
ones.

When Paley discovers that her kindergartners, like the black
birds, think that Tico should give up the golden feathers, she initi-
ates a class discussion: She says that she thinks Tico should be
allowed to keep his golden feathers and that she is surprised so many
people seem to disagree. The five-year-olds confidently explain why
Tico is wrong to make his friends jealous in this way.

In our TE-101 class, Sarah argued that "racism is a big problem
in our society, and Paley had a duty to tell them that Tico *should* be
allowed to keep his golden feathers, that everyone has the right to
be different, and that everyone should respect the differences of
others." Other students agreed or disagreed, explaining what they
thought insistence would have accomplished. When Featherstone
pressed students to analyze what Paley *had* said, and how her students responded to her stated opinion, they considered the text
thoughtfully. The ensuing discussion seemed to deepen and enrich
both students' understanding of Paley and their insight into their
own assumptions about teaching.

Both the discussion of the "its" in Marva Collins's classroom
and the discussion of Paley raise questions about the care with which
these sophomores read—no student in the second discussion pointed
out that Paley *had* told her students what she thought. The discussions, however, focused on very different kinds of problems. In the
first instance, the problem was a matter of definition: What does
David Hawkins mean by "it" in his essay "I, Thou, and It"? In
the second instance, the problem involved a teacher's moral and
professional obligation in a discussion about values. The first text is
written by a professional philosopher; it is difficult and abstract,

although highly rewarding. The second is written by a teacher; although some of the language is abstract, all ideas are illustrated with classroom vignettes. Students probably found the second problem both more interesting and more accessible. They connected to it more easily and more successfully.

But these observations do not solve the dilemma of the TE-101 instructor, for even if she manages to select "problems" on the right level of difficulty, the exploration of teaching will not stand still, circling obediently around these satisfactory problems. Instead, teachers will find that one question leads to another, and students will need sometimes to probe the complex and inaccessible in order to move forward.

Our students often identify a parallel between the way Vivian Paley teaches kindergarten and the way we teach TE-101. Like her, we ask a lot of questions. Like her, we encourage our students to work out their own answers to the problems that arise in discussion and to share ideas with others. For the most part, our students approve of Paley's approach because they feel that she is encouraging social development, which they regard as a legitimate function of kindergarten. Sometimes her restraint worries them; they would prefer that she "stand and deliver." Similarly, although they like the open-ended discussions they have in TE-101, they would often like us to tell them whether they are right or wrong.

And we, at least, have also found that when the teacher takes the discussion from the hands of the students — when she decides to stand and deliver — she ends up refocusing the class on herself, and losing some ground in the struggle to convince students that they themselves possess the resources to make sense of the questions before them.

DILEMMA 3: CRITICAL THINKING VERSUS PARTICIPATION

The TE-101 instructor, like any discussion leader, depends heavily on students. Unless they think hard about the readings and issues of the course and share their ideas with their classmates, nothing much happens. The instructor rarely lectures, so if the students fail to volunteer in discussions and in group time, an awkward silence will prevail. Even though students may learn as much from hearing two or three thoughtful students debate a complex issue, as instructors we usually *feel* more successful when arms wave and many students contribute their ideas to a discussion. Knowing that many students hesitate to speak in front of a group, and that only a minority believe confidently that they have valuable ideas to contribute to a discussion, we feel a strong impulse to encourage all the brave souls who volunteer comments with praise of one sort or another.

This impulse, however, conflicts with our usual ways of accomplishing one of the course's explicit goals: We want to help students to discover and examine their own ideas about teaching, learning, and schools. In order to do this, we push them to seek evidence for the opinions they voice (see Chapter 6 for a discussion of this point).

When a student volunteers that "Paley teaches by asking questions," her instructor asks whether Paley's kindergartners learn anything from her questions. When a TE-101 student responds to this query, her teacher may ask the class to examine the text for evidence that Paley's students actually learned something from the conversation. These questions, as Wilson points out in her chapter, violate the conventions of social conversation, where "Why?" often signals disagreement. Sophomores may find the questions of their TE-101 instructor rude, unsettling, embarrassing, or even frightening. In one way or another, many of these college students tell their TE-101 instructors that the questions and challenges sometimes inhibit their willingness to speak out in a class discussion. Most instructors can recall variants of the following scene: A student raises her hand and then lowers it part way; when her teacher asks whether she has something to say, she shakes her head, "No, because I know that if I said it you would ask, 'Why?', and I don't know why." One of us recalls a young woman who, having sat silently through the first 10 classes, finally observed during a discussion, "I think there's too much attention to diversity." When her instructor asked her to explain why she thought this, she clammed up. Later she sent her teacher a note complaining that "when I finally worked up the nerve to say something, you snubbed me."

If we discourage participation in full-class discussions when we push students to examine and justify the ideas they put forth, we deprive our students of important educational goods. To begin with, we limit their active participation in learning: For although students may engage mentally with the discussion without speaking, their involvement is surely less *active* when they remain silent through a protracted discussion. In addition, we reduce the resources available to their classmates: We know from individual conferences that students who remain silent often have stories or ideas that could help others to learn. Third, we decrease the likelihood that they will get help from articulate classmates in examining their ideas.

And yet, as this last point indicates, if we fail to push for evidence, we reduce the value of discussions for all concerned. For the TE-101 instructor attempts to model in discussions the kind of critical thinking that she hopes students will learn to carry on without her, in small groups, in individual papers and journals, and in the large group. Unless she teaches her students to examine the empirical basis for ideas about teaching, learning, and schooling, she will accomplish very little by exposing them to the ideas of their peers for three and a half hours a week.

Group Work

When a TE-101 class breaks into small groups, participation increases dramatically. Conversation becomes animated, with students who rarely speak in a full-class discussion offering opinions and asking questions. (In analyzing one group exercise, several shy students reported that, in a small group setting, they felt entirely comfortable asking a fellow student to repeat or explain a difficult point but would hesitate to put their puzzlement on display for the full class.) We value the active involvement we see in group work, but sometimes, as we listen in on the conversations, we feel that we have bought participation at the expense of critical thinking. Some TE-101 instructors worry that, in order to minimize stress, many groups keep discussion at the level of their least capable member. A second excerpt from Featherstone's TE-101 journal illustrates the problem many of us feel we are seeing. The incident described below followed a class exercise in which an instructor had asked her students to solve the problem "$1\frac{3}{4} \div \frac{1}{2} = \underline{\quad}$." All students had gotten the correct answer: $3\frac{1}{2}$. (See McMahon, Chapter 8, for further reflections on this exercise.)

> When I watched Section 2 work on $1\frac{3}{4}$ divided by $\frac{1}{2}$, I saw group work as many of us had suspected it went. The instructor asked each group to create a story that would help a class of fourth graders to understand what this problem meant. One student in the group of four sitting near me took the lead, saying, "O.K., what shall we use?" They quickly decided that pizza would engage the interest of fourth graders, and formulated the story like this: "There are $1\frac{3}{4}$ pizzas in the refrigerator and your mom has left you a note saying that you

can eat ½ of what you find there. How much pizza can you eat?"

They were not stopped by the fact that what you could eat was ⅞ pizza — even though they had all agreed that the "answer" to 1¾ divided by ½ was 3½. They simply noted that the pizza had to be divided into quarters, and that you got to eat 3½ pieces. Their *collective* attention was entirely directed at creating a "cute" and engaging problem with charming human dimensions. But when they finished — which they did fairly speedily, but not long before the 10 minutes allotted for the activity was up — the woman whose back was to me apparently looked dissatisfied. The leader kidded her because she seemed to be taking it all too seriously: "What's the matter? You're making it more complicated than it is. It's only a math problem." Earlier, the woman seemed troubled by the fact that the answer they were getting did not really fit the calculation they had begun with and she had made soft, tentative noises suggesting that something wasn't quite working. But the others sailed ahead, certain that she was "making it all more complicated than it [was]."

Apparently, the group had within it the resources to discover the mathematical challenge they were facing. One student — let us call her Melissa — suspected that the representation they had selected did not actually fit the mathematics problem. But neither Melissa nor her classmates were disposed to pursue Melissa's uncomfortable feeling. Their impulse to see their task as simple and straightforward, and their disinclination to analyze or argue, limited what they were able to learn from the exercise and from their somewhat more probing classmate.

Although not all groups operate in this way, many do. In the exercise described above, for example, three or four groups out of five usually arrive at some variant of the pizza story: They use food or candy that will be familiar and attractive to fourth graders and that can easily be divided into fourths and then halved. The fate of the fifth group varies. One of us recently taught a section in which the fifth group announced, with considerable confidence, that the problem could not be solved. They had, like the other groups, considered a pizza or candy representation, but one of their number — an older student who had leapt eagerly into every challenge the course presented and had led her moon group in developing a sophisticated discovery unit on the lunar cycle — had seen that this story illustrated 1¾ $\times$ ½, not 1¾ ÷ ½. After some effort she convinced other members of her group that this was so. When all their efforts to develop a better representation carried them up the same creek, they concluded that the task was insoluble. They were wrong, but we were heartened to see them thinking and arguing in this way.

Managing the Dilemma

TE-101 instructors find a variety of ways to manage this dilemma, often varying their approaches over the course of the quarter, and balancing other goals as well. Many find that role-playing activities allow students to try out new ways of talking along with new positions. Thus, for example, in the school board debate (see Chapter 7) teachers assign students both roles and positions—for example, parent of a gifted student who favors tracking—for which they must construct defensible arguments. This sets them in conflict with other class members whose arguments and evidence they must analyze and evaluate. Other instructors model in their responses to student journals the sort of critical thinking they want students to use (see Chapter 8).

We have said that when we send students off to work in groups, we often feel as though we are trading critical thinking for participation: Students who remain silent in full-class discussions offer opinions and ask questions in their small groups. After reflecting on this observation with other TE-101 instructors, we have begun to wonder whether we might not be inadvertently undermining the quality of group work by the way in which we structure group tasks. This has led us to question two aspects of our current practice.

First, on many occasions we break the class into four to six groups and give each group a somewhat different task. (For example, on the morning in which Fran Bridges's group decided that the "it" in Marva Collins's school was "the structured situation," other groups were analyzing "I", "thou", and "it" in the classrooms of other teachers we had met earlier in the quarter.) Perhaps giving different groups different jobs sets up a situation in which it seems rude, difficult, and dangerous to challenge another group's analysis. It is rude because the students who are reporting have just worked on this problem and are, by virtue of this visible investment of time, the legitimate experts on the subject. If you challenge them you seem to say, "without either thinking about this for 15 minutes or consulting with my peers, I have a better answer to this question than you do." It is difficult because, in fact, you *haven't* had a chance to think this problem through, so the chances of your being able to answer it well are small. It is dangerous because, when your own group reports, others may later challenge you.

If we want groups to challenge one another instead of reporting out expert testimony, we might do better to give all groups the same question to ponder. If all groups work on the same question, challenging becomes far easier and less rude. And if challenges from other groups are likely, it becomes less rude and counterproductive to challenge *within* the group: When one student asks another to justify a position, she helps the group arrive at an answer that will not crumble when exposed to outside scrutiny. Students can begin to say, "*They're* sure to ask us . . . , so we'd better think it through" (as McMahon reports they did in her section). Thus, by increasing the chances of external challenges to a group's conclusions, we may change norms and task perception within the group and increase the likelihood of critical thinking there.

This brings us to our second question: When we ask for a group report, are we, perhaps unintentionally, suppressing dissent and therefore critical thinking? The notion of a group report suggests group consensus; if students believe that we are asking them for consensus, it would not be surprising if they avoided controversy. Yet disagreements are almost inevitable when people think hard about difficult questions. Perhaps we need to value disagreements explicitly, and to ask groups to report their disagreements as one valued product of group work.

We hope that in doing this we would encourage within groups the sorts of conversation that promote critical thinking. We might also generate more provocative group reports. For disagreement provides more snags and corners for others in the class to seize and react to than does the smooth surface of a consensus report. Intellectual disagreements, like playground fights, evoke reactions and draw in observers. They provoke tangential observations and sometimes, at least, they beckon the diffident and unconfident, signaling to them that "right" answers are not obvious here, and that if they stick their necks out they are unlikely to look stupid.

CONCLUSION

The more closely we look at teaching mathematics for understanding and teaching TE-101, the more parallels we find. The writings of Ball (1990), Lampert (1985a), and Heaton (1991) help us think about managing dilemmas that stem from who we are as teachers and what kind of classroom we want. Despite differences in subject matter and students, we all want to create learning communities in which students believe that they have the resources within themselves to ask their own questions and figure out what answers make sense.

And so our suggestion that college teachers can learn from elementary and secondary teachers has a concrete referent: We continue to learn both from the practice and from the reflective writing of our colleagues who teach elementary school math. The lessons go beyond insights about asking questions and nurturing learning communities — we have also learned from the ways in which they have studied their practice and shared the results of that study with a wider public (Ball, 1990).

This book is about the improvement of college teaching. It records the efforts of its authors and their colleagues to grapple with vexing problems of undergraduate teaching and improve on their own practice. It is also part of an effort to legitimize and nourish the inclinations of college teachers to work collectively to improve their teaching. For although professors in colleges of education write and talk at length about the need for *school*teachers to talk about pedagogy, and to strive together to understand and improve their teaching, few universities provide any formal mechanisms for collective efforts to study and improve college teaching. Yet there is good reason to believe that college teaching needs help equally urgently.

The authors of these essays write in order to make their teaching, and their thoughts about this teaching, visible. In inviting the scrutiny of members of our professional community, we hope to provide grist from more conversation about the education of undergraduates in general, and about the preparation of preservice teachers in particular. For we see such conversations as essential to the improvement of college teaching.

Educational reformers are now asking how to change the place of teaching in the professional lives of the professoriat — how to make college teaching valued and visible. We offer the example of TE-101, which, like David Riesman's famous Soc Sci 136 at Harvard, we have succeeded in making the focus of ongoing conversation. Although we teach differently and structure our sections differently, our shared goals and our shared interest in improving our practice and in helping novices enable us to spend an hour and a half a week in productive talk. These conversations feed our knowledge of our subject matter, our students, and our pedagogy.

With this book, we invite others to join our conversation, to tell us about their courses and the teaching communities that they are fostering. We hope to learn about the dilemmas other college teachers face day to day, the strategies they have crafted for managing these dilemmas, and their efforts to see their practice more clearly. This sort of public dialogue, linked to ongoing study of the teaching itself and to conversations about public school teaching, can improve the quality of the work all of us do in classrooms.

Appendix

Here is a sample syllabus from Sharon Feiman-Nemser's section of the course. Other instructors have developed their own versions of the course within a similar framework.

TE-101: EXPLORING TEACHING

Purposes of the Course

This course is designed to help you begin thinking about teaching in new ways. As a pupil in elementary and secondary school, you have probably formed ideas about what teaching is like, what schools are for, and what teachers need to know. Now that you are thinking about becoming a teacher, you should examine your ideas about teaching and schooling and consider what you need to learn to become a good teacher.

TE-101 is an opportunity to participate in a professional conversation about teaching, to clarify your thinking about what teachers do, to test your thinking against others' views, and to assess your seriousness about preparing to teach. The course will not teach you how to teach; building a repertoire of ideas and practices takes years. Rather it will provide opportunities for you to participate in an informed and focused conversation about teaching that could contribute to your repertoire in time.

Overview of the Course

The course is organized around three questions:

1. What does it mean to teach?
2. What does it mean to teach school?
3. What do teachers need to know?

The first question focuses on the *activity* of teaching. What do good teachers do? How can you tell when teaching and learning are going on? Can there be teaching without learning? Where does subject matter fit in the teacher–student relationship?

The second question focuses on the *setting* of teaching. What are schools for? What do students really learn there? Do teachers, students, and parents want the same things from their schools? How do the multiple and often conflicting purposes of schooling affect what teachers do and what they ought to do?

Finally we will examine what teachers need to know and how they acquire and develop the necessary knowledge and skills? What do teachers need to know about their subjects? Their students? Their school, community, and country? What can teachers learn from firsthand experience in classrooms? From teachers and other educational professionals? From books and articles? What should you be learning to prepare for teaching?

Course Requirements and Grading

Attendance and Participation. The learning that we aim for in this course (clarifying, testing, justifying ideas) depends largely on your attendance and active participation. It is particularly important that you complete readings, journal entries, and other assignments *on time*, because class and group discussions will generally be based on them. Hence, attendance, timely completion of assignments, and participation in class will count in your grade.

Journal. Throughout the term you will keep a journal where you will respond reflectively to readings, class discussions, or questions raised by classmates or by me. Sometimes I will suggest a focus for your journal. Other times, you can write about whatever intrigues or puzzles you from the readings or class discussions. I will collect the journals to read and respond to your entries.

Study Questions. To help you focus on important ideas in the readings and make connections among ideas and examples of teaching, I will distribute study questions. Some study questions will be the topic for class discussion. You might use the questions to focus your journal entry.

Moon Project.   During the course you will participate in a project designed to help you study your own learning and teaching. First you will keep a moon journal where you record observations of the moon. Then in groups you will pool your knowledge and work together to answer your own questions. Finally you will plan a lesson about the moon and teach it to someone out of class. Your second paper will be based on the moon project.

Folder.   Each student will have a folder (with two side pockets) for keeping journal entries and in-class "fastwrites." Please put entries that you want me to read on the left side and old work on the right side.

Papers.   The ability to communicate ideas clearly in writing is an important prerequisite for teaching; getting feedback from others and revising your first thoughts are critical steps toward good writing. You will write two papers during the quarter. The first paper will take the form of a conversation. You will exchange a draft of this paper with a member of your group who will provide you with written comments. You will then revise your paper in light of those comments. The second paper will be based on the moon project. I will give you detailed information about the papers and how they will be graded.

Final Exam.   There will be a take-home exam. Questions will be distributed at the last class. Exams are due during finals week.

Grading.   Your final grade will be determined as follows:

First paper	20 points
Second paper	25 points
Participation, journal, projects, group work	30 points
Final exam	25 points

Required Readings

Required.   A packet of readings is available at Copygraph (at the corner of M.A.C. and Grand River, East Lansing - 337-1666).

Kohl, H. (1984). *Growing minds: On becoming a teacher.* New York: Harper & Row.

COURSE OUTLINE

Part I: What Does It Mean to Teach?

SESSION 1: INTRODUCTION TO THE COURSE
1/7 Introductions; preview course content and policies; assign
groups and distribute study questions for Part I readings.
View, write about, and discuss portraits of teaching.

SESSIONS 2 & 3: IS THIS (GOOD) TEACHING?

Readings
> Plato. (1982). The geometrical experiment with Meno's slave.
> In *Protagoras and Meno*. New York: Penguin Books.
> Paley, V. (1984). Excerpt from *Wally's Stories*. Cambridge, MA:
> Harvard University Press.
> Kohl, H. (1984). *Growing Minds: On Becoming a Teacher*. New
> York: Harper & Row. Begin reading now; complete by
> 2/25.

Written Assignment
> Journal due 1/14.

Class
1/9 Analyze excerpts from Paley as instances of teaching; Introduce
moon project.
1/14 Discuss "The Geometrical Experiment" and Socrates' role as
teacher. Compare Paley and Socrates.

SESSIONS 4 & 5: TEACHER, STUDENT, AND
SUBJECT MATTER: I-THOU-IT

Reading
> Hawkins, D. (1967/1974). I, thou, and it. In *The informed vision:
> Essays on learning and human nature*. New York: Agathon
> Press.

Written Assignments
> Journal entry due 1/21.

Class
1/16 Discuss "I-Thou-It" in relation to Paley. Consider Hawkins's
ideas about the teacher's role. Discuss *paper #1*.

1/21 View videotape of Deborah Ball's mathematics teaching and discuss in terms of Hawkins's ideas.

SESSION 6: THE RELATIONSHIP OF TEACHING AND LEARNING

Readings
Jackson, P. (1986). The uncertainties of teaching. In *The practice of teaching* (ch. 3). New York: Teachers College Press.

Apelman, M. (1980, Spring) Red-shifted by a factor of a thousand. *Outlook, 38,* 22–27.

Lortie, D. (1975). "Intangibility and Assessment." In *Schoolteacher* (pp. 142–148). Chicago: University of Chicago Press.

Written Assignment
Exchange draft of paper with buddy, write comments, and meet to discuss comments during week.

Class
1/23 Discuss relationship between teaching and learning; consider Jackson's and Lortie's arguments about the "uncertainties of teaching" and the distinction between "knowledge reproduction" and "knowledge transformation." Compare with Apelman's ideas about learning, "teaching by instruction," and "teaching by facilitation."

SESSION 7: SYNTHESIS OF PART I: WHAT DOES IT MEAN TO TEACH?

Written Assignment
Bring moon journals to share in class.

Class
1/28 Analysis and synthesis of topics treated in Part I; discussion of students' conceptions of what teaching and learning mean; review vignettes of teaching.

Share initial data from moon journals.

Part II: What Does It Mean to Teach in School?

SESSIONS 8 & 9: THE HIDDEN CURRICULUM

Reading
Jackson, P. W. (1968). The daily grind. In *Life in classrooms* (ch. 1, pp. 3–37). New York: Holt.

Written assignments
Paper #1 due to Erickson 116-P on 1/30.

Class
1/30 View and discuss videos of Marva Collins and Leslie Stein in terms of the I-Thou-It triangle.

2/4 Discuss the sources and characteristics of the hidden curriculum. What is it? Where does it come from? How does it shape students' experiences of school? How does it connect to the explicit curriculum and the outcomes of schooling?

SESSIONS 10 & 11: WHAT (AND WHO) ARE SCHOOLS FOR?

Readings
Powell, A. G., Farrar, E., & Cohen, D. K. (1985). The shopping mall high school. In *The Shopping Mall High School* (pp. 8–38). Boston: Houghton Mifflin.

Anyon, J. (1981). Social class and school knowledge. *Curriculum Inquiry, 11*, 3–41.

Written Assignments
Journal entry due 2/11.

Class
2/6 Discuss purposes of schooling implicit in readings and films. Meet in groups to clarify confusions about moon and plan lesson.

2/11 Relate purposes of schooling to issue of who controls schools, different publics; discuss historical development of tracking and the effects of the "shopping mall" curriculum; discuss individual experiences with tracking.

SESSIONS 12 & 13: MANAGING STUDENT DIVERSITY

Readings
Oakes, J. (1986). Keeping track (Parts I and II).

Cohen, E. G. (1987). *Designing groupwork: Strategies for the heterogeneous classroom* (chs. 1, 2, 3, 11). New York: Teachers College Press.

Adler, M. (1983). *The Paideia proposal* (chs. 3, 4). New York: Macmillan.

Featherstone, H. (1987). Organizing classes by ability. *The Harvard Education Letter, 3*(4), 1-4.

Written Assignments
Journal entry due 2/18.

Class
2/13 Discuss rationale for tracking; effects of tracking; pros and cons of tracking—why are some teachers and parents in favor. Jigsaw exercise.
2/18 In-class writing based on readings. Synthesis of Part II.

Part III: What Do Teachers Need to Know?

SESSIONS 14 & 15: WHAT DO TEACHERS NEED TO KNOW?

Readings
Kohl, H. (1984). *Growing minds: On becoming a teacher,* Part III. New York: Harper & Row.

Written Assignment
Moon journal due 2/20.

Class
2/20 Group presentations on moon lessons. Distribute and talk about paper #2.
2/25 Analyze lessons in Kohl, Part III. Discuss teacher knowledge and speculate on where teachers learn what they know.

SESSION 16: THE ROLE OF SUBJECT MATTER KNOWLEDGE IN TEACHING

Reading
Wilson, S. M., Shulman, L. S., & Richert, A. E. (1987). '150 different ways' of knowing: Representations of knowledge in teaching. In J. Calderhead (Ed.), *Exploring teachers' thinking.* London: Cassell.

Class
2/27 What is involved in transforming subject-matter knowledge for purposes of teaching; what does it mean to "know" ones subjects? Group exercise.

SESSIONS 17 & 18: LEARNING TO TEACH

Readings

Kohl, H. (1984). *Growing minds: On becoming a teacher,* Part I. New York: Harper & Row.

Wigginton, E. (1986). Excerpts from *Sometimes a Shining Moment.*

Written Assignment

Paper #2 due 3/4.

Class

3/4 Discuss process of learning to teach; What kinds of knowledge do teachers acquire through experience? How did Wigginton and Kohl's ideas about teaching change and what contributed to those changes?

3/6 Reconsider teaching and learning; revisit videos. Discuss final exam. Course evaluation.

Final exam: Take-home exam due on Wed., March 6.

References

Anyon, J. (1981). Social class and school knowledge. *Curriculum Inquiry,* *11,* 3–41.

Apelman, M. (1980, Spring). Red-shifted by a factor of a thousand. *Outlook, 38,* 22–27.

Ball, D. L. (1988a). *Knowledge and reasoning in mathematical pedagogy: Examining what prospective teachers bring to teacher education.* Unpublished doctoral dissertation, Michigan State University, East Lansing.

Ball, D. L. (1988b, April). *Prospective teachers' understandings of mathematics: What do they bring with them to teacher education?* Paper presented at the annual meeting of the American Educational Research Association, New Orleans, LA.

Ball, D. L. (1989, March). *Breaking with experience in learning to teach mathematics: The role of a preservice methods course.* Paper presented at the annual meeting of the American Educational Research Association, San Francisco, CA.

Ball, D. L. (1990). *With an eye on the mathematical horizon: Dilemmas of teaching elementary school mathematics* (Craft paper 90–3). East Lansing: Michigan State University, National Center for Research on Teacher Education.

Ball, D. L., & Feiman-Nemser, S. (1988). Using textbooks and teachers' guides: A dilemma for beginning teachers and teacher educators. *Curriculum Inquiry, 18*(4), 401–423.

Ball, D. L., & McDiarmid, G. W. (1990). The subject matter preparation of teachers. In W. R. Houston (Ed.), *Handbook of research on teacher education* (pp. 437–449). New York: Macmillan.

Barnes, H. (1987). The conceptual basis for thematic teacher preparation programs. *Journal of Teacher Education, 38*(4), 13–18.

Bennett, W. (1984). *To reclaim a legacy: A report on the humanities in higher education.* Washington, DC: National Endowment for the Humanities.

Blake, R., & Verhille, C. (1985). The story of O. *For the Learning of Mathematics, 5*(3), 35–46.

Book, C., Byers, J., & Freeman, D. (1983). Student expectations and teacher education traditions with which we can and cannot live. *Journal of Teacher Education, 34*(1), 9–13.

Boyer, E. (1987). *College: The undergraduate experience in America.* New York: Harper & Row.

Brousseau, B. A., & Freeman, D. J. (1989). How do teacher education faculty members define desirable teacher beliefs? *Teaching and Teacher Education, 4,* 267–273.

Brousseau, B., Freeman, D., & Book, C. (1984). *Comparing educational beliefs of teacher candidates and their non-teaching counterparts* (Program Evaluation Series No. 3). East Lansing: Michigan State University, College of Education, Office of Program Evaluation.

Brown, A. L., & Palincsar, A. S. (1990). Guided, cooperative learning and individual knowledge acquisition. In L. Resnick (Ed.), *Knowing, learning and instruction* (pp. 393–451). Hillsdale, NJ: Erlbaum.

Buchmann, M. (1985). *Improving education by talking* (Occasional Papers 68). East Lansing: Michigan State University, The Institute for Research on Teaching.

Buchmann, M. (1987). Teacher knowledge: The lights that teachers live by. *Oxford Review of Education, 13,* 151–164.

Burnett, F. H. (1962). *The secret garden.* New York: Lippincott.

Calderhead, J. (1988). Learning from introductory school experience. *Journal of Education for Teaching, 14*(1), 75–83.

Carnegie Task Force on Teacher as a Profession. (1986). *A nation prepared: Teachers for the 21st Century.* Washington, DC: Carnegie Forum on Education and the Economy.

CBS News. (Producer). (1983). A "60 Minutes" segment on Marva Collins [videotape]. New York: CBS News.

Cohen, D. K. (1984). The American common school: A divided vision. *Education and Urban Society, 16,* 253–261.

Cohen, D. K. (1988). *Teaching practice: Plus ça change . . .* (Issue Paper 88-3). East Lansing: Michigan State University, National Center for Research on Teacher Education.

Cohen, E. G. (1986). *Designing groupwork: Strategies for the heterogeneous classroom.* New York: Teachers College Press.

Crow, N. A. (1987). Preservice teachers' biography: A case study. Paper presented at the annual meeting of the American Educational Research Association, Washington, DC.

Cuban, L. (1984). *How teachers taught: Constancy and change in American classrooms, 1890–1980.* New York: Longman.

Davis, P., & Hersh, R. (1981). *The mathematical experience.* New York: Houghton Mifflin.

DeShino, M. (1987). The many phases of growth. *Teaching and Learning: The Journal of Natural Inquiry, 1*(3), 12–28.

Dewey, J. (1904). The relation of theory to practice in education. In C. McMurry (Ed.), *The relation of theory to practice in the education of teachers* (3rd Yearbook of the National Society for the Scientific Study of Education, Part 2, pp. 140–171). Chicago: University of Chicago Press.

Dewey, J. (1929). *The quest for certainty: A study of the relation of knowledge and action.* New York: Minton, Balch.

Dewey, J. (1983). *Experience and education.* New York: Collier Books.

diSessa, A. (1982). Unlearning Aristotelian physics: A study of knowledge-based learning. *Cognitive Science, 6,* 37–75.

Duckworth, E. (1986). Teaching as research. *Harvard Educational Review, 56*(4), 481–495.

Duffy, G. G., & Roehler, L. R. (1987). Improving instruction through the use of responsive elaboration. *The Reading Teacher, 40*(6), 515–520.

Duffy, G. G., Roehler, L. R., & Herrman, B. A. (1988). Modeling mental processes helps poor readers become strategic readers. *The Reading Teacher, 41*(8), 763–767.

Feiman-Nemser, S. (1983). Learning to teach. In L. Shulman & G. Sykes (Eds.), *Handbook of teaching and policy* (pp. 150–170). New York: Longman.

Feiman-Nemser, S., & Buchmann, M. (1986a). The first year of teacher preparation: Transition to pedagogical thinking. *Journal of Curriculum Studies, 18,* 239–256.

Feiman-Nemser, S., & Buchmann, M. (1986b). Pitfalls of experience in teacher preparation. In J. D. Raths & L. G. Katz (Eds.), *Advances in Teacher Education* (Vol. II, pp. 61–73). Norwood, NJ: Ablex.

Feiman-Nemser, S., McDiarmid, G. W., Melnick, S., & Parker, M. (1989). Changing beginning teachers' conceptions: A description of an introductory course. (Research Report, 89-1), Michigan State University, East Lansing, MI: National Center for Research on Teacher Education.

Floden, R., & Clark, C. M. (1988). Preparing teachers to teach for uncertainty. *Teachers College Record, 89,* 505–524.

Florio-Ruane, S. (1989). Creating your own case studies: A guide for early field experience. *Teacher Education Quarterly, 17* (1), 29–41.

Florio-Ruane, S., & Lensmire, T. (1990). Transforming prospective teachers' ideas about writing instruction. *Journal of Curriculum Studies, 22,* 277–289.

Fotiu, R., Freeman, D., & West, B. (1985). *Undergraduate follow-up study Spring, 1985* (Program Evaluation Series No. 11). East Lansing: Michigan State University, College of Education, Office of Program Evaluation.

Freeman, D. J., & Kalaian, H. A. (1989). *Profiles of students completing teacher education programs at M.S.U.: Fall, 1986 through Spring, 1988* (Program Evaluation Series No. 25). East Lansing: Michigan State University, College of Education, Office of Program Evaluation.

Gomez, M. L. (1988, April). *Prospective teachers' beliefs about good writing: What do they bring with them to teacher education?* Paper presented at the annual meeting of the American Educational Research Association, New Orleans, LA.

Good, T. (1987). Two decades of research on teacher expectations: Find-ings and future directions. *Journal of Teacher Education, 38*(4), 32–47.

Goodlad, J. (1984). *A place called school.* New York: McGraw Hill.

Gray, D. (1989, Fall). Putting minds to work: How to use the seminar approach in the classroom. *American Educator,* pp. 16–23.

Grumet, M. R. (1988). *Bitter milk: Women and teaching.* Amherst: University of Massachusetts Press.

Hawkins, D. (1974). I, thou, and it. In *The informed vision: Essays on learning and human nature* (pp. 48–62). New York: Agathon. (Original work published 1967)

Heaton, R. (1991, February). *Continuity and connectedness in teaching and research: A self study of learning to teach mathematics for understanding.* Paper presented at the University of Pennsylvania Ethnography in Educa-tion Research Forum, Philadelphia, PA.

Hiebert, J. (1986). *Conceptual and procedural knowledge: The case of mathematics.* Hillsdale, NJ: Erlbaum.

Holmes Group. (1986). *Tomorrow's teachers: A report of the Holmes Group.* East Lansing: Michigan State University, College of Education.

Holmes, N. (Producer and Director). (n.d.). *We all know why we're here.* [Film of Leslie Stein teaching second grade in Central Park East Elementary School]. New York: Charlie/Pappa Productions.

Jackson, P. (1986). The uncertainties of teaching. In *The practice of teaching* (ch. 3, pp. 53–74). New York: Teachers College Press.

Jackson, P. (1986). Real teaching. In *The practice of teaching* (Ch. 4, pp. 75–97). New York: Teachers College Press.

Jackson, P. W. (1968). The daily grind. In *Life in classrooms* (pp. 3–37). New York: Holt.

Kalaian, H. A., & Freeman, D. J. (1988). *Dimensionality of specific measures of teacher candidates' self-confidence and educational beliefs* (Program Evalua-tion Series No. 23). East Lansing: Michigan State University, De-partment of Teacher Education and Office of Program Evaluation.

Katz, L., Raths, J., Mohanty, C., Kurachi, A., & Irving, J. (1981). Follow-up studies: Are they worth doing? *Journal of Teacher Education, 32*(2), 18–24.

Kennedy, M. (1991). *Teaching academic subjects to diverse learners.* New York: Teachers College Press.

Kimball, B. (1986). *Orators and philosophers: A history of the idea of liberal education.* New York: Teachers College Press.

Kimball, B. (1988). The historical and cultural dimensions of the recent reports on undergraduate education. *American Journal of Education, 96,* 293–322.

Kline, M. (1977). *Why the professor can't teach: Mathematics and the dilemma of university education.* New York: St. Martin's Press.

Kohl, H. (1984). *Growing minds: On becoming a teacher.* New York: Harper & Row.

Kowalski, T. J., Weaver, R. A., & Henson, K. T. (1990). *Case studies on teaching*. New York: Longman.

Lampert, M. (1985a). How do teachers manage to teach: Perspectives on problems in practice. *Harvard Educational Review, 55*, 178–194.

Lampert, M. (1985b). Mathematics learning in context: The voyage of the *Mimi*. *The Journal of Mathematical Behavior, 4*, 157–167.

Lanier, J. E., & Little, J. W. (1986). Research on teacher education. In M. C. Wittrock (Ed.), *Handbook of research on teaching* (3rd ed., pp. 527–569). New York: Macmillan.

Lortie, D. (1975). *Schoolteacher: A sociological study*. Chicago: University of Chicago Press.

McDiarmid, G. W. (1989, February). *What do teachers need to know about cultural diversity: Restoring subject matter knowledge to the picture*. Paper presented at the meeting of the Policy Conference of the National Center for Research on Teacher Education, Washington, DC.

McDiarmid, G. W. (1990). Liberal arts: Will more result in better subject matter understanding? *Theory into Practice, 29*(1), 21–29.

McDiarmid, G. W. (1991). In M. Kennedy (Ed.), *Teaching academic subjects to diverse learners* (pp. 257–270). New York: Teachers College Press.

McDiarmid, G. W., & Ball, D. L. (1987). *Keeping track of teacher learning*. Unpublished manuscript, Michigan State University, National Center for Research on Teacher Education, East Lansing.

McDiarmid, G., Ball, D., & Anderson, C. (1989). Why staying one chapter ahead really doesn't work: Subject-specific pedagogy. In M. Reynolds (Ed.), *Knowledge base for beginning teachers* (pp. 193–205). Oxford, England: Pergamon.

Merseth, K. (1991). The role of the case method in the education of teachers. In J. Shulman (Ed.), *Case methods in teacher education*. New York: Teachers College Press.

Neufeld, B. (1988, April). *Why do I have to learn that? Prospective teachers' ideas about the importance of the subjects they will teach*. Paper presented at the annual meeting of the American Educational Research Association, New Orleans, LA.

Oakes, J. (1985). *Keeping track: How school structures inequality*. New Haven, CT: Yale University Press.

Oakes, J. (1986a). Keeping track, Part I: The policy and practice of curriculum inequality. *Phi Delta Kappan*, p. 17.

Oakes, J. (1986b). Keeping track, Part II: Curriculum inequality and school reform. *Phi Delta Kappan*, pp. 148–153.

Paine, L. (1990). *Orientations toward diversity: What do prospective teachers bring?* (Research Report 89-9). East Lansing: Michigan State University, National Center for Research on Teacher Education.

Paley, V. (1979). *White teacher*. Cambridge, MA: Harvard University Press.

Paley, V. (1981). *Wally's stories*. Cambridge: Harvard University Press.

Paley, V. (1986). On listening to what the children say. *Harvard Educational Review, 56*(2), 122-131.

Peterson, P. L., Fennema, E., Carpenter, T., & Loef, M. (1989). Teachers' pedagogical content beliefs in mathematics. *Cognition and Instruction, 6*(1), 1-40.

Posner, G., Strike, K., Hewson, P., & Gertzog, W. (1982). Accommodation of a scientific conception: Toward a theory of conceptual change. *Science Education, 66*, 211-227.

Resnick, L. B. (1983). Toward a cognitive theory of instruction. In S. Paris, G. Olson, & H. Stevenson (Eds.), *Learning and motivation in the classroom* (pp. 5-38). Hillsdale, NJ: Erlbaum.

Reynolds, M. (Ed.). (1989). *Knowledge base for the beginning teacher.* Oxford, England: Pergamon Press.

Richardson, V. (1987). *Educator's handbook.* New York: Longman.

Rorty, R. (1982). *Consequences of pragmatism.* Minneapolis: University of Minnesota Press.

Rosenshine, B., & Stevens, R. (1986). Teaching functions. In M. C. Wittrock (Ed.), *Handbook of research on teaching* (3rd ed., pp. 376-391). New York: MacMillan.

Ryle, G. (1949). *The concept of mind.* New York: Barnes and Noble.

Schoenfeld, A. (1983). Beyond the purely cognitive: Belief systems, social cognitions, and metacognitions as driving forces in intellectual performance. *Cognitive Science, 7*, 329-363.

Schon, D. (1983). *The reflective practitioner.* New York: Basic Books.

Schram, P., Wilcox, S., Lanier, P., Lappan, G., & Even, R. (1988, April). *Changing mathematical conceptions of pre-service teachers: A content and pedagogical intervention.* Paper presented at the annual meeting of the American Educational Research Association, New Orleans, LA.

Schwab, J. (1954). Eros and education: A discussion of one aspect of discussion. *Journal of General Education, 8*, 54-71.

Schwab, J. J. (1976). Education and the state: Learning community. In *Great ideas today* (pp. 234-271). Chicago: Encyclopedia Britannica.

Schwab, J. J. (1978). The practical: A language for curriculum. In I. Westbury & N. J. Wilkif (Eds.), *Science, curriculum, and liberal education: Selected essays* (pp. 287-321). Chicago: University of Chicago Press.

Shulman, L. S. (1986). Those who understand: Knowledge growth in teaching. *Educational Researcher, 15*(2), 4-14.

Shulman, L. S. (1987). Knowledge and teaching: Foundations of the new reform. *Harvard Educational Review, 57*, 1-22.

Smith, F. (1964). Prospective teachers' attitudes toward arithmetic. *Arithmetic Teacher, 11*, 474-477.

Smith, L. (1988). From our readers. *Harvard Education Letter, (4)*, 2, 8.

Suina, J. (1985, Winter). . . . And then I went to school. *New Mexico Journal of Reading, 5*(2).

Tabachnick, B., & Zeichner, K. (1984). The impact of the student teaching experience on the development of teacher perspectives. *Journal of Teacher Education, 35*(6), 28–42.

Tolkien, J. R. R. (1965). *The Lord of the rings: Vol. 2. The two towers.* New York: Ballantine.

Waxman, H. C., & Walberg, H. J. (1986). Effects of early field experiences. In J. Raths & L. Katz (Eds.), *Advances in teacher education* (Vol. 2, pp. 165–184). Norwood, NJ: Ablex.

Webb, C. (1981). Theoretical and empirical bases for early field experiences in teacher education. In C. Webb, N. Gehrke, P. Ishler, & A. Mendoza (Eds.), *Exploratory field experiences in teacher education* (pp. 12–37). Washington, DC: Association of Teacher Educators. (ERIC Document Reproduction Service No. ED 205 482)

Weinstein, C. (1989). Teacher education students' preconceptions of teaching. *Journal of Teacher Education, 40*(2), 53–60.

Wilson, S. M., Shulman, L. S., & Richert, A. E. (1987). '150 different ways' of knowing: Representations of knowledge in teaching. In J. Calderhead (Ed.), *Exploring teachers' thinking* (pp. 104–124). London: Cassell.

Wittrock, M. C. (1986). Students' thought processes. In M. C. Wittrock (Ed.), *Handbook of research on teaching* (3rd ed., pp. 297–314). New York: Macmillan.

About the Editors
and Contributors

Deborah Loewenberg Ball is associate professor of teacher education at Michigan State University. She received her PhD in 1988 from Michigan State University. She teaches third-grade mathematics at Spartan Village Elementary School in East Lansing, Michigan, as well as courses for undergraduate and graduate students at Michigan State. She was a primary author of the new National Council of Teachers of Mathematics *Professional Standards for Teaching Mathematics*. A senior researcher with the National Center for Research on Teacher Learning, Ball is especially interested in the multiple factors that affect the practice of teaching in elementary schools and how teachers learn to teach mathematics to diverse learners. Together with Magdalene Lampert, she coordinates Mathematics and Teaching Through Hypermedia (M.A.T.H.), an NSF-funded research and development project that aims to explore the use of new technologies to create tools for use in elementary teacher preparation as well as research on teaching.

Tom Bird is an assistant professor in the department of teacher education at Michigan State University, where he teaches undergraduate courses, supervises student teachers, and works with experienced teachers in a professional development school. He received his PhD in 1990 from Stanford. He is interested in the day-to-day practice of teacher education in those contexts and participates in research being conducted by the National Center for Research on Teacher Learning at MSU. He contributed a chapter on "the schoolteacher's portfolio" to *The New Handbook of Teacher Evaluation*. Formerly, he studied professional relations in schools while working at

215

the Far West Laboratory for Educational Research and Development in San Francisco and at the Center for Action Research in Boulder, Colorado. He had a previous life as a trainer and consultant on programs to prevent juvenile delinquency.

Helen Featherstone (EdD, Harvard University, 1973) is associate professor of teacher education at Michigan State and a senior researcher with the National Center for Research on Teacher Learning. She has written extensively on elementary and secondary schooling, and on preschool and special education. She was the founding editor of the *Harvard Education Letter* and of *Changing Minds*, the bulletin of the Michigan Education Extension Service.

Sharon Feiman-Nemser is a professor of teacher education at Michigan State University and a senior researcher with the National Center for Research on Teacher Learning. She received her EdD from Teachers College, Columbia University in 1972. Involved in the study and practice of teacher education for over 20 years, she has contributed chapters to the *Handbook of Research on Teacher Education, Handbook of Research on Teacher Education*, and written extensively about teacher development, learning to teach, teacher centers, teacher education curriculum, and mentoring. Besides teaching undergraduate and graduate courses, she also works with experienced teachers in a professional development school.

G. Williamson McDiarmid received his doctorate from the Harvard Graduate School of Education in 1984 after teaching secondary and elementary school for nine years — primarily in Greece and Alaska. He worked at the Center for Cross-Cultural Studies at the University of Alaska-Fairbanks and started a post-BA teacher education program to prepare teachers for Alaska's small rural high schools. Since 1986, he has been associate director of the National Center for Research on Teacher Learning at Michigan State University where he is also an associate professor of teacher education. His work includes studies of how teachers are being prepared to teach culturally diverse learners, the role that prospective teachers' beliefs about teaching and learning play in their professional preparation, and what prospective teachers learn about their subject matter and teaching it in arts and science courses — the latter work commenced as a Spencer Fellow of the National Academy of Education.

Susan McMahon received her PhD in literacy education from Michigan State University in 1991 where she taught undergraduate and graduate courses in areas of reading and writing, and teacher graduate courses in areas of reading and writing and teacher preparation. She is interested in literacy acquisition and explores this through collaborative, classroom-based research. McMahon has taught English in grades 6 through 12 in Michigan and Kentucky at both public and private schools. She is currently an assistant professor teaching graduate and undergraduate courses in reading at the University of Wisconsin, Madison.

Susan L. Melnick (PhD, 1978, University of Wisconsin, Madison) is associate professor and assistant chairperson in the department of teacher education and senior researcher in the National Center for Research on Teacher Learning at Michigan State University. A former secondary English and Spanish teacher, Melnick has been actively involved for nearly 20 years in the education of both prospective and experienced teachers. Her primary research interests are reflected in her scholarly writing on professional knowledge for teaching; policy issues in teacher education and in learning to teach; and concerns of race, class, gender, and educational equity, both domestic and crossnational.

Margery D. Osborne is currently teaching Science Methods as well as TE-101 at Michigan State University. She is also teaching first-grade science at Spartan Village Elementary School, a professional development school associated with MSU. She previously taught geology and crystallography courses and has an extensive publication and research record in crystal chemistry.

Michelle B. Parker is a research assistant with the National Center for Research on Teacher Learning, where she studies how beginning teachers learn to teach and the role of experienced teachers in supporting that learning. For 3 years she has been working in high school and elementary professional development schools, examining how they can serve as laboratories for teachers in all career phases to learn about teaching. She has also been engaged in classroom action research about how high school students learn and understand social science. Parker has taught TE-101 for eight terms.

Linda J. Tiezzi (PhD, 1991, Michigan State) is an assistant professor at the University of Wisconsin, Milwaukee. While a doctoral student at Michigan State, she served as assistant coordinator of the Heterogeneous Classrooms Teacher Education Program and as coordinator of an elementary professional development school. Across these contexts, she pursued her interest in teacher learning at both the preservice and inservice phases of teaching. Her particular focus is on the evolution of students' thinking and the ways in which teachers facilitate the changes. Also a veteran TE-101 instructor, Tiezzi taught the class for eight terms.

Suzanne M. Wilson (PhD, Stanford University, 1988) is associate professor of teacher education at Michigan State University. She is a senior researcher with the National Center for Research on Teacher Learning and the Center for the Teaching and Learning of Elementary Subjects. As part of her current work, Wilson teaches third- and fourth-grade social studies daily in an elementary school in Lansing in order to learn more about elementary school teaching. Her research and writing involved the examination of the role of subject-matter knowledge in teaching, the assessment of teachers' knowledge, and the effects of state level policy on changes in teaching practice.

Index